THE
WALK-ON

THE WALK-ON

By W.L. McClain

ISBN: [979-8-218-03746-8]

With the highest praise, I dedicate the chapter titled "Five after Seven" to my late wife, Marilyn. She was a bright-eyed, happy, magnetic person, who could spread joy, enthusiasm, and spirit, lifting love in an entire room filled with people young and old. Her unmistakable passion and love for the Lord, like an angel, showed that she was truly a child of His.

My beloved gallantly fought the good fight but eventually lost the battle to cancer on December 1, 2017—five minutes after seven.

CONTENTS

The pitch: "JUST CATCH THE BALL." REVERBERATED EUPHEMISM FROM A DISTANCE PAST. FADED GLORY IS MY THOUGHTS AS I SAUNTER PAST AN EMPTY TROPHY STAND.

INTRODUCTION

A red breasted Robin perched on my sister's bedroom window ledge. Its wings had a touch of royal blue near their ends and were trimmed in gold. It arrived every year at about the same time to bask in the refreshing, aromatic spring air. To us this was a great indication that the harsh, seemingly never-ending winter was finally over. The weather on this ominous, sacred holiday had a soft, welcome breeze, sunny with an aqueous, blue background.

The smattering of cumulus clouds added flavor to the tropical and complementary temperature that those who resided in Southern California enjoyed daily. The sky reminded me of a landscape painting that could easily have been created on the canvas of Rembrandt, Monet, or Michelangelo.

The one ritual that almost the entire population in the city participated in, besides the good eating and egg hunting, was showing off their extravagant formal dress wear. Ladies, men, girls, and boys were shining bright and smelling like a rose in the summer or a fragrance like Faberge, Brut, Old spice, Chanel no 5, and whatever other perfume young and older ladies wore in that time period. Their apparel was purchased from Hudson's, Macy's, Lane Bryant. And youngsters looking good in Kings Way department store Bargains.

But first before going inside of the store to shop, the children had to ride on one of four plastic horses that were located outside of the store at twenty-five cents a pop. Then they hit up the gum ball machines. And finally, they put a penny in the scale that not only told you how much you weigh but also predicted your fortune for the next five years. In different way, it read that you would live long and receive an inheritance of lots of money. Children strutted like proud peacocks as if they were on a fashion runway. The plush, majestic movie theaters were packed with children as were the beaches and parks, and the delightful smell of barbeque filled the air in every neighborhood this holiday season.

My younger brother and cousin were dressed in matching blue pinstripe suits with vests, light blue silk shirt, and oxford shoes with blue- and red-lined windowpane socks. Some of the neighborhood boys were dressed in gabardine suits and penny loafers.

Others wore mohair sweaters with silk pants. I was draped in a gray Italian sharkskin suit, a vest, a white silk shirt, and gray thick and thin socks. My shoes were suede double monk straps: two leather straps with a metal buckle closure.

It was around 3:45 p.m., and my mother seemed to be levitating on the gate of a worn, galvanized chain-link fence. Screaming my first and middle name, "Willie Lamarr," at the top of her lungs. Why was she yelling? She caught me with my hands under the center. We were behind the house in the alley, playing hard-hitting, two-hand touch football, still decked out in our Sunday best.

My name is Willie Lamarr McClain Jr., and I was born October 3, 1954, in Detroit, Michigan. My mother, Sarah, was basically a homemaker who worked when she wanted to obtain something of importance. My father, Willie Mose McClain, was a Georgia migrant who retired after twenty-five years from of working at General Motors as a boiler engineer and relief man. He didn't engage in contact sports like all his children. He loved golf. In the garage was a golf bag filled with all the clubs and irons he used.

He often wore golf gear at picnics. He loved his family more and sacrificed his game by spending family time. In his late seventies, that dreaded illness called dementia reared its ugly face in his final days, he watched the 1986 Masters Tournament, won by Jack Nicklaus, over and over in his hometown of Augusta, Georgia. He was excited every time the tape started over.

Sarah and Willie had four boys and four girls. They adopted one other boy from birth named Corby Dee. I was the second whippersnapper in the family and had an older sister named Maria.

I remember that gas was twenty-six cents a gallon. As a family we spent a considerable amount of time traveling to unspoiled outdoor destinations where you could ride a horse and/or rent a canoe. We hit the beaches and hidden fishing holes as far south as Tennessee and north on King's Highway 401, all the way up to Toronto, Canada.

My parents were the opposite of helicopter parents. They did not cuddle us or have us on a leash. It was mostly my mother who helped packed our bags, kissed us on the cheek, and said, "I love you. See you later."

The travel bug made 7of her 8 children, plus our adopted brother, do a stint in an different state Job Corps facility for six months or more, except for our younger brother, Clifford, who was located at the Job Corps center in Dayton, Ohio. At 5:00 p.m. he took off from the center to work with a pit crew inside the Daytona 500 racetrack. He really started slipping away from his Job Corps obligations and began spending the whole weekend with the Dayton 500 pit crew, only to show back up at the center on Monday mornings. He was a repeat offender, making more money over the weekend than the other corps students made in a month. After four months job corps kicked him out.

Cliff was quite the Cade. When he reached drinking age, he kept a bottle of wine with him, even though he didn't work. He made his money by telling jokes and making his prey laugh until they gave up their money. His antics worked even on me. And yet he was always going to pay you back on Tuesday. I don't think anyone ever got a penny back from him. Cliff preformed his getting a free drink con in every club that we hit, and there were so many in Detroit before the no smoking law decimated them.

As soon as we entered the joints, Cliff would shout out that it was his birthday. His ploy worked, and he got a free drink on the house every time.

My youngest sister, Step, we called the brat. With the assistance of our parents and older siblings, she left home and was able to move into the upstairs of a two-family flat that was fully furnished, when she was only sixteen. Mom's children still make their homes in different cities across the globe.

When we were growing up, our house was the party house where relatives, friend, and coworkers started drifting on Thursdays after work to unwind. Friday was the sit-or-stand-where-you-can night. And, as usual, like the part in a family movie where the nine-year-old kid is called to entertain the crowed by dancing or telling a joke, I was summoned to spin the forty-five and thirty-three size disk records. Only my mother and I enjoyed classical music printed on thick seventy-eight speed disks.

I could visualize the seating arrangement and instruments as the orchestra played in our heads. But for the rest of my kind folks, it was the music of Motown, Stax Records, and Chicago's Blue Notes Records. And they loved those Rolling Stones.

I used to trip out watching guys with thick chains tied to eight-inch wallets sticking out of their back pockets dance with a few of the ladies, who lifted one side of their dress to show their underwear whenever they were feeling it. The hypnotic drum beat that precedes the words "hey, hey, hey" from the song "I Can't Get No Satisfaction." My fascination with dancing females was, on Saturday nights, entertained by *The Honeymooners'* Jackie Gleason. On his self-named variety show, he had about thirty female swimmers who mesmerized me with their perfect synchronous dancing in the pool.

All the visiting adults drove brand-new cars. The showing off day was Saturday. This was a regular event because it seemed that every time a couple of jugs of Moonshine arrived from Georgia, someone tore up their automobile. Then they brought a brand new "stylish car that only cost $5,000" back then. And a few weeks later, they'd come by the house on Saturday afternoon to show it off.

Another reason our home was an attraction for visitors was to peek at the family dog. His name was Ladd, a short-legged English Cocker Spaniel. He had silky, black fur with a white mane and white paws. And if someone didn't know better, they would think that this dog was human.

My father loved chewing bubble gum on Saturday, the kind that was rectangular, not Bazooka Joe. We liked the comic in Joe. Anyway, the kids, and sometimes myself, would gather around the TV set in the front room along with the dog after my father had given him a wad of bubble gum. Ladd would chew, pop, and blow bubbles while watching at his two favorite shows: *Lassie* and *The Adventures of Rin Tin Tin*. The household was used to seeing this, but an outsider would get a kick when they checked out the attentive dog transfixed, looking at what was on the tube.

My mother, who grew up for a spell on the east side of Detroit in the perilous Brewster Project, lived in the same building complex as one of Motown's most famous singers. Both had the exact same fiery-hot temperament and aggressive demeanor when it came to fighting. Mom was a few years older, but the youngster didn't care about the age of her opponents. Neither one wasted any time talking. In the hallway they bumped into each other, and dresses were torn, and hair was pulled.

I'm not sure that the scuffle had anything to do with it, but our entire kinship—which consisted of over 300 plus relatives, eight children being the average number in multiple single-family homes (seventeen brothers and sisters raised in one household was the max)—was always invited to anything the record company sponsored: backyard house parties, reviews, New Year's Eve, and, my favorite, The Motown Picnic.

On Fridays, even when I was in college, I would visit my mother's house and watch her favorite TV shows, which were The *Price Is Right* and *The Young and the Restless*. I watched the Newman kids grow up on TV. That Jack Albert was my kind of guy. I think that I was in love with the character name Drucilla and her doctor sister.

Anyway, we used to go out on the town a whole lot. Mom was good at finishing her store shopping so that we could catch the fifth inning of the baseball game at Tiger Stadium. The gate attendees would let us in for free, but some days we would just pay the two dollars to sit in the bleachers. Sometimes we moved down close to the dugout, but during bust times we just enjoyed the outing, munching on a three-dollar hot dog with a coke. I even used to take her to the clubs, dancing.

I loved Big Time Wrestling and went to the arena in Windsor, Canada, and Detroit to take in some great entertainment. The champion at the time—whose name was The Sheik and whose cheating sidekick was named The Weasel—faced off against my favorite wrestler, the charismatic movie star and formal wrestler The Rock. His father was named Rocky Johnson, and his thing was flying around in the air, drop-kicking his opponent into submission. He and Flying Fred Curry could really elevate with springlike legs while dropping their targets in the ring with exciting flair. Back then the wrestlers had to wrestle some before someone hit the mat for a three count. The Fabulous Kangaroos were probable best when preforming real wrestling.

My mother had never been to Cobo Arena. She never wanted to go to watch. For a whole month, I had to convince her to go with me. It was harder on the night of the event when I finally got her to attend the championship match with me. We had floor-level seats and she complained until all, but the bright ring lights darkened. The Sheik was losing the match until The Weasel, his manager slipped him sparkles to blind Rocky Johnson and pin him to the mat. Throughout the night she barely said a word. I felt that she must have been miserable that evening as I drove her home. I thought that she would never let me take her there again.

A month passed, and this time the championship match at Cobo Arena was with a fan favorite Bobo Brazil, along with his patented headbutt, and he was to battle with The Sheik. I truly wanted to attend the match; however, it's not that fun when you are by yourself, so I didn't buy tickets. I dropped by mom's house that night, and she was getting dressed. Being a little curious, I inquired about her night plans. She was being evasive, and she told me that "I didn't have to go with her" and kept pushing me to leave.

But it wasn't like her to go out at night alone. It just so happened that on my way out of the front door, I looked down at the small end table where her purse rested, and I saw something that looked like wrestling tickets. "Mom!" She broke down and said, "Oooooh! All those big muscle men. All that chest and legs." She was taking her best friend named Charlotte, and she was attempting to sneaking back to Cobo Arena to watch the men wrestling without me.

My entire family was constantly mingling with future hall-of-fame superstars during their teenage years. However, to us they were just neighbors. The pot of talent boiled over because 80 percent of Detroit's population could sing, dance, and a put on a talent show that had the masses coming back for more during those years. Most of us kids learned how to sing lead and back up in any setting. The worst of the worst could bang on bongos or play a musical instrument. We youngsters were taught to use a pitch or tuning fork.

What I really loved about those times was that kids could eat food from any of the entertainer's table.

The mothers and aunts of the singers would gladly fix you a plate. I remember coming back from my hangout in the thick woods, and as I passed by the table belonging to Martha Reeves' family, one of the ladies saw me staring at a piece of chicken. She asked if I would like a piece. For that kind of question, there is only one answer. But, instead of just the chicken, she fixed me an overfilled Styrofoam plate loaded with the works. At this picnic,

Ladd, our dog, who always travel to Belle Isle with the family. Sometimes he would take off through the woods, streams, and wet marshes with us kids. And other times he would go off on his own. But, no matter what, he would show up when we start packing up the cars to leave. There was a feel-good atmosphere and great weather that started off the day. After everyone ate heartily, it was time to head to the Bandshell to be entertained by one great singer or group after another. As usual the Funk Brothers held down the fort and jammed with the future hall-of-fame icons flawlessly.

The crowed was in a festive mood. And, on cue, when too many Black folks got together, one or two egotistic foolish performers needed to have all the attention on themselves. I was seated on the grass near the last row of ground-level Bandshell seating. I turned my head when I heard some commotion. A group of Black guys had a hold of singer David Ruffin, pulling him backward. I did not see what caused it, but I did see singer Tammy Montgomery, stage name Tammi Terrell, falling backward quickly toward the ground.

The female singing group that was on the Bandshell stage at the time was called The Marvelettes. They abruptly stopped singing. The band started unplugging their instruments and the shell-shocked spectators, who didn't know what was happening, started dispersing. As we helped clear off the picnic tables and packed the car, we noticed that something missing.

The dog. He did not show up as usual. Oh no! Four car loads of family started searching the island, looking for him. For hours, long after the happy times were over and the crowd had thinned, we combed the known places where he hung out. That night the moon-lit sky was the only bright enough to see jerky deer scampering about. We called it a day and went home, a car full of heartbroken, shocked family members.

Our home was some six miles away from the island. After a major public event that had a large crowd, a person crossing the street faced all kinds of stampeding and weaving drivers on the side streets and major highways. There was always someone trying to be the first to get home with a drink in one hand, a lit cigarette in the other, steering with the palm of the hand holding the cigarette. And all while driving with suspended license. The avenues, no doubt, were an obstacle course.

As we turned the corner on our block, I noticed a small, black shadow balled up on the front porch. As we got closer, it moved. When we parked, Ladd leaped off the porch and ran towards us. Whew! And that was the very last picnic that Motown threw at the Island. And with the end of the Motown picnics went the relaxing trail horseback riding, cruising the waterways in a canoe, and bicycle rental rides.

Running was in my blood.at seven I started running for no apparent reason to every location where I was supposed to be next. It could be less than a mile, or if the grocery store was three miles away, I ran all the way there and back if the load was light. At the same time, I started taking apart machines, toys, electrical equipment, and motors, anything that was held together by nuts, bolts, electrical wire, and screws. Then I put them back together, and they worked just fine.

I was a regular at Lafayette Electronic and Radio Shack, which was located downtown on Broadway Street in Detroit. Radio Shack used to specialize in kits for putting together the then popular Ham Shortwave Radios, replacement vacuum tubes, and resistors.

My earth father, who shoes I could never fill, his conduct and character were more like Christ. He was the forgiving, kind, and compassionate and quick to walk away from a heated disagreement. He practiced what was called unconditional love—emotions that are still a work in progress for me.

When I was eight, my father, who was a co-owner of two brand spanking new Bays Shell gas stations, had me work with him under a 1960 Chevrolet Bel Air. He really placed heavy importance on safety and the different tools, stating that the right tools make the job at hand a whole lot easier.

I learned their sizes, purposes, and how to torque down screws and bolts. He had me take out the transmission on that Chevrolet at nine years old. When I turned ten, I could tune up the points, plugs, and carburetor of any automobile or truck. I could also tune up and make an engine hum by sound.

I won my first foot race on an Easter Day at Chandler Park, on the east side of the city. It was a thirty-yard race for nine- to twelve-year-old children. We walked to a fence, took our shoes off, and then walked thirty yards back. In order to win, you had to put your shoes on then get back to the starting line. I won a beautiful, realistic, functional red-and-white fire truck, as well as a football. Well, in my entire life, I've never had any desire to run into a building on fire, especially when the crackling wood adds the soundtrack of flames arching out like a solar flare.

As a crazy kid with a whole handful of loose screws in my head, I used to run a three-hundred-and-sixty-degree circle around our house at dusk right before we had to come inside for the evening. I wanted to see if I could do it faster than the night before. My mother always took the clothesline down after she finished washing, and I took it for granted that this was always the case. So, one night at dusk, I take off around the house at full speed. I turn the corner to the backyard, and I hit the ground so fast that I didn't have time to think. Every star in the universe brilliantly zoomed in; they seemed to sparkle and pop like champagne. That one was on me. My mother did not take the clothesline down that evening.

The Walk On is a chronological, true, underdog story about how I am also known simply as Lamarr, an extremely gifted and humble individual in the eyes of the Lord. I am also a twenty-two-year veteran of the Minor League Football who was given two shots to join a professional football organization after I retired. During my interesting journeys, I had the strength and fortitude to become a member of just about any football team whenever I felt like it, even at the end of their training camps. As always, I got flak from and was called by resentful players who had been working out there months before I arrived.

During my football-playing years, most of the time I hid how fast I really was. I lost foot races on purpose, mainly due to a syndrome I called "the-fastest-gun-in-the-west" syndrome. I did this mainly because once people find out who's the fastest or best in anything, then here they come, out of the woodwork, to challenge you to a foot race at all inconvenient hours of day and night. Even Billy the Kid would travel all the way from Kansas City, put his fast-draw six shooter aside, don a pair of sneakers, and challenge you to a showdown race at sundown.

One day the most popular guy at school, who lived on our block, challenged me to bike race the length of a city street. He could not believe he lost. And from that day, it seemed like every other day after school someone wanted to bike race. Sometimes during a foot race, I would forget about that syndrome and turn on the afterburners until I got near the finishing line, and then I would think, *oh, wait! If I win, someone else will challenge me tomorrow.* I would pull up, let them pass, and watch them gloat. And all the while, I'd be thinking, *Good. And now they can bother you.*

The three sections that divide the chronological chapter are based on real events in my life, and I titled these sections "The Best of the Best"— situations where many others concurred that I was acknowledged to be a member of the best, had the highest quality, and greatest ability of a class. The first of the three sections titled "Best of the Best" is about my role as an involuntary athletic director of a Job Corps center. The second is about what occurred on the rugged Zugspitze Mountain in southern Germany. And the third is about the owner of one of the most popular and successful football franchises in the National Football League (NFL).

Around the early 1990s, I used to jog around Central Park every other day, when I lived in four of the five boroughs of New York. They were Bronx, Queens, Manhattan, and Brooklyn. I was about 120 meters from my finishing spot when a Tour de France biker decided to race me on his very expensive bike. Because I jogged slowly but steadily, he thought that he was, for sure, going to beat me in front of the crowd of bikers and spectators.

Looking dejected afterwards, he said that "his speedometer registered twenty-three miles per hour." And as I did with everyone else, I didn't let him pass the back of my ear. I could sense where and how close someone was behind me. The bikers and crowd of spectators could not believe that he lost. After that, every time I came to the park, other bikers wanted to race. I ran listlessly and lost on purpose so that they would go away and let me jog in peace.

At training camps anywhere—once I demonstrated my hundred-and ten-yard zip staring from the back of the end zone to the other goal line— after coaches on the field finally closed their mouths after gasping in awe, the result was always the same, no matter my age or the part of the season. At the end of my run, the coaches would always say, "Go get that man a uniform." But that was only the corporal side of the story.

As for the metaphysical spiritual side, that part of my life was hidden until I started writing. I had a very good reason to lie low and live incognito among my relatives, neighbors, and friends. The terror I experienced would freeze a normal person's soul. The most frightening thing that I found out firsthand that the Devil is real and not a metaphor. It would have done them more harm than good to know something that's evil will seek them expeditiously because of who they know.

At the questioning-everything age of twelve, my adventures and misadventures lay primarily in the wholesome, addictive sport of football. Ever-increasing mystifying encounters with those residing in the supernatural, came into my life about the same time as football.

One relaxing Sunday morning, curiosity made me pick up a piece of a broken mirror in the alley behind our house. I pointed the sun's reflection toward an empty twelve-ounce root beer can, and it moved. The events that happen afterward I can only describe as feeling like opening a portal that lets you see the invisible man.

When I stuck my hand between the reflection and the mirror, I felt nothing. However, the trinket stopped moving. I removed my hand and then targeted larger and larger objects—they also moved. This remarkable metaphysical awareness blew my young scientific mind. At the same time, I became extremely skeptical about things that I classified as wizardry or witchcraft. I would look for hidden ropes and trap doors, anyway, and suddenly the lessons that I repeatedly heard at Sunday school about unseen elements, which used words such as principality, spirits, and powers, began to make sense. The more I was exposed to loved ones who communicated with me as they made their convert to the other side, the less I questioned the teachings that I received in the church service.

The chapter titled "Zephaniah: What the Lord Hid" reveals the sighting of thousands of mysterious, divinely aligned stars, whose configuration was designed to display an extremely large stellar crucifix. The Holy Spirit did not want my writing to be worded with diction and language so sophisticated that only a literature scholar with two PhDs could understand.

The Spirit did not want only true believers because, believers can already distinguish between a worldwide virus and a light drizzle of the fore told plagues. Unless there is an unlikely total repentance of mankind, the light mist will surely progress into a destructive monsoon.

The Holy Spirit did want my writing to be identifiable with nonbelievers who I hung around with—those that society labels as undesirable and incorrigible and the enterprising friends that they call roughnecks—so that they could be aware of the focal point of the cross. The way, the truth, and the only place in the universe that encompass life, death, and resurrection all in one.

On the evening of December 24, 1985, I witness a stellar phenomenon located in the southeastern sky. It was a mammoth cross. It was a breathtaking sight. It was a crux-shaped constellation of stars that was sparkling like a bunch of polished diamonds, majestically designed and on display the entire duration of that glorious, revealing Eve.

For years I wrestled with wondering why I could see an apparition that nobody else could. I consistently questioned myself asking, *why me? Who am I? What does it mean?*

I was relieved when a messenger revealed that I was not the only one who witnessed that astronomical beauty. The Spirit made it known that there are too many realities that lie beyond our senses. I was chosen to be one of the eleven who saw it. To this very day, I still contemplate whenever I think about why so few people. However, it felt much better knowing that I was sane and not considered megalomaniac when I was thinking for a while that if I was the only one who saw that, then perhaps it didn't happen.

Sunday mornings in the city use to be relatively serene, peaceful, with very little human movement or traffic as if time was frozen around 4: 45 in the morning. A time before the greedy fat cats decided to squeeze the labor force for every second on the 24 clock, seven days a week. Walking outside the empty streets felt like you had the world to yourself as if you were in a scene in the movie call "Omega Man." Staring Charlton Heston. With my mind on thoughts that were a million miles away a young lady appears in my vision from out of nowhere. For no known reason she stirred up some hidden emotions that were dormant inside of my heart. Her appearance seemed to satisfy a longing for something that I wanted. I had a sudden urgency to speak to her and yet, when I tried to walk faster to catch up to her, she vanished to thin air.

This damsel who you could tell came from a perfectly blissful dwelling. She was around twenty-two years old, petite, had a size six waist, stood about five feet two inches in height, and was about one hundred pounds. Her surrounding aura emitted that her upbringing was pleasant. She was a happy child, a radiant beauty whose light tan complexion suggested that her earth home was somewhere near the Mediterranean Sea or perhaps the island of Capri. Her thick brows highlighted the mystery woman's almond-shaped, hazel-brown eyes that complemented her shining, raven black waist-length hair. She was draped in an elegant but not formal just-above-the-knee black dress with black sheer stockings. And she glided in black two-inch high heels that had a strap around her ankles.

Those soft brown eyes said "come" as she smiled and said, "Follow me." And for years I did but, I never could catch up with her. As always, I was astonished. I thought, *how could I lose her again?* I was never that far behind her. *Impossible. Where did she go?*

The males who were two of the three guardians appear, at times, from out of nowhere. Or so it seemed. Usually, they joined me in an open grass field, right in the middle. They talked and walked with me. They mostly wore football jersey, blue jeans, tennis shoes, and a sports cap.

The conversations were pretty much small talk about nothing significant. Maybe a little chatter concerning the weather or types of food we liked. We hardly talked about anything deep.

When I suddenly saw or heard a distracting sound, I looked away from my acquaintance, and when I turn back toward them, they were gone.

This was not a random once-or-twice occurrence. I realized much later in life that all that time they were preparing me for something I felt was going to be a soul-shaking moment that had yet to come. Regular humans do have the Lord Jesus Christ who is always present in their lives, whether they believe it or not.

My earth mom wasn't over-bearing, but I did have three helicopter parent cherubs in my life, who made me always aware that they were there. Mostly they admonished me repeatedly, over the span of my lifetime. I was aware of their presence, and I was still hanging out with gangsters, the Crips, the Bloods, MS-13, and motorcycle gangs. The cherubs have had to repeatedly reiterate where I was on the spiritual hierarchy. They told me that I was born slightly above regular humans. They insistently divulged that I walk with the prophets, preachers, and saints. This is the reason I call them all brothers and sisters.

The one thing that I do know is the Lord calls me one of his favorite sons, the prodigal one I feel. More times than I can count, I have found a large wad of money and squandered away the good fortune on wine, women, and a good time. Then I'd go home broke.

I was almost involved in three dead-center car accidents when someone jumped their traffic lane. There was no way out to avoid impact. I could only brace myself and close my eyes. And nothing happened. Each time when I opened my eyes, the approaching vehicle was moved a whole car length out of the way.

Why? I spoke of this to very few people because mainly the close family members and friends that I did enlighten about the conversations I had with the advocate and helpers didn't comprehend. In the beginning of my phenomenon meeting with the angels, I did constantly inform friends and acquaintances that I was close to the Lord.

A pastors and saint, such as Father William Cunningham, founder of Focus Hope, knew that I was a man of God. Most of the true Christians who I met instinctively knew. But the day-to-day population tends to be enveloped in spiritual blindness and could only see what was directly in front of them, believing only what they want. My attempting to enlighten them fell on deaf ears. Due to reasons of their own, they could not possibly register what I told them with their basic cut-and-dry thinking.

Another reason why I didn't was that growing up in the Detroit, if a person was thought to have something missing upstairs, they were shipped off to Northville Psychiatric Hospital. Those who came back were worse off than a zombie, with a blank stare on their faces, oblivious to their surroundings. People told me that crazy people were treated by way of electroshock therapy.

I kept my mouth closed about what was happening to me with the transcendental travelers because if they sent me to that Northville and a straitjacket was the newest addition to my wardrobe, I surely presumed that I would become a doped-up guinea pig. I would be reduced to a medical number, one of those who is lacking a whole bundle of nuts and bolts. To me, electroshock therapy was the first cousin of something that belong in the hair-raising, shocking family of electrocution.

Many times, my encounters with angels and unclean spirits were night-marish. On a normal, supernatural day, they mostly appeared in triplets. They communicated with me in different fashions. For the most part, I saw them as a normal transcendental cherub. Another kind of meeting was through a person who was talking to me. They would not change their appearance but speak through them, exactly like Professor Xavier from the X-Men movies and comic book series.

Another way the advocate appeared to me was by transfiguration, changing the outward appearance of the host. There was nothing to it over time; I wasn't even startled when I could recognize the transformation immediately. Sometimes something pertinent that I have forgotten like direction or information could be communicated for me to remember by an animal, such as a bird walking five meters in front of me. In most cases, when they caught my attention, I become aware that the spirit was with them. And the almost-scary way that they communicated with me was about thirty-five meters up in the sky. Their voices startle me every time when they do that. It's like a booming voice that is clearly spoken through a microphone.

However, instruction can come from an old man. Or the one that gets to me is when a small child's aphorism makes me stop in my tracks; unless they been here before, the information they provide or subject they speak of could not possibly have been learned.

I was repeatedly warned that the Lord would take His hand off me if I did not stop engaging in mischievous activities. I did bodyguard work for people who a peace officer might want to speak to. I believe that one time I was punished because I hung out with those gangsters and bad girls much too much for heaven's sake.

I ventured into a pickup football game when I was twelve. During this era, any kid could walk fifteen blocks in any direction or go to just about any park or recreation area, and there you would find guys and girls playing football.

In that game I was assigned to maintain the left tackle position, and I got the heck beat out of me. That pulverization was instrumental in molding and developing my hitting abilities on defense. I became a disciple of football Hall of Famer and tackler Dick Butkus. And a two-way player like the Philadelphia Eagles linebacker Chuck Bednarik. I stayed at the left-tackle position voluntarily because I could throughout my semipro career and enjoyed the numerous times when I blew up a linemen or linebacker trying to come through to roughly visit my quarterback.

With all respect, I mirrored another ageless sports hero. My playing in just over 350 football games is probably equal to playing in 2,000 baseball game. The other ageless wonder was born in Mobil, Alabama and was named Leroy "Satchel" Paige.

Blaring TV commercials, medical experts, and sports doctors all say that when a football player turns thirty, that's it. The body start hitting an invisible wall that slow players down to mall walking. He's already hit his prime, and the athletic body is heading south. Even non-sports, common folks bought into it. At first, I even bought into it for a hot minute as I saw ex-teammates physically change into coach potatoes. Some even blew up, changing into unrecognizable specimen.

Those elite thinkers had me looking at my legs as I ran. Thinking, "Am I losing a step? What's that? Oh man, it's starting." Turning thirty was pure hell. When I hit the age of thirty-five, every team that we faced, I got a heckling from the coaches whenever I was near their sidelines. They said that I was too old to be playing football or that with one good hit, I was going to be knocked out of the game. This sort of player hating continued all the way until my second to last semipro football game. It stopped on my very last game before retiring.

I smiled when they said made up, untrue things about me. But by the second quarter, they always had to change their game plan and put an extra man on me. The first major mistake that humbled opposing coaches was that I was the one doing the hitting.

At the advanced age of forty-nine, I was still literally exploding twenty to twenty-five yards off the line of scrimmage, like I was shot out of a cannon. In San Diego, when the scouts came to a pickup game to evaluate my younger opponents, they thought that I was around twenty-five to thirty because of the way I played.

I felt that I really didn't slow down until I reached fifty-five. At that age I could still do a halfway decent backward flip. I dropped down from warp speed factor three to warp speed factor two, a speed that was still a blur to those big, old linemen who were attempting to tackle me. The drop of my quickness occurred after I stopped doing my regiment of running six miles every other day. I pulled back on the 600 sit-ups and the 200 push-ups, in between hitting the gym every other nonjogging day.

I grew up in the area of Detroit called the Black Bottom, and most homes were built with cheap wood and no insulation or drywall to block those blasting cold winter nights. We heated that house with a cast-iron, potbelly stove. I surely remember pulling my Radio Flyer red wagon to fill the two farmer's baskets at the coal yard for twenty-five cents apiece. I fetched the coals mainly because my father was at work, and I truly did not want to get sick.

If you were an unfortunate one and became ill, it was either a bottle of Father John's medicine syrup or castor oil down the pipes. You never tasted anything so horrible in your life; nevertheless, we were still some of the fortunate ones because others lived in the bottoms, inside of tin roof houses. Sometimes I knew that a family was huddled up inside, but I saw no smoke coming out of their chimneys.

Physical disputes started way too early in my life for my taste. I was only in the second grade when another second grader confronted me with battle words on a Friday after school. I remember thinking about how my schoolwork always turns out while sitting at my desk that had an inkwell on the upper right corner. The problem was that I was left-handed and dripped ink from the pen all the way across my notebook paper most of the time.

On that Friday, a brave and misguided boy came into my view. In front of the whole class, he got his self-annihilated. This insane action continued in my school life from elementary school until I finally reached Kettering High School. By then I believed that after-school fighting was a normal way life.

Bad neighbors and gang riffraff replaced the vacated Friday spot left by former grade-school opponents who always insisted that they get beat up in front of their own homes. I did not waste time. If they told me to knock the wood chip off their shoulder, I flicked it off quickly or crossed the line as soon as they drew it in the dirt. I always baited them into swinging first. No one ever returned for a second round because I became the provoker once I was approached by the instigator. They started it, and no matter what, I would not let them back out.

There is a chapter in my story titled "What I Hid," and it is one of the three hidden gems scattered throughout this novel. This one is the ultimate nightmare. For me these were riveting and, perspective wise, life-changing encounters that I constantly replay in my mind over and over as if I were locked up in a jail cell. It was going over and over the events that brought me back in jail.

In spring of 1992, I was confronted by and challenged to do battle with one of the most dangerous, ruthless, and devious opponent mankind has ever known. There was one memorable pickup football game in that story that was a bona fide thriller. That was the game when all of those sharply dress boys were caught playing ball in their Sunday best on Easter. That was twenty years ago. The same players had turned into forged, hardened tempered like steel and dip in blood football players.

Collectively, the combined players from the alley never lost any pickup game. We never took our foot off the gas pedal. Our team played clean and error free and understood down and distance football. We played precision football like the 1983–2006 Detroit Red Wings played hockey, always mindful of the competition's athletics and physical abilities, never underestimating any opponent, not even if we played against fourteen-year-old Boy Scouts.

We modeled our playing styles after large college football programs during the times when all of the major university like the Big 12, Big Ten, Pacific Conference, and Notre Dame sucked up all of the best football players with scholarship programs.

The little colleges received one or two of the blue-chip leftovers. And the little teams always got blown out by scores of seventy-seven to three. When we faced a bloated wishbones running offensive, our scores were always in the high seventies, mostly when I was at the quarterback position.

Those dapperly dressed alley football players became elite, and with the kind of scouting system that evaluates draft choices these days, they would have ranked eight of our players to be taken in the very first round. And three of us would have been gone in the first ten slots. Out of the fourteen of us, no one would have lasted past the second round.

Here's a case in point: In spring 1979, I walked on the minor league football team named the Detroit Jets. Shortly after a brief interview, coach Holmes, ascertaining all the positions that I was versed in on the field, gave me the title of utility player. The roster was composed of various sized players and was built like a professional football team.

This organization was feared around the league. Playing against them meant you better be on your best game, or you were toast. In my opinion, the Jets could have easily replaced the professional football team in Pontiac, Michigan. As a replacement team during their strike years, the Jets collectively would have put up a better and more entertaining fight.

A professional football player dropped by the Detroit Jets semipro football practice field located on Southeastern High School football field right after he was drafted first in the second round of the 1980 NFL draft by the New York Jets. Out of the university of Michigan, semipro ballplayers usually must hold down a job or two, so most showed up late to practice and sometimes were not able to make it at all. The team was two players short to complete a full complement of players on both sides of the line of scrimmage.

They let my younger brothers, Zack and Cliff, fill in for the missing players. Two of the three young boys besides coach Leonard Holmes' son, who we called "third" and was always hanging around the team. The coaches allowed them to play corner and safety at this practice.

I tore my ankle ligament completely in half running full speed before stretching so that a sportscaster from ABC could shoot a sport segment. Our female trainer, who doubled as the head cheerleader, wrapped my leg, and it looked like a mummy. I walked with a cane until game day, when I still started on a very bad ankle. In football, playing on a severed ankle was still less painful then playing with turf toe. And I still made the quarterback look somewhere else to get a completion. But this day I watched my brothers play in the practice

I hear that the New York Jets draft choice became prominent and has done wonderful things throughout the community where he lives. However, that day at the Jets' practice, the running back, who also played receiver, lined up on my brothers' side of the field. And that day he did not get a completion. My brothers batted away everything that came their way. They blanked and stuck to him like wallpaper. He did not get a step on Cliff or Zachary. He never got open to catch a pass.

When practice was over, he stood on the sidelines with an astonished and bewildered look on his face as if it was saying, "But...but...but...I'm an NFL second round draft pick. This...this...is not supposed to happen." His facial expression displayed the feelings of a person who was so deeply disillusioned that I truly wanted to walk toward him, put my arm around his shoulder, and tell him, "Don't worry about it. You are all right. They do this to everybody."

BEST OF THE BEST I

PURPLE REIGN

I had a very different account of the 1967 Detroit Riot then what was published in newspaper and "Life Magazine." The hoodlums and conmen in my neighborhood, plus a few unscrupulous cousins and friends of mine, were still my homies. What anybody else did wasn't ever any concern of mine. For some unknown reasons, the bad boy in the hood always seems to befriend my brothers and me. During the uprising, I was introduced to two syndicate members of the notorious Detroit Purple Gang. They were the last of the Mohicans.

It was in the predawn hours of Sunday, July 23, 1967. The time was around 4:45 a.m. A soft knock on my basement bedroom window interrupted my joyous flight over the landscape where, from an air-born view, there always appeared to be square. As a youth at night, I regularly flew around in my dreams. And I could hardly wait to go to sleep so that I could get the peace and tranquility of flying. It took me a year or so before I learned how to land. I usually woke before I hit the ground hard, tumbled over, or belly flopped, but when I did learn it, it was a piece of cake.

The knocker was my late cousin Clarence. I opened the window, and he explained that he had an important phone call to make, and our telephone was one of the few that didn't have party line where someone else could listen to your conversations.

I opened the back door and let him in. The household was not disturbed because I normally had a paper route. In those years, young kids could freely walk around outside in the predawn hours because people back then acted halfway civilly and did not try to molest or kidnap every child who was hustling delivering newspaper.

After Clarence stayed on the phone for about fifteen minutes, he appeared to be excited and filled me in on the details. He explained that the people were tearing 12th Street apart. He said that they were breaking into stores and businesses, then carting home all the steaks and hams, TVs, radio appliances, boxes of liquor, and cartons of cigarettes that they could carry on their backs. He said that it all started in an after-hours club, or as other called it a "blind pig," located on Baron and 12th Street, above a printing shop where my cousin Clarence was drinking and gambling at the time. I got my information below from interviewing witnesses who were on the scene.

There were two police detectives from the 10th Precinct, vice squad, a tall man and a short man. One of the men named Frazer started the whole scenario by knocking the mother of the Mason gang down the steps. Granted, she had a sassy attitude and gave the peace officers a wicked tongue lashing so much so that she pushed the right buttons, got under their skin, and they gave her a push right down the stairs. She called her sons.

The gang acted, mixing it up with the police. The police could not handle the gang and called in for more reinforcement. That action cause rival gang members called the Shakers and the M&M gang to join in the fighting. The looters, in addition to battling with three different gang sects, overwhelmed the police force. They had no choice but to call for help from the governor's office—enter the National Guard who set up shop on the west side of the John C. Lodge Freeway, making the hospital where I was born in their headquarters. The hoodlums from the Martin Scorsese movie *Goodfellas*, were not the only hoodlums stealing from loaded tractor trailer trucks.

After my cousin completed the phone call, we took all backroads and drove behind a department store. In these times, the major department stores were gigantic. The scenery outdoors was starless and pitch black; the stillness of the night blended in with the total darkness that comes right before dawn, perfect for sneaking around.

Other vehicles also were pulling in. The pillaging trucks were of various sizes—anywhere from two-and-a-half tons to homemade truck beds made of dilapidated two-by-four wood beams tied with rope. I saw very old trucks that you only saw in 1930s Mexican movies still running, ready to be stuffed with goods and flatbed trucks with no siding.

Because of the calamity that engulfed the city, instead of backing into the dock as usual, the truck driver was told to pull their truck in so that it was facing forward to save time and get the hell away from the madness as soon as possible. In the center directing traffic were two men who I was told were Jewish, not that it mattered to me, anyway. A short, graying, middle-aged, unidentified Black man climbed on the backend of the two trailers with great big bolt cutters and severed the locks with ease.

The trailers were emptied out in no less the twenty-five minutes. And the twelve to fifteen loaded vehicles with washing machines, brand name TVs, refrigerators, long stereo consoles, and you name it were all still packaged in boxes as people scattered, fleeing the area in different direction. During the whole event, I was thinking, *why am I here?* I had to remain calm because I had to think positive and tell myself that I was going back home. Should doubt creep in and invite the Big Four unit to the party, even though I was just sitting there, I would have gone to jail as fast as everyone else.

The next day, Monday, July 24, 1967, the city was in anarchy. Later I found out that it was the city's 266th birthday. At around the same time as the previous day, my cousin knocked again. And once again we took the backroads, dodging military jeeps and rumbling tanks. Once again, we finally stopped behind a huge department store, only this time the location was much closer. How the heck did I wind up in this situation again? The two Jewish men were in the center, directing traffic. The same man as before cut the locks. And as they got ready to unload the trailers, there seemed to be some confusion between the organizer and the movers.

They were discussing something for about fifteen minutes. Astonishingly, one by one, the vehicle's gloominess looking drivers drove away empty hand-ed. When I found out the reason, I felt the whole situation had become comical. I wanted to laugh. It was not the National Guards that had deterred these pillagers. The deciding factor was that they had stolen so much the day before, they had nowhere to store any items. All their garages were filled, their basements, attics, and storage containers were also full to the brim. After they cut the lock, they had nowhere safe to take the goods.

The two very old Jewish guys were rumored to have taken part in the St. Valentine's Day Massacre in Chicago. My thoughts and feelings after seeing them over the past two days were that they were too well organized and really knew what they are doing. You could tell by their demeanor that they were cutthroat and ruthless back in their day. To me it was no rumor—I was positive those two did take part in the massacre.

Tuesday, July 25, 1967, was the third day of the uprising. I woke up early and left the house just in case my cousin came by again with another dangerous plan to take me to a hotspot where none of us were supposed to be, watching but not getting a dime. Usually at five in the morning, right before dawn, I sucked in the tranquil and unpopulated brisk, clean air.

However, that day I thought, *ugh*—the air smelled like burned wood and looked dark, filled with smoke. To top it off, noisy, heavy military tanks continued to shake the ground all day as they rumbled down the main highway.

I went to the newspaper staging station. I just love the fresh smell of ink on brand new papers in the morning. On that day there was union problem with the delivery of the city's two major newspapers, the *Detroit News* and the *Detroit Free Press*. So, with nothing to do at five in the morning, I heard of some newspaper work at a councilman's house. Once there, I made a few dollars selling a newsletter that I believe sold for fifteen cents a copy.

I went to the first house on the corner of Crane Street and met with a vibrant, brash young man name Nicholas Hood. He gave us the assignments and locations of where to go. Back then, as I mentioned before, a preadolescent paper boy, or sometimes girl, could go house to house without being enticed into—whether voluntarily or involuntarily—winding up an unforgivable statistic. It was a good day's work. We youngsters came back unharmed and with all the money.

Wednesday, July 26, 1967, was the fourth day of the uprising. Burn, Baby, Burn was the background sights of the city. One of my favorite uncles picked me up to work in his garage. I helped with the body work on cars, bumping out the fenders, bonding, and sanding with different pads on the circular drill. My uncle left the garage for a few hours, which was normal for him. And since the days in the city all felt strange, the day seemed to have the makings of a typical rioting morning. But I was badly mistaken.

My uncle hurried back to uncharacteristically close the body shop and take me to his house. *Something isn't right*, I thought. As he went to his closet and pulled out a long-barrel shotgun. *What now!* I though. He was sawing off the barrel, and I saw the long part hit the floor. He grabbed a bunch of small boxes off the top shelf, put them in a bag, and told me to come. Man! And I thought we were going to an early breakfast, not to the O.K. Corral.

We pulled up directly in front of the Black Panthers headquarters where I saw men dressed in black with black berets, going to-and-fro around the building. Oh no! I'd seen that picture before. They were fortifying the building, sand bagging the windows so that a small peephole to shoot out of was all that was needed.

Those brothers were getting ready for war. It was that dark, black tension and everyone there could feel it was in the air, the kind of tension you feel when a depressed person comes into to a room filled with partying people going full tilt. Everyone's mood changes from happy to sad. No one sees the color the person brought in, but each would describe it as dark.

They were carrying all kinds of weapons across their bodies, machine guns and handguns. Their facial expressions exhibited anger to the tenth degree. I thought that I saw thick streams of smoke coming out of their nostrils and ears. After talking to the headquarter director named Frank D., my uncle tells me that the word on the street was that the three men were killed in the Algiers Motel on Woodward Avenue late the night before. They were reported as members of the Panther Party. Why, oh why did my family have to stick their noses into every damn thing? These folks were not only having problems with the local police force. At night when I watched the news, I saw that countrywide the entire Black Panther Party was losing all the skirmishes they had with J. Edgar Hoover and the FBI.

Numbness swept through my whole body as I thought about those frightening images of people in Mississippi getting hosed and beaten. As my dumb butt sat right in the front of the building in a pick-up truck, right in the line of fire for hours, paralyzed because of the way events were unfolding minute by minute, things were not looking good at all.

Around 11: 45 a.m., Frank and his gang got the word that the three men killed at the motel were found to not be Black Panther members at all. I asked my uncle to take me home, where I became unglued, almost shaking as I always do after I get far away from an area where a heavy backsplash of consequential action could get you killed or locked up.

It was Thursday, July 27, 1967, and the human storm was subsiding in Motor City because the all-you-can-carry free shopping was over. The gloomy smoke that had enveloped the streets for day was clearing. Things were beginning to cool down in the city. Instead of hearing the more-than-normal firing of machine gun bullets throughout the night, the crickets' chatter started to be loud and bothersome as usual and sometimes disturbing, especially if they were right under your bedroom window.

After sweating and concentrating very hard not to give into paranoia during the tractor-trailer heist and my involuntary hanging out with the Panthers, I wanted nothing more to do with the uprising. If anyone knocked on my bedroom window, I was not going to answer. I was not home to answer the phone or take short drives anywhere, not even with my own father. I'd had enough. I thought about concentrating on doing something easy and safe like hanging out with my sisters and a few other longtime neighbors for our annual ritual of climbing the back of eight-feet-high razor and barbed-wire fences to harvest and fill our big brown bags with all kinds of delicious fruits from apple, cherry, peach, and pear trees. We hardly ever missed hitting the ripe mouthwatering juicy green grape vines.

During that era, I read lots of publications that said that the Detroit Riot was the main cause of white flight from the city. Perhaps, but not in my neighborhood. The whites that left already had the intention of moving, anyway. The Korean store owners did not move because they were treated by the peace officers the same way Blacks were. Their businesses were not touched. I was bewildered by the white flight narrative because I saw just as many U-Haul's in front of the houses where black people with money lived. They were also hauling tail.

In school I heard more of their children talking about their families moving to California. And some folks had no reason to leave the city. They stayed in their houses, avoiding the melee all together. Something good did come from the city's unfathomable chaos: that Focus: HOPE organization, canned goods, and cheese was right on time and meant so much for families struggling with no finances, having only prayer that kept them standing up as they waited in those extremely long food lines. But better yet was my memorable two-year relationship that I cultivated with Focus: HOPE's founders—Father William Cunningham and the classy, wonderful, and elegant lady name Eleanor Josaitis. To me one was a prophet, the other an angel.

JOB CORPS

The complex was an abandon military base. I joined the recreation services department in our dorm, which was dorm 1010. I was between assignments, so I figured I would only have to pass out fliers given out by the athlete director. The corpsman with the different color badges gets to sleep in and catch a late breakfast. Boy oh boy, was I ever wrong. Three days later, the dorm's sports director, who was also a Golden Gloves boxing champion, had a sudden unscheduled boxing match out of state and named me the athletic director, an occupation I knew absolutely nothing about. Six weeks later, when the dust cleared, our dorm won first place in every event. And just my luck, for six weeks I hardly got any sleep at all.

How I made my way to job corps was because of two reasons, one my older sister was already placed in a outer town job corps.

Transferring from middle school to high school there was nothing except that math became harder as I was introduced to algebra. You were allowed to choose your own curriculum as my guidance counselor name Miss Hadley, who was also my elementary music teacher that followed 80 percent of that class onwards to middle school. And then once again into high school with my junior high classmates that had matriculated as 65 percent of the class remained intact. She also worked as a counselor and music instructor at the high school. She lived in the neighborhood and often invited student that were behind in music lessons to her home for individual tutoring. I know because I was one.

At Kettering I joined the Reserve Officers' Training Corps (ROTC), and I loved the uniforms, the organization skills bestowed upon us, the discipline, the weapon training, and the parade marching in step. I learned the whole book of Uniform Code of Military Justice (UCMJ) and the Army Regulation 15 handbook, when I was fifteen years old, I was happy with the direction that my life was taking, until coach Tucker kicked me off the football team.

The high school gave me options to make money once I turned sixteen. The counselor that followed the class all the way from elementary school also served as a career counselor. I really appreciated the experiences that my uncles gave me working in their automobile repair garages and gas stations, but high school kids' fashion sense changes, and clothing costs more.

I could no longer spend all my free time after school working in my family's garages. Miss Hadley first discussed joining the Peace Corp—traveling to the jungles of other impoverished countries, places where I already knew about the undrinkable water but, more so, the bug bites, jaundice, snakes, malaria, and other creepy, crawly things. Why go way over there when I didn't like getting bitten by bugs here?

"What else do you have, counselor?" She talked about joining Junior Achievement, but that didn't ring any bells. And then there was the Job Corps. After six months I could get my General Educational Development (GED), be done with high school, and learn a profitable, skilled trade like welding, carpentry, or become an electrician, all careers that all paid well. I would get back money that they put aside for me, plus I could purchase U.S. Saving Bonds. My father had stacks of those, and they came in handy when your funds were low. I was sold on this one.

In February of 1970, away I went. That was the very first time I traveled alone without other family members—ten kids in the backseat of a car that was made to seat three-and-a-half passengers. I caught the Greyhound to downtown Indianapolis and was later picked up in an old brown Ford station wagon. That drove me to a once-abandon military base called Camp Atterbury located in Edinburgh, a rural area of Central Indiana. I got settled in one of the old military barracks. It was in dorm number 1010.

One of the first people that I met from my hometown called himself "Grave Digger." I shook his hand and continued with my tour of the base. Later that day I met a corpsman, a local who was lucky enough to be assigned in his home state. He had the nickname "Country."

So far so good. After dinner, and as dusk approached, guys started showing their true colors. First Grave Digger invited me to come with him to get out of the barracks and get some air. I asked him, "What are we going to do?" He answered by telling me that we were going to the burial ground and dig up caskets. What? He got excited, laughing constantly as he showed me some of the goods that he had pocketed from two nights before. I thought that it was morbid and way out of my league. I said, "Grave Digger, I am tired from the journey here. I must pass." He laughed while grabbing his digging tools, and he headed out the door.

Raging puberty was hitting most of the adolescent corpsmen. Some developed in different ways, exploring their newfound sexuality. Walking ahead of me one day, while I was making my way to the mess hall, were at least six young men in a group. They were colorful chaps that made me wonder if I may have been mistaken, but, to me, they looked like they had female mannerisms. And I didn't stare at them for too long, but I could swear that they were wearing makeup.

It was around seven in the evening, and I was lying in the top bunk, relaxing and reading some old edition of *Popular Mechanics* and *Psychology Today* that I found in the camp's library. Unexpectedly, the one called "Country" stuck his head in the doorway. He invited me to come with him. He spoke of a nearby farm that had sheep roaming. "So what?" I asked him. He goes on to explain the anatomy of the sheep to. *That's sick*, I think. "You go on and enjoy yourself. I will see you later." He departed.

My bottom bunkmate came in a few hours later, and he liked to wrestle. However, he was not satisfied until I let him win. On the weekdays, lights out was at ten, when the campus retired for the evening. I drifted into sleep thinking, "Man oh man. What in the hell have I gotten myself into?"

I do sometimes have the same two disturbing, recurring dreams, even into middle age. One is in a jungle where I am surrounded by snakes. The other nightmare is one where I am running as fast as I can, sweating and breathing hard, tramping through the woods as the branches of the thick trees brush up against me. I am trying to get away from an angry mob of white-hooded sheet-wearing KKK members. It is always the same dream. I wake before they catch me. While I am looking back as they try to pursue me, I reach the exact same conclusion: "Damn. I must have done something bad. I must have gotten caught sleeping with one of their women." The nightmares rarely come, but when they do, it consumes me for the whole day as I try to interpenetrate why I have the same bad dreams.

The following day we woke and did things to get ready before and after breakfast because at 7:30 a.m., from Monday through Friday, all of us had to catch the big yellow shuttle bus with hard lather seats, except for one bus that everyone tried to board. The rest of the busses had very bad suspension systems that tossed us around like we were breaking on a black stallion.

It was about a mile ride away from the barracks, and we traveled through the frost-covered landscape where there was nothing to see except for this one man from the state of Alaska. You could tell that this specimen hit the gym regularly because he was buff. How did we know this? Because it was seven degrees outdoors, and he wore no coat or shirt. Every day he walked all the way to school like that, with bare skin. Everyone had an opinion about him, anything from he is special to he is crazy. I had the chance to speak with him a few times, and he said that he was uncomfortably, burning hot. My thoughts were that even if I were from Alaska, I still would not walk around like that.

The complex that we drove to be an educational and skill-trade facility where a person could finish high school or leave the Corps with a valuable, money-making occupation. I obtained enough credits to be awarded a GED in three months, so I moved on to learn a trade.

The base's career counselor showed me the kind of money that a welder could bring home every week. *Cool, I will try it,* I thought. And for a month, things were going well; that is, until I had to do vertical, overhead welding. Fire was jumping all over, burning the hell out of me. Every day I tried to pad myself with more and more clothing that made me move around like Frankenstein. How those sparks got inside my thick insulation I'll never know.

One day I called the instructor over to my booth and told him that I'd had enough of being deep fried. To make matters worse, I'd sat my live welding stick behind me, and I forgot that it was there. While I was talking to the instructor, I had my eye shield up, and I pointed something out to the teacher and spun around. My arm knocked over the hot stick, and I looked directly into the blinding white arc.

They covered my eyes with an ice-cold cloth and took me to the infirmary where the doctor dropped all kind of fluids in my eyes and gave me extremely dark glasses to wear. I was nearly blind for a whole solar day. I toiled in disgruntlement limbo for a few weeks because I was not going back to the welding shop, but I still had to leave the housing area until three thirty—that's when the stormy-sea busses brought everyone back from school. If you were caught in the barracks sleeping before that time, you were heavily fined and put on restriction. Plus, you had to do extra duty.

But wait! I noticed that a few corpsmen were going to breakfast late, and some were still sleeping in their bunks. They wore a different color badge. I accidently bumped (wink wink) into a sleeping head, waking him for a few minutes. I asked him, "How do you get to sleep in?" He answered, and I was on my way to the recreation department.

A cheerful and bright young man answered the door of a small but functional office. It had the gray standard office desk, and in front of it were two gray folding chairs for visitors to sit in. Pictures of boxers were plastered all over the walls. In the top center was an old wooden clock with numbers so large that you could see them all the way from downtown Indianapolis. I could never forget his name—Mr. Eddie Griffin. We introduced ourselves. He then gave me the rundown on operations. He walked me around, showing me the different recreation areas and the equipment. I was photographed and given a different color badge. And all I had to do was pass out tryout flyers about the upcoming tournament between the dorms. Easy money, I got to sleep in, life was good.

For two days I ran around the entire campus with my flyers, trying to convince my fellow dorm members to come to the tryouts that started the following Monday. The Sports were soft ball, basketball, boxing, flag football, volleyball, and tossing horseshoes.

It was Friday. I ate a late breakfast and leisurely walked to the dorm's office. Weirdly, the door was open, and Eddie was there emptying the desk draws and removing some pictures from the wall. He then packed all his thing in boxes. *There goes my badge*, I was thinking. *After only two days.*

"What's up, Eddie?' I asked. He was extremely excited as he said that he was leaving. *Well, I can see that*, I thought.

He continued with, "I have been invited to the Golden Gloves finals down in Kentucky. I will be leaving this afternoon."

"Wait, what?" During our first meeting he explained that he was a boxer. "Eddie, who is going to meet with the complex administrators?"

"You are. You are the new athletic director." I was thunderstruck!

The tournaments between the dorms were designed to last a month. It was the eight northern dorms and the eight southern dorms fighting it out between each other. From eight to four to two, then one. It was down to the number one left from the north versus the number one from the south. The conference had to outright win at least four of the six events to be determined the campus champions.

Tryouts Monday. I had never done anything nearly close to being the head of one sport's department, let alone six in one. I did not have a clue what I was doing, and what was worse was that the starting time of each sport was back-to-back. This was a formal military base, and it was huge. The tryouts were held some great distance apart. I started at the volleyball court. I had exactly thirty minutes to get to the baseball tryouts. It was surreal as I reasoned that if I didn't know what the heck I was doing, then I better find some good people that did.

What was surprising was that at every event location, there were enough bodies present that I did not have to forfeit any games. The volleyball players primarily governed themselves. I simply had to choose a leader to meet with. But, during the meetings, they all came. I jogged to the baseball diamond with a golf club bag on my back, filled with bats, gloves, helmets, chalk, and bases. I arrived just slightly ahead of the players. I didn't have a problem managing the sport because even our sisters were great in that. I knew how to play winning baseball. For some reason I was always chosen as the leadoff hitter. And for the record, I all ways managed to get on base. I was no home-run hitter, but I could hit the ball to any alley that I chose. If the pitcher was throwing some serious heat, I bunted just far enough to make it legal. I have always beat the throw to first. Then I Lou Brock-ed it to second. In this lifetime, my on-base percentage is 1,000. No matter the game, I was always called safe at first.

One player stood out from the rest. He was from a rural country area somewhere down in Nebraska. He was a thick white boy, built exactly like the Baltimore Orioles' Boog Powell. He was powerful, chewing tobacco as he was knocking every pitch thrown his way for massive home runs. I pulled him aside and picked his brain with baseball scenarios. He was knowledgeable and spoke with a southern drawl. He passed my interview. I said, "Good, now you are the manager."

Up next, I had to go to the outdoor basketball court located a quarter of a mile away. I jogged at half speed to get there on time. Once there, I had the players go through basic drills:

dribbling, passing, and shooting. I noticed this player that was hustling, stealing the ball away from other players. And what really stood out about him was that he was smaller, perhaps about five feet two inches tall, which is small for a basketball player. He reminded me of a professional basketball player who played for the Atlanta Hawks named Spud Webb. But forget that—when I saw him elevate and his hands just barely touched the basketball rim as the ball swooshed in the net, I knew that I going to pick his brain. He performed and directed the team like he was a little general. After I said, "Good, now you are the coach."

I had no problem with the horseshoe players. They were jiving and talking smack between themselves. It was good for a heated competition. I picked one thrower to lead and told them about the next practice time and let them be. It was getting toward dinnertime, and I was exhausted and needed a break. I still had two more events to cover the next day: flag football and boxing.

When I arrived at the football field, there were a few players there. I oversaw every bit of equipment that was now scattered through the campus. I broke out the footballs and had the players stretch before the tryouts began. Oh no! There was a problem. As I went through drills, many youngsters had the physical abilities, but no player had the fortitude or solid knowledge of football to coach the different units on the teams. I had no brain out of the bunch to pick that time. My solution, even though I was running around ragged, was that there was no better coach than myself to preform both as a player and as a coach. Problem solved.

The boxing field house was located half a mile on the east side of campus. The heavyweight boxing champion George Foreman was a product of Job Corps, and he and the rest of the boxing world constantly reminded the public of this fact. I didn't have any problem recruiting a fighter. The problem was that no one knew how to work the corner. There was no brain to pick for this event, either. They were robotic as if they knew how to give and take a punch but nothing more.

George Foreman had various adolescent kids from all walks of life trying to box. This one boxing trainee had me perplexed. He had a breathing problem in the ring. He would swing a few times, mostly misses, then come to his corner to get a whiff from his inhaler and go back to center ring. I felt sorry for him. The kid had heart, but in an actual fight, you don't get a break to top off with air. My plate was past full, and I was living off fumes. What else could I do? Damn. I reached the only viable option available: I had to make time to manage and train the fighters myself. The month was April of 1970, and the games began the following Saturday afternoon. Outside the weather was sunny, cloudless, mild, and the visible pollen floated loosely in the air. It had those who were allergic sneezing.

The boxing matches started in the evening, and we all had to catch the standard yellow bus to the boxing arena. At the field house, the fights were televised by way of cable, all the way to Naptown. Most of the events started about the same time. I also briefly caught the George Foreman fever and attempted to make a go of the sport a little more than a month later

Indianapolis in the late sixties was tiny and basically still rural. It had only the three major TV stations that were so small that during the week, they went off the air at midnight. That's when you saw a test pattern on the screen. Except for the race car venues, especially the Indianapolis 500, the town had no major sports. The local amateur boxing was filmed from our field house because it was one of the only live sports broadcasted in that area.

I had two amateur fights. The first I easily won. The second made me quit the sport because it was loaded with riffraff. During the very short time that I indulged in the sport, I saw and heard so much about payoff, rigging, and corruption, which I hadn't witnessed since *The Untouchables* went off-air. I had always scouted my next opponent and trained for his style of boxing. While we were entering the ring, I made the mistake of telling him that he was dead meat. On the spot, he chickened out, so they substituted the frightened young man with a bigger, out-of-my-weight class fighter.

In the middle of the third round the crowd erupted as we traded blows. For some unknown reason, in a surreal fashion, frame-by-frame, people moved about so slowly, like a robot who's running out of juice. I looked around at the crowd, then turned my head back to my opponent. Then I thought, *why am I here?* I witnessed other fights being fixed—the fighter down on the mat had his hand lifted as the winner because promoters wanted it that way.

To heck with this, I thought. I walked away. I was disqualified for turning my back.

I got mad because the substitute boxer was two times out of my weight class. And he got a few good licks in only because I had no scouting information on him. I wasn't prepared for his style of fighting. It is very important to know if the fighter was right or left-handed. What was his tendency when he got rocked? Did he grab and hold, or did he duck out of habit? Did he lie on the ropes?

One of the real reasons I stopped was that the rulebook stated that if a fighter is unable to partake in the match, then the opponent wins by forfeit. What I did learn from my two battles under the lights was that the live matches in the ring, those three minutes in the round, felt like an unreachable, grinding thirty minutes. And the old, fixed lights that hung above oven-baked you like a roast. You were also quickly drained from the television and camera lights. I used the little knowledge that I had to train my four fighters: welterweight, lightweight, featherweight, and middleweight.

Every other day I got them up before breakfast to run four miles. The fighters were serious about what they were getting into. They did what was asked of them and never once complained. On the in between days, I had them at the boxing gym, working on repartition and speed, not the heavy bag. I did this to build endurance for the longest three minutes that they would ever know.

The first thing that you notice when entering a boxing gym is the unmistakably musky stench that slams into an unexpecting nose. It is an odor that you won't smell anywhere else other than a poorly ventilated boxing gym. In the gym, I put the boxers in the sweat box for twenty minutes to get them used to the burning hot arena and camera lights. This box had a little round stoop in the center to sit on and had at least fifty hot light bulbs inside. With a white towel wrapped around their necks, their heads stuck out of an opening at the top.

On fight night, the matches were exciting and intense. I found out later that all four of my fighters won their close-call bouts on points. The other fighters were good, but something told me that someone from their camp had scouted mine. I did see their boys hitting the heavy bag and lifting heavy weights. Too much power over time reduced their mobility and agility. As the corner man I made my fighters dance around and stay away from the ropes to make their opponent swing and miss as much as possible. My guys simply wore their counterparts out. When I saw them start dropping their elbows near their waist, I told my fighters that this was it—unload with everything you've got.

The month was May. It was a planned festive day with barbeque. There were water balloon tossing contests, chess matches, and sack-racing games. Souped-up cars were on display and, most importantly, the Job Corp women who were also located in Indiana were invited to the all-male campus to attend the cookout. Many of the big wigs that had anything to do with the Corps' success were there. The Job Corps campus director called for a meeting only in our dorm—number 1010. Most of the kids in our barracks thought that we'd done something wrong. *Why single us out?* they were mumbling and grumbling. I was too because we were missing the barbeque. With many events to attend, I could not be everywhere. Running with my 4 boxer early mornings and flag football practices mainly accounted for most of my time. The administration folks did not want to reveal any of the units' game results until the day of the picnic. I had no idea how the other events made out. We sat in one of the two large bays at each end of the building and waited for the big man.

The director and four other people were introduced, and they took turns talking about the accomplishments and successes of this Job Corps. When it was the big man's turn to speak while still standing in the doorway to the hall, he asked for the athletic director to stand up and come stand where he was.

He gave me a sheet of paper that had the results of all the event between the dorms. He told me to read it out loud. It read, "In the final tally of the volleyball tournament, dorm 1010 finished in first place. In the final tally of the baseball tournament, dorm 1010 finished in first place. In the horseshoe tournament, dorm 1010 finished in first place. In the basketball tournament, dorm 1010 finished in first place. In the boxing tournament, dorm 1010 finished in first place. In the flag football tournament, dorm 1010 finished in first place."

The bay was past full capacity. People were sitting on top of beds, tables, heaters, and every inch of space on the floor. They were stunned, like a graduating high school student who was told to go to the garage and finds a brand-new car there waiting for them. I have never seen that many winners in one place before. Something strange was happening in the air. It was a rainlike mist hovering above everyone in the bay. The color was a light vapor whisper; that looked like white rain it reminded me of electric energy. *What was this thing?* Then I noticed that I was thinking, *Hey! It's coming from this thunderstruck crowed...*

But that wasn't the end. Running down the hallway to the bay were two more corpsmen. They held in their hands a sheet of paper, which they promptly gave to the big guy who read it. Then he gave it to me. Unbeknownst to me because of my hectic schedule, two late, additional events were added to the tournament, and they were bowling and table tennis. I read that we also came in first place in those events as well. Suddenly, every corpsman in the entire bay went into a phenomenal shock. That light rain mist color cloud that hung over everyone turned to a waxing, dark black. It was powerful, and as I was standing next to the complex director, I was thinking, *What in the hell?*

This phenomenal cloud unexpectedly, forcefully, and shoved only me, not the program director who was standing next to me, a foot length into the hallway. The head's belonging to the young men in the bay slowly came down from the clouds. Little by little they started drifting back outdoors to the food, fun, and the bussed in young females from a nearby Job Corps center. My thoughts were *That cloud was there. I saw it.* And I knew that I would forever be haunted by it because I knew that in the back of my mind, I would obsessively attempt to make this head-scratcher of an experience happen again.

KETTERING HIGH TAKE TWO

I first wore a helmet, mouthpiece, and pads for an organized football team in the late summer of 1970. My best friend, Sam Cannon, and I tried out for a spot on the junior varsity football team for Kettering High School in Detroit. There were 120 teenagers who was ran around the field in mid-August's ninety-degree temperatures until their thirsty tongues hung outside of their mouths. Then came seventy-five push-ups for all who were trying out for about fifty slots. Sam quit on cut-down day. I was placed in the middle of a large circle of 120 teenagers to see how many blocks I could endure before I was knocked down. Coach Tucker sent one after another, and it took thirty-seven hits before I was worn down and folded.

We broke off into an offense-against-defensive practice. I was a quarterback/running back, and coach Tucker called a play for a tight end. He turned toward me and asked me what position I played. On this set of downs, I was a running back. He said, "You ain't sh*t. Get off my field. If I call you a tight end, then you better be a tight end".

All that body conditioning that I had obtained by running in the blazing summer's heat before coming to tryouts suddenly went down the drain, and my thoughts simultaneously went down south to Job Corps; When Coach Tucker said that I was an example to the players who did make the cut. A little more than six months passed, and I reached the qualifying time for me to leave Job Corps with my benefits, penalty free. I did get my GED, and I left with some saving bonds and some money in the bank. However, I was still sixteen years old. When I came home, every one of my peers was still going to high school.

I spoke with the high school counselor and music teacher that followed my classmates and me all the way from elementary and junior high school. Because my peers were still in school, I had no one around to hang with, and life seemed to be a boring drag. She suggested that I return to high school and start taking classes to prepare for college.

I took her advice. This time I got real deep into the ROTC. I was the guidon bearer, "the guy in the front of the platoon who carried the flag." I also joined the special drill team. Sam, my best friend, along with spit-and-polish me, made the rank of sergeant in the space of three months. As a member of the special drill team, we were invited to do our thing in parades, schools, and community events. We were sharp with slick in-and-out precession steps that would have had the Motown singing group the Temptations smile with admiration.

Somewhere along the line, I caught the attention of a U.S. Army recruiter who promised me the world and some parts of Brooklyn if I joined. He said that since I already had my GED, if I took the entrance examination and scored good, I could finish college and name my own career in the service. I was only seventeen and a starter on the junior varsity football team. The recruiter said, "You can sign up now with the buddy plan. Then you and your best friend can go into the service together, after the football season."

Sam's father fought in the Korean War. He did not want any part of the Vietnam conflict. My thing was that death will find you no matter where you try to hide. If it's your time, there is nothing you can do to prevent it. I signed up for the delayed entry program and did not have to report for duty until the following year of January 1972.

After graduating from Job Corps, I tried out for the junior varsity football team again. That time, before coming, I read and studied every football book in the library for hours and days. Since I was fifteen years old, every year I bought the latest edition of *Street and Smith's Football* magazine, which was very masterful in instructing on basic formations and how to play in every football position. I could have gotten a cot, moved into any library, and read my life away. I was always an autodidact on any subject that I wanted to know.

There I was again on the sparse grass playing field located on the street of Van Dyke and Georgia. And, purely by chance, once more I was the only one sent to the middle of the circle of 120 hopefuls. That time around I knew how to play every football position, and it took fifty-six of coach Tucker's hitman attempts before my legs gave way. I ran two kickoffs back-to-back for scores. I made the final cut and was promoted to the starting position of running back. We played in a late afternoon football game on a Thursday. The quarterback started because he was the son of the coach's fraternity member and fellow schoolteacher. He was a glory grabber, something that I never cared about. He wanted to look good in front of the girls. He wasn't that good of a passer.

It was the second quarter, and he dropped back to pass. The play called for pass protection, and as the running back, I had to watch out for the blitzing linebacker. And he came flying toward the line of scrimmage. I engaged him. I also saw the defensive end riding on his right shoulder. I pushed the linebacker into the defensive end and cut them both down. I was thinking, "This should give the quarterback plenty of time to look downfield."

I looked back as the two defensives linemen, and I hit the deck. Instead of stepping up into a perfect pocket, he took off running for no reason. He tripped over his own two feet and fumbled and lost the ball to the other team. The coaches are in an uproar as we come to the sideline. Well, I'll be darned—the coach blames me for the quarterback's fumble. Coach Tucker takes off his belt and starts whipping me across the rear end. The stadium was packed with spectators and my mother, who was also in attendance. I was so embarrassed in front of all these people that I wished I was on the other side of the planet. In that very moment, my career thoughts and plans turned to the U.S. Army.

THE AWAKENING

Mr. Hunt, the assistant coach, tried to talk me out of leaving the team. He stated that coach Tucker only did that to people that he cared, about, that it was his way of showing love. I still turned in my borrowed shoulder pads because I didn't need that kind of love.

In January 1972, there wasn't snow covering the scenery, but there was ice, so much of it that when you stepped outside, the floating, cold mist looked like you had just opened the door and walked into a deep freezer. The recruiter pulled up in an olive-green military Sedan.

He was clothed in his decorated green, drab dress uniform as he exited the vehicle and walked up the steps where my mother and I were standing. Then she handed me my suitcase and kissed me good-bye.

The staff sergeant drove me to the bus station where I caught the morning Greyhound bus heading southeast to Louisville, Kentucky. Once the bus arrived at the station in downtown Louisville, about a half hour later, a green-painted school bus picked up the many deerlike, staring eyes belonging to the mostly eighteen-year-old men who'd never been away from home and were wondering how in the heck they got themselves into this.

As we drove past the United States Bullion Depository, location of Fort Knox it appeared calm and pleasant to look at. The open, green, neatly trimmed landscape appeared to be easy to access. But that was hardly the case. My impression of the base was that it looked exactly like it did in the James Bond movie *Goldfinger*. We arrived at the reception center, disembarked from the bus, and were promptly indoctrinated by a yelling, foaming-at-the-mouth drill sergeant who was skilled in the art of brainwashing and character assassination. I thought that I saw tears in the eyes of the recruits during the hair-cutting phase. The ones who wore their hair long had watery eyes as they watched their locks hit the barber's floor.

Once I joined, I would have automatically been given a strip because of my time in ROTC, and I would have to functioned in a leadership role. But I declined to tell them of this because it would be like the blind leading the blind. I did not know what in the hell I was doing either. I learned more actual military procedures by observing for a while and getting my feet wet. Somehow, I still wound-up marching in front of the platoon, carrying the flag.

They shocked us greenhorns awake, banging on the top of a garbage can very loudly at 3:30 a.m., telling us to fall outside and get into formation, only to talk about nothing important. That was one of the first tests of our character. Yelling and screaming at 4:30 a.m. to jog four miles was just as nerve racking. I was still in football shape, so the running didn't bother me. Marching up the fearsome Agony and Misery hills didn't bother me. The zinging sound of live bullets passing over your head during the low-crawling drill in wet, gooey mud didn't bother me, and removing our gas masks in the tear-gas chamber didn't bother me either. I had thick snot floating like a river out of my nose, but the rest of the soldiers were totally discombobulated, pulling on and falling over each other. Trying to find the backdoor to get out of there was purely comical. I made it worse for myself and couldn't get out because I was holding my belly and laughing so hard. However, not eating breakfast before starting all that insane break-the-man-down-then-build-them-back-up indoctrination truly was getting on my last nerve.

In February of 1972, it the third week of basic training, and the taskmasters were beginning to tone down their brainwashing and reconditioning just a little. That weekend we were allowed to bring back one civilian clothing outfit. On day one, we had to strip down and send all our outerwear back home in boxes. There was nothing but military items stored in our lockers.

That week we were also allowed to have some form of music, a small radio or what have you. I chose a cassette player. I had brought a few cassettes from the Post Exchange to satisfy the aesthetic part of my soul. I basically played only one special tape that I liked over and over throughout basic training. It was Marvin Gaye's "What's Going On." It seemed to answer a lot of questions about the happenings back home, and the events that surrounded the base. We were still not allowed to leave the base unless we attended church services. Still, that was better than looking at troops marching and earth-shaking tanks roaming around.

Night fell at 5:30 p.m., and those who decided to go to the service boarded the green bus. From a window seat I stared out to scope downtown Louisville, which didn't look like a big city. The town still looked like the outskirts of a farm county. I was mainly looking for anything with my idol, boxer icon, Muhammad Ali's name on it. I didn't see anything. We pulled up to a small house which had a steeple on top. We disembarked and headed inside. There was nothing out of the norm during the service, nothing that I didn't experience in Sunday school back home.

On Sundays my father and mother gave the children, perhaps, two dollars and fifty cents, enough to cover our expenses for bible study and regular church service where we had to put only twenty-five cents in the basket. And finally, we had enough to get popcorn and candy while attending the various movie theaters scattered throughout the city. We kids knew that our parents sent us away on Sundays so that they could have the house to themselves, at least one day of the week. Back then, the movies were double features.

Back in midtown Louisville, we had reached the part in the services where we were invited to come to the alter to pray. This was nothing that I hadn't done before hundreds of times. Three of us slowly walked to the alter, kneeled, and prayed. I was only a few minutes into my prayers when I sprung to my feet because I felt like I was being electrocuted. The jolt was extremely powerful. I had been shocked so many times by 120 volts working on TVs and radios that it tickled me and didn't even bother me.

This was different. It felt like I had stuck my finger into a 440-volt outlet. I was dizzy, the Church was spinning, and it turned dark. I felt like I was passing out as I stood there watching the other two still down on their knees, praying. This was a whopper; I was staggering as I tried to look cool, walking back to my seat. After the benediction, we wandered around socializing while drinking coffee and eating doughnuts.

My thoughts were deep about that unusual, mystical experience. As we rode home on the bus, I spoke to no one as I tried to figure out why all these strange occurrences were happening to me after I picked up that mirror in the alley. The muster call at 5:00 a.m. to run broke me out of my line of thought.

Tension was thick throughout the whole military machine. On one side, as the causality list grew, so did the fed upped public who hated the unpopular war. And on the other side of the isle was the way the Vietnam conflict was haphazardly fought. There were a lot of frowning faces in between the ranks. Many thought that they were fighting with their hands tied behind their backs. Training companies Alpha, Charley, Delta, and our company, Bravo, were summoned to the parade field where we were surprised to find out that the USO Troupe was there to entertain and break the icy tension.

There were big bands playing the latest top ten tunes. Singers, comedians, and the glamorous 1972 Miss Black Kansas had most all the soldiers forgetting about everything. We didn't have Bob Hope, but we had a great time. When the show was over, I caught up with Miss Black Kansas whom I spoke with for a few minutes and got her to sign her name on her three-by-five photo. She told me that she was still in college and was preparing to enter the Miss USA Pageant. Yes, that was a great day.

The yelling at 4:30 a.m. the following day once more shocked us out of our sleep. We were told to fall in formation with all our TA-50 gear—that meant our tents, sleeping bags, rations to eat, gas masks, gun belts, first aid kits, and extra underwear. And, of course, our weapons, cigarettes, and, most important, no one forgot their P-38—can opener.

The drill sergeant inspected our gear and told us to put our steel pots on our heads and everything else on our backs. We were going on a three-day camping excursion called bivouac. This is where those fearsome hills named Agony and Misery came into the picture. As we marched up the very steep hills during the six-mile night walks, it was make-it-or-break-it time for a few big guys who could not make it up the hills with full gear on. They were given a ride in the trailing safety vehicle back to base and discharged from the service. We were involved in fire fights, which, to me, was a thing of beauty because of the tracers lighting up black nights on its deadly trajectory. Then we had to run the obstacle course and crawl on the ground in full gear. I marched in front, carrying the unit flag as the guidon bearer throughout basic training. After we took the evening meal break, the company then had to choose one person as the point man.

This position is very important because you are primarily the advance scout and the first person to walk into dangerous situations where you might get shot, gassed, or blown up. You had better be mindful, listening to the sounds in the environment and paying attention to the broken branches that sometimes indicate the directions of human and animal movements. This person had to be especially well-versed in different kinds of paw prints to be able to determine if a mountain lion, fox, deer, or wild boar was in the area. Then they had to quickly alert those who trailed behind them of the dangers.

A stirred-up group of critters usually meant something didn't belong or someone was in the area and/or was approaching. The point man was responsible for stopping the entire company from walking into imminent danger like mine fields, inventive traps, and ambushes. I'd heard many times of a point man warning their trailing platoon brothers of danger the hard way, by accidently stepping into a bamboo trap or a land mine. Somehow, I knew that I would be chosen as the point man!

There was another school of thought concerning leading the way. I had always studied wars that reached back as far as the beginning of mankind, when, for example, a couple of cavemen threw rocks at each other, fighting over the girl who lived in the four-family rock flat near the base of an active volcano. And later in history, there was Helen of Troy.

I will read anything in print concerning military strategy and tactics from ancient times. In any cases, and in mostly all ambushes, the enemy left the point man alone. The reason being that if you shoot the point man first, the rest of the troops had a chance to run for cover. Should you let the fourth and fifth wave of troops pass, it created a log jam where they could not turn back or run for cover, and the approaching troops had no choice but to assist their comrades in trouble. So, what the heck? I was in front carrying the unit flag.

On the first night of bivouac, the weather wasn't bad for winter. The wind behaved, and it wasn't freezing cold. It may have been, but with all that equipment on your back, who could tell the difference? It was pitch black, the sky was totally covered in clouds, and the moon and stars took the day off. That, in turn, resulted in poor visibility for us. We could barely see as we silently walked along in the muddy side of the road trench. We made good use of the reflective light from the passing vehicles that were awfully noisy, rumbling on the tank trails.

Because we were told in advance to expect to be caught in an ambush during this part of the maneuver, the anticipation had our adrenalin pumping blood strenuously throughout our veins, so much so that our audible heart beats sounded like the slow pounding of a drum. As the night deepened and the stars had yet to shine, we stealthily moved forward on the tank trail.

Over time I learned that there were way too many realities that lie beyond our senses. After the visit to the church in Louisville, if my world wasn't strange enough already, I started becoming sensitive to unseen feelings like gravity emitting from people, feelings like gluttony, deception, pride, greed, selfishness, lust, and envy. I could not see them, but the feelings grew stronger as time passed. There were two specific emotions that tingled in me like the bells of a five-alarm fire. I became super perceptive of danger and evil.

Back on the side of the tank trail, we stopped for a hearty c-ration dinner, where we all learned that the steel pot, we wore on our heads had many uses. One of them was that you could use it to bowl water for bathing and shaving. In the daylight, we had classes in the field. At night we moved out on patrol. An hour into our patrol, I suddenly started having that tingling sensation.

The more we walked, the more severe the tingling became, and it bothered me so much that I raised the company's flag higher in the air to signal that we needed to stop our movement. I just happened to look down at the out-of-place foliage that was an eighth of an inch from my boot's shoelaces. I took out my red lens flashlight, and lo and behold, it wasn't grass at all but a fish line that was all but invisible on the trail.

I signaled for the drill sergeant to look. We discovered that it was a ten-foot fish line alright; however, on both ends were two grenades tied to a tree. If whole the platoon was sluggish after dinner, they were wide awake now. One more step and we would have been blasted to pieces. About forty-five minutes later, we approached a barren, open field that looked harmless. I was still a little paranoid because of the fish wire, but I was still in front leading. I told myself to calm down and pay attention to the environment.

I started having those tingling sensations again. I could not afford to second guess myself because it could get us all killed. I noticed that the field was smooth and flat. There were no tire or tank marks. That was very strange for an active, heavily traveled vehicle area. Once more I stopped the platoon and summoned the drill sergeant. He asked, "What is it?" I said, "I am not sure." I removed my bayonet from its sleeve and softly poked around the dirt. I received an A in demolition and bomb-diffusion classes. Claymore and land mines were easy for me. I may have been half-asleep in other not as pertinent field lessons but, learning how not to get blown up kept me wide awake.

Eureka. I very carefully remove the dirt that surrounded a land mine. Phew! I removed the fuse and looked around with the sergeant, only to find that the field was loaded. We detoured around the field and headed toward a tree line, but the tingling didn't stop or subside. My body was still on high alert. The evening clouds had started to dissipate, and a full moon was illuminating our paths. The light was good enough that we could walk with force, instead of gingerly tiptoeing away from the mines.

There were two more skills that the platoon leader must have: One was the ability to know which direction to walk in, in the dark, by looking up and finding Polaris, the North Star. You do not always have the luxury of having a compass or map. Another crucial skill for a point man was to be able to look at the position of the sun in order to tell the correct time and have a reference point for when you had to get to a location at a specific time. One did not have the minutes to stop and take off layers of gear to keep looking at a wristwatch.

As I first entered the tree line, the buzzing inside of me grew as loud as an air raid's bombing siren. I noticed that it was too quiet. Since I was a child, I have roamed through the woods, day and night. What was missing in that moment was the sound that the nocturnal animals make when their land is being invaded by strangers. They tell on us by signaling to each other. Still ahead of everyone, I saw a small, green metal-ammunition container on the ground, leaning on a tree. It looked like maps, important papers, and dollar bills were hanging out of it, giving it the appearance of someone having just fled the area.

I raised the company's flag, signaling us to stop. The drill sergeant approached. I pointed to the metal box while I explained my theory about the absence of sounds from the night animals. I said, "If it's too good to be true, then, sir, I believe that it's a trap." I'd never seen the sergeant smile before, but when he looked at me, he had a wide grin that was perfect for a toothpaste commercial. I knew then that I had just saved the platoon from impending disaster.

The exuberant sergeant blew a whistle, and all kinds of lights came on. The men were camouflaged so well that had the moon not appeared, there would have been no way to prevent the bush whacking. The colors they had on blended in perfectly with the foliage, grass, and trees. We all became happy when they told us that we had the rest of the night off. Plus, we didn't have to walk anymore. Agony and Misery didn't just affect the worn-out fat boys. We caught a much need break because the top dog (the sergeant major) allowed us to make camp right there, on the spot.

After attending the basic training graduation ceremony eight weeks later, we were given our next assignments. True to the military's motto which says, "Yours is not to reason why, yours is but to do or die," You were sent where you were needed. Forgetting about what fantastic location where you were told you may go to at the recruiter station. For my Advance Individual Training (AIT) occupation, I was supposed to be training to repair transmitters and other communications devices. What's more, the training was supposed to take place at a paradise location I picked, like California or somewhere in the Pacific Islands. Looking conflicted with wide eyes, I tried to figure out why in the heck I got orders to show up in the Arizona desert?

In April of 1972 I showed up at the doorsteps of Fort Huachuca, located in southeastern Arizona. My orders assigned me to the Intelligence Electronic Warfare division as a radar operator—17K20. I got a real kick of that place because it was the base for the Buffalo Soldiers 10th Cavalry Regiment and was also home of the great Indian chief Cochise, who seemed to be the leathery, tough rascal in all the old Western cowboys versus Indians movies.

Besides the extremely hot temperatures, that place was hugely different from the rigorous training instilled at Fort Knox. We leisurely strolled to breakfast where we had more choices for grub. Even better, we had to get to classes on time on our own, no marching in a group. We were taught to calibrate and operate various kind of radars: land, sea, and air. We trained in difficult scenarios so we would know when it was time to call in heavy artillery and when it was necessary to reach out to all the other branches of services.

I specifically memorized how to communicate with the Air Force when we were in trouble. If I were to get into a stressful situation, I wanted my equalizer to get to us on the double. Teaching the class about the radar's hardware was the basic core of my occupation.

Because we would be worked less than a few meters from the communist borders, we were drilled on what to do and how to act while carrying out our duties whenever we were captured. We learned about the Geneva Conventions, specifically how to locate the American Embassy in the event we were caught and put on ice. Other than passing the lectures regarding the how-to function in foreign countries as a United States ambassador with flying colors, I began traveling to Nogales, Mexico, regularly for vocational relaxation and recreation.

In May, after graduation, all the troops stood in a long line to receive our destination orders. One by one the soldiers ahead of me were sent to Vietnam. In the line, I was only two bodies before the dispatcher started calling out that duty stations would be in Germany. After a two-week vacation home, I was to report to a combat support company in the 3rd Armored Division in Erlangen.

Once I arrived home, the very next day I had to take my sister, who is two years younger than I am, to court in St. Clair Shores, Michigan. Her name is Rachel. She was the black sheep of the family. At thirteen she was hanging out with the hoodlums in the neighborhood, smoking, drinking, and writing bad checks. She is the reason I learned the word and meaning of incorrigible. She went missing from home for three days. When she finally did show up, after both extremely worried parents had called all the hospitals and jails, she received an old-fashioned whipping, the kind that would make me never do that again. However, later on that very same night, my mother asked me to check on her, and she was not in her bed. She had climbed out of her bedroom window and was gone.

In any event, she'd had a few drinks before I took her to court. She said, "If I go to jail, I am going drunk." And so, we went. We arrived and took our seats. I heard cases of crooks who had really started being stupid and getting caught on cameras that they knew were there. Then it was my sister's turn to face the judge. The prosecuting attorney had her client stand up. The judge repeatedly started clearing her throat, as if breakfast was lodged in it, as she read out the charges.

She lowered her head and hid behind the folder. I noticed that she was acting strange and giggling. I thought, *What kind of judge acts like this?* She lifted her head and continued to clear her throat of something. She tried to get it together, but she couldn't, and she let loose a hearty laugh. The words "what the hell" entered my mind. *Why was she laughing?* The judge had a hard time reading the charges in between trying keep it together. I finally looked at the person who pressed charges against my sister.

He stood about six feet five and weighed about two-hundred-and-forty pounds. I looked harder at him, and he had a black eye with a big cheery-red knot in the center of his forehead with grotesque bumps on the other side of his face. I just happened to look at my fifteen-year-old little sister who stood about five feet and a harmless one-hundred-and-ten pounds. However, she beat the heck out of the security guard because he tried to detain her for writing bad checks.

The judge held it together long enough to dismiss the charges against my sister. They simply didn't want a Black girl in their St. Clair Shores jail. But what was really unusual, and a change of pace was that she reprimanded the security guard. She warned him to not ever tell anyone about this, about getting beat up by a little girl. As we traveled home, I was amazed because she was lucky. The court would have shackled me and given me chain gang detail for the same thing. My sister was a handful most of her young life.

EL GATO

Our next-door neighbor named Miss Steven was a voluptuous freckle-faced redbone who hailed from Louisiana. She birthed nine beautiful different shades of daughters. She was familiar with the practice of Voodoo. It was in the wee hours of a Sunday morning when she approached me because of a critical situation that developed. Her car had been stolen. The car was ahead of its time. It was a '60 Chevrolet in mint condition. What stood out about this vehicle was that she put fancy chrome mags rims on all four axes. The grill was chrome as were the engine's air filter and carburetor. The body had chrome trimming all around.

Back in this era, teenage car thieves would borrow the vehicle for the night or until the gas ran out, and they would leave the ride where it stopped moving. They had swiped it Friday night, and because of its appeal, they had no intention of giving it back to the owner. She and a female member of her family found the parked car on that Sunday about twenty blocks from her home, in front of a house overseen by six hoodlums. She had other sons-in-law, but she asked me to go with her to retrieve it.

I asked her to park on the street, away from the six mean-mugging teen-agers that stared at us. She gave me the spare keys to the prized Chevrolet. As I walked to the vehicle, all the while looking directly at the car thieves, those young men scattered on different sides of the porch. I wanted to see what their reaction was going to be when they were relieved of the stolen ride. I was thinking that I was going to knock some religion into the very first person who jumped off the porch, started the car, and fled the scene. They seemed frozen, stunned as though they thought that either I was crazy because it was six against one or I was packing a gun. I uneventfully drove the car back to Miss Steven's house as she followed in the other car. After that day, I was always invited into her home, and she continued to try and fix me up with one of her daughters. I didn't date close to home. I always needed a hiding place to take a break from romance.

She had four felines that, one by one, started making their way over to our house to hang out with my three brothers along with me. My sisters and my father's lived in lady friend did not like them around. The first cat that visited we named Tiger because of the striped fur he had on his body. He tore the top part of the screen door so he could enter our house when he wished. All the females that lived in the house protested his visiting and demanded that my father fix the screen door. He did, but Tiger undid the repair work the very next day. Four times my father repaired the screen, and four more times Tiger ripped it apart so much so that my father gave up and didn't fix the screen anymore.

The cats never wanted food or any special treatment; they just loved hanging out with us sharply dressed, wine-drinking brothers. They walked around like they owned the place. I watched them for months, jumping off furniture and tables without looking. It occurred to me that they processed total spatial recall because there was no way they could blindly jump from one different height and distance to another unless they knew exactly how far away and where their landing point was in their minds.

In any event, I don't remember when, but I started acting like them. I could jump over a five-foot fence without coiling or springing. When I ran with the ball, I just changed direction for absolutely no reason whatsoever, but it would be the right time to shift. If humans had a cat alias, then I would be called a cheetah because I could run long distances very fast without tiring. Anyone could point to a building or object in the distant horizon and say "Lamarr, run to that spot," which could be six or ten miles away. Back then I could run all the way there without stopping. For most of my life I had to run at least three-and-a-half miles before my carburetor would open, and I caught my first wind.

In a hundred-and-twenty-yard run, from zero to forty yards, it took 1.1 seconds for me to cover every ten yards. For the next forty yards, it took me 1 second to cover every ten yards. For the last forty yards, I always joked that my warp speed engines kicked in because from that point on it was around .9 seconds for me to cover every ten yards.

On the playing field, I hit like a leopard. In the early eighties, I watched a movie called *Gallipoli* with Mel Gibson. In the beginning scenes, there is this runner being coached by a wise old fox.

He asks the runner, "What are those?" As the runner pumps his legs up and down at the starting line.

The runner answers, "They are steel springs."

The coach then asks him, "What are they going to do?"

He answers, "They are going to hurl me down the track."

The next question that the coach asked him was, "How fast are you going to run?"

The runner says, "As fast as a leopard."

"How fast?" he asks once more.

Again, he answers, "As fast as a leopard."

"Then let me see you do it." And the runner jets down the track.

At the end of every six-mile run, I went through this scenario in my head or every time I started at the two-hundred-and-twenty mark on the field. When I reached the one-hundred-and-twenty-yards mark, I'd say, "Let me see you do it," and then I'd take off like a leopard. That was one of the best motivations and reasons why I had a lot of great hundred-meter timings.

The strangest mimicking of all that I inherited from the cats was that one day, before the semipro football season started, I jumped up and grabbed ahold of the cross bar of the team's football goal post and looked at the playing field while sitting on the bar. I rested one of my shoulders upright to study myself. I was one of those ballplayers who hung around the playing field when there was no one was around. I found out that if I hung upside down with the back of my knees on the cross bar, it was really relaxing. I could meditate and still could look at the field. I did this for twenty-two years until I had retired from organized football. And no one ever knew that I did this.

THE RINGER'S GAME

On Saturdays those players who played football in their Sunday best played a football game, sometimes two, on the far side of the city. We kept beating the Grosse Pointe football players on their own trimmed, nice, immaculate playing field. What no other team was aware of was the fact that we felt every football field was our field. It was always a home game to us. When we got to their fields, someone on our team would say, "Did anyone pay the rent for the field?" We always answered, "Paid them yesterday."

My younger brother's best friend, Kelvin, strangely kept coming over to our apartment for a month, asking us, "Are we still going to play in the upcoming game that we all have planned?" We would play football in the dark on rocks. Those well-to-do Grosse Pointe's kids got tired of losing to us. When game day arrived, we were shocked by the types of expensive trucks and cars pulling up at the beautiful playing field. My eyes got wide when so many professional, football-sized lineman disembarked from their trucks. We had only three legitimate linemen available on this day. Later we found out that they were ex–Michigan State University football players. The quarterback, the brutish 245-pound running back, and the speedy pass catchers all were on the roster of the powerhouse Lansing semipro football team. We were set up.

The playing field was located behind a high school in the city of Grosse Pointe, Michigan. The season was fall. The temperature was around sixty-two degrees with a slight breeze and a blue sky that was sparsely clouded— perfect weather for football. We were all astonished because of their size as the opposite team dismounted from their vehicles. My younger brother's friend, Kevin, had set us up good.

Out of all the three hundred games that I played in my life, this was the most memorable, thrilling, and the catalyst in the ways that I evolved in my playing style and how I viewed the game of football. This game completely altered the way I played football from then on. We were out gunned, out-matched, and overwhelmed in every head-to-head squad. On our side of the field was a feeling of destruction, as if three touchdowns were posted on the home team side of the score board even before we had played the game.

They won the coin toss and decided to receive. They started the game with the 245-pound tailback gaining fifteen yards on a dive play, something that had never happened to us. They gashed us three times on this play, which we were unable to stop. The quarterback completed a thirty-yard pass on the left corner of the end zone to start the scoring. Our cornerbacks had never been beaten with this kind of speed. They continued to score by running tailback power plays and sweeps. I had never seen any of my teammate's whiff on their tackling. They looked so discombobulated, like this was a slow-motion, surreal dream. But it much closer to a nightmare.

The score was thirty-five to seven at half time. Not only was this score rare, but other teams hardly ever reached thirty-five points on us this early in any game. We had our water break, and I got mad. I was upset with my teammates because this was not the way we played. Even in those tough, defensive, low-scoring games that we previously played in; we always collectively kept our composure. I was never the exhilarating cheer leader type of character. The people who worked with or for me always saw a calm, easygoing type of person, when productions were going right. However, mess up with me, and folks just did not believe that I could change into a mean, haven't-eaten-for-three-days bulldog.

I did not yell at my teammates; instead, I spoke strongly and forcefully. I said that I didn't know what in the hell was going on. But I told them that "this sh*t had better stop. And it better stop right now." This was a rare, unexpected tongue lashing from me that caught them totally off guard. It woke them up.

We discussed the numerous problems we had in our coverage and our glaring holes in our run defense. We decided to do something that we had never done before: we went to a zone defense where a player stayed in his area during coverage. I went back to quarterback because when I played in any other position on the field, I didn't need to think much about how others handled their parts. But when my hands were under center, I changed into a chess master, positioning all the pieces on the playing field. My chess skills are way above average, so much so that I rarely lose. I once beat a computer in a game, and the computer turned off, rather than declare it was a checkmate.

Together we decided that we would take what they gave us, and from that very day, we had chosen "take what they give us," as a motto. However, I was still furious that we were set up, and I took our new motto even farther. I said, "To hell with that. Taking what they give us is for losers. We are going to take what we want." Half time was almost over, so I had the team stretch. As quarterback, I figured that since we were losing anyway, we were going to abandon our normal game plan and put a hurt on them. We were going to hit them so hard, like those old, hard-hitting Detroit Lions versus Pittsburgh Steelers games, knocking people out of the game back-to-back. And we did. At my disposal, at running back, I had the equivalent of NFL superstars Marshall Faulk, Dave Meggett, Tony Dorsett, and Earl Campbell. If I wanted to beat up on the other team, I unleashed the hounds.

Our running back got the ball down to their twenty-yard line, and while the other team was still catching their breath and expecting another run, I called a post-corner pattern to begin on the first sound. If anyone who loves the game of football ever wanted to see a beautiful end zone pass, I had one in my arsenal, —it had an arch that dropped straight down, just outside the outer bound lines, where only the receiver could catch the ball and pull it inside for a touchdown. It had absolutely no chance of being intercepted. We scored.

They received the kickoff but got only to the twelve-yard line as the returner was hit hard and gang tackled by four players. They were not fazed, and on the first play, they went back to the tailback dive like at the start of the game, only this time four of us hit him. After the break I told my teammates to forget about the other players and just keep hitting the running back. He didn't even get back close to the line of scrimmage.

They tried a fake dive on the next play. The running back didn't have the ball, but three players hit him as he entered the line of scrimmage. He started complaining that he was getting hit even though he did have the ball. The quarterback backpedaled for a five-step drop-back pass. I stayed at a rover position even though we were in a zone defense. I was on him before he could lift his arm, and I dropped him to the ground.

This was not unusual, but to my surprise, as I got up, I was more than happy to see that one of my teammates also tackled and had a hold of him on the ground from the other side. They were now backed up to their own five-yard line. Kelvin's team went back to the tailback dive, and he got hit so hard in the back field that he fumbled the ball in the end zone. My guys fell on the ball. The score now was thirty-five to twenty-one. They received the kickoff and made a reasonable gain to the twenty-yard line. Our opponents decided to try their passing game, and on the first play, the quarterback rolled away from to the right hash mark and got the pass off. On our way to the passer, we continued to hit the running back as we rushed past, and he started crying, saying that he was not supposed to be hit that many times.

I didn't think that it was possible, but we somehow turned up the heat on our hitting. On one tackle, I felt the ground shake. My guys were hitting them so hard that they were causing seismic disturbances. Spectators heard the popping sounds of human bones slapping together as we were determined to make sure that even if we lost, they would never want to play us again. They were unaware that we went into a zone defense, and I assigned an extra rover to their very fast receiver.

When the ball reached his hand, he was hit synchronously high and low by two men. His head went east, his feet went west, and the ball bounced off his hand into the hand of a trailing player who ran it all the way back for a touchdown. The score now was thirty-five to twenty-eight. On the very next series, their quarterback was leveled by a wicked hit, and he also fumbled the ball, which we recovered.

I saw that they were tired. Some players were on their knees, and others had their hands on their hips. I mainly used my punishing runner, Earl Campbell likeness on the drive. When we reached their 25-yard line, I called for a strong side power, and he easily shook off the worn-out tackler like a bowling pin on his way to the end zone.

My teammate's names were Michael Clark, Brothers Derek, Robert Courtney, Jason Lewis, Pig, Corby Dee Thompson, and my brothers Zachary and Clifford McClain. There were three other regulars whose names escape me, but their contributions were memorable.

The score tied at thirty-five. It was suddenly a brand-new ball game. The other team that was once puffing out their chests as they initially put on a display of dominance and power was now engulfed in desperation, seeking ways to cope with the adversity that resulted from the recoil of switched momentum.

We played well into the later hours, and because of the desperation and gloom the ballplayers would have faced going back to Lansing area having lost to a smaller, underdog team, the game turned into a slug fest. They started hitting just as hard as we did. Both teams decided that the last team to score would win the game. At that point, nothing came easy. Kelvin's team starting blitzing on every play. At first, they sent one extra man after me, the quarterback. Then it was two.

Near the end of the game, they had totally sold out, besides leaving the two corners to cover the wide receivers. They sent nine players that hovered around the line of scrimmage to deck me. Blitzing linebackers never rattled me. My guys easily recognized that defensive strategy. On cue they knew how to sit in the just-vacated area, and we'd burn them every time on that play. Since junior varsity way back in high school, I would simply call a screen pass to the running back. I used misdirection plays to slow down versus pursing defensive players on time, as if I were reading their minds. And they both worked. But in this game, they really threw the pots and pans at me, so I didn't have the time.

Still under sunny skies and no breeze, we won the coin toss and decided to receive our version of a kickoff. A deep pass was the kickoff. Our returner gained decent yardage to about the thirty-five-yard line. Now moving the ball became rough. In the game you had to have two completions or move the ball ten yards to gain a first down. They stopped us on three downs, and we had to go for it on fourth and ten, which was out of the ordinary.

Because this was the first time in the extra quarter that they were even able to halt our drives, their team and the spectators on their sideline were fired up.

While at the shot gun position, I motioned for the running back to widen his gap, close to the left hash mark. On the second hut, the other team roared through the line of scrimmage like it had Swiss cheese holes. I pitched the ball back to the running back who took two steps as if he was going to run a sweep. I paused and acted like I was out of the play, and as the hungry wolfs rushed past, me I took off. I ran a three step inside arrow pattern across the line of scrimmage as the runner delivered a perfect pass back to me. I didn't know that the visiting team coaches had a linebacker shadowing me. As I turned to run, he was right in my face with his arms stretched out to tackle me for a minimum gain well short of the first-down marker. In midair, waist high, I motored to the left side of the linebacker, then to the right side, and then back to the left side of his waist, which spun him completely around, three-hundred-and-sixty degrees. And I saw nothing but space.

Nevertheless, the panicking linebacker gave his all and made a shoestring tackle after I gained seven yards. I stumbled going down for two yards and pushed off with my legs an inch before I touched the grass and landed right at the first-down marker. There was no touchdown, but we kept the ball alive for another series. I don't know how I did that left-right-left thing in midair, and I never did it again. I attributed that shiftiness to hanging out with Miss Steven's cats.

Every play and every movement on the field was heavily contested as we neared their goal line. My teammates and I were totally spent and exhausted as we pushed onward to their ten-yard line where for three downs, we ran into a brick wall. We had to go for it on fourth down again because it was for all the marbles. The tension and nervousness on both sides of the field felt like an ocean swell. I had my tight end run a ten-yard square in at the goal line while on the first sound I rolled left. I was hit hard as I put a tremendous amount of heat on the pass that drilled into the belly of the tight end. The ball arrived so hard at the receiver that he had a choice to "catch it or have the air knocked out of you."

Their whole sideline erupted with relief as one of my newcomers took a serious blow in the back and dropped the ball for an incomplete. They had dodged a proverbial bullet. For the very first time since the well dress guys playing football ball on Easter collectively played together, we turned the ball over on downs. The hitting had worn us out to the point where they started moving the ball again, mixing up their runs and passing. They got the ball to midfield and pulled a fast one over me. Instead of using their fastest receiver up the field, they dragged him seven yards across the field, knowing full well that I would follow him. They sent their flanker up the field behind me, who caught the tired backs off guard. The receiver caught the ball and was off and running.

Oh no! The defensive back was losing that race as I saw the runner gain more and more separation from the back who was in between me and the receiver. I dropped my coverage and was directly behind my teammate. I could not reach the speedy runner through him. Once again, I thought about the cats. But that time I was thinking of a TV commercial of a black leopard soaring in the air, leaping toward the back of his frightened dinner.

This was one of the finest tackles that I executed in my lifetime. I soared over the head of my five-feet-nine teammate and wrapped my arms around the head and neck area of the breaking away receiver. He went down at our twenty-five-yard line. Their crowed went silent. Our side let out a sign of relief. They still had a fresh set of downs to work with, and we had hope. Winning was contagious for us. It buoyed us for the daunting challenges that we encountered. There was something inside of us that said we would find a way to pull it off. As time slipped away, our pride kept their running game to little or no yards, so they had to go for it on the fourth down.

That was it: the scenario that every ballplayer dreamed of being in. The make-it-or-break-it occasions for a hero to step up in the game. Our focus and understanding of the moment were sharp. No one could make any mistakes on the line or in coverage. We didn't, but they did. Their mistake was fatal. They went back to that play where they had the fastest receiver run a shallow route, and they once again knew that I would follow him. My stepbrother, Corby Dee, was a bona fide NFL first-round draft choice. He excelled in every sport or activity that required dexterity. Anyone who went against him had better bring their A game. Corby had great speed and football instincts. He always seemed to make the difficult look easy as the visitors found out. Their coach had two backs and the tight end in the back field for maximum pass protection. They ran the flanker once again behind me as the quarterback hit the ground but got the pass off. However, this time Corby Dee did not bite. As usual, he got his second interception of the game, and as usual, he ran it all the way back for a pick-six game winner. Yea, baby.

High fives, fist pumping, and head slapping was happening all over on our jubilant side of the field. Their sideline looked like they'd just come back from a funeral, quiet and melancholy. Packing up our gear and heading home, we were totally exhausted and completely dehydrated. We had to help carry each other off the field. The way we were dragging reminded me of the 1981–1982 playoff game between the San Diego Chargers and the Miami Dolphins. We all looked like Chargers tight end Kellen Winslow at the end of the game. I was thinking that if Clara Barton saw us, she would approve of the three-pints-of-blood special from the Red Cross.

Exiting the field, we were the beneficiaries of the most touching moment that I ever experienced in most of my years of playing sports. Banged up, sluggishly walking, and holding each other up, we hear voices coming from behind us. The voices became a little louder, and we stop at the fence opening. Sore and hurting, we labored painfully just to turn around and see. It was Kelvin and at least eight players from the visiting team, running behind us and saying, "Hey! Hey, you guys really are good."

THE PLAYER'S CLUB

I was initiated by a highly selective group of Black soldiers into a brother-hood. They were a small group of playboys with sensibilities, tact, and polished dating skills. These skills were refined enough to serenade women and cultivate affairs with well-to-do ladies who lived in luxurious homes, drove expensive cars, and had a passion for the nightlife in cosmopolitan cities across West Germany and targeted areas of Europe.

They named the nightclub where we met "The Player's Club." The real name was The Rendezvous, located in the heart of downtown Erlangen, Germany. There were three requirements for membership: First, the member must be Black. Second, the member must come from one of the major cities in the United States (New York, Chicago, Miami, Los Angeles, Atlanta, Memphis, or Detroit). And third, the member must be charismatic.

I was introduced as the youngest of the twenty members. No one knew that I was only seventeen years old. We met twice a month on a Friday at 7:00 p.m., that's if the whole base wasn't suddenly frantically alarmed at 4:00 a.m. and called in to go to the boondocks. We were dispatched in pairs to check out the clubs and nightlife in select vibrant, major cities and then report our findings at the meetings. We were scattered to cities such as Stuttgart, Hamburg, Berlin, Frankfurt, Madrid, Amsterdam, and Munich. There were five bylaws in the charter that governed our actions, laws that we were tested on in the handbook. They are as follows:

- Rule #1: etiquette

- Rule #2: wardrobe / looking the part

- Rule #3: treatment / being attentive

- Rule #4 A: the strike out—when to stop working the clubs.

- Rule #4 B: do not sleep with all of them

- Rule #5: marriage = run

In the spring of 1974, I took a civilian driver's license examination at the driver's registration office (Fuhrerscheeinstelle). located in Nuremburg, Germany, to qualify for an international driver's license. The license allowed me to operate a motor vehicle in almost every country in the world. I passed because I drove so much; however, that wasn't the only thing about me that was international. By the time that the dust had settled, I had lived with or dated females from all over the Asian continent and just about half of the Caribbean region.

But these were mostly short because over time I learned that quick, intense attractions in most relationships between the sexes don't guarantee a happy outcome. I have experienced quite the opposite, in fact, to a great degree. They quickly yield to an intense emotional deprivation such as detachment, fear, anger, and, the number one relationship spoiler, jealousy.

An adorable young lady from Cambodia attached herself to me. She was trying to get rid of her competition from Ethiopia who did the same. We were classmates. As I walked to school and from class to class, I had the lovely Ethiopian who was covered in clothing from head to toe on one side of me and the cute, short Cambodian on the other. Jealousy from both turned into chaos as they tried to outdo each other, squeezing into the seat next to me and disrupting the classes.

I spent the night with a gorgeous, insatiable Russian named Grace. She was the second lady from Russia that I worked my debonair charm on. Both were beautiful tempestuous that could always seem to turn up my body heat, but this one had a vigorous menagerie of lustful cravings. She had me crawling on my knees to get to the refrigerator, searching for any kind of nutrition. Once there, I labored to make a jelly, hot dog sandwich.

She worked as a hostess in a major hotel in downtown San Diego. And she ran out of time to straighten out her work visa. She wanted to get married way too quickly for my taste and ended up in my relationship rearview mirror, another victim of the player's handbook rule number five.

While 87 percent of the soldiers on the base centered their recreational engagement in sex and romance around the local Fraulein's at 2:00 a.m. Friday night, when they were back in the barracks sleeping, I was in Munich at 4:30 a.m., living it up and saluting while tossing back drinks. I clearly remember the fancy Italian restaurant where a plate of spaghetti cost 100 marks, and at the time, that was thirty-five American dollars. What stood out was that the pasta had no meatballs or sauce on the plate. I had a lovely date with me from a top ten nightclub at an after-hours restaurant. I got to play the role of, "Garcon, please bring me two." In that place, we were hanging out with the worldly, wise night lifers, theater actors from Greece, and breathtaking Scandinavian airline stewards.

My very first European girlfriend in Germany was born in Ankara, the capital of Turkey. Her name was Vorushka, and she was a beautiful, voluptuous young lady. Her parents were both born in Greece. What was unusual about her folks was that they called themself Gypsies. They dressed liked they did in the movies. Some were fortune tellers and had a crystal ball with the usual paraphernalia.

I was introduced to her by a theater actress that had a part in the musical *Hair*. Her name was Donna Gaines, and she was a firecracker that whirled throughout the top ten nightclubs in downtown Munich, like she was a Tasmanian devil. She was a little older than I was, but she was a popular Black beauty that was rare in that part of the country. For me, she came under player's handbook rule number four B: do not sleep with all of them.

I still remember Vorushka's and my fourth date. We had a third wheel with us on that pleasant, slightly breezy moonlit autumn night in Munich. The other lady who was with us was also a Gypsy. We decided to go to the cinema to watch the talked about Mario Puzo movie called *The Godfather*. The theater was a huge, old, grandly designed piece of architecture, with balcony and side-box seating. It had one great big white screen on the back wall of the stage, where the projector's colorful rays came to life.

The movie was dub in German, so I had to read the subtitles that ran across the bottom of the screen. I really didn't understand what in the heck Michael Corleone was doing. What I did know was that the movie was a little too long. Perhaps three quarters into the picture, Vorushka said, "We should start discussing our marriage plans." For some reason, I felt a sudden jolt in my heart.

The number five in the player's handbook seemed to appear sublimely on the screen. It also suddenly became very hot in the theater, so much so that I had to loosen my top three collar buttons on my shirt to breath. I thought about Snagglepuss, the saber-toothed tiger. The stage looked exactly like the one on which the cartoon character always said his famous words: "It's time to exist stage left." Mr. Snagglepuss knew when it was time to cut out.

The player's brotherhood members got dropped off back at the base in expensive European cars such as Porsches, Maserati, Jaguars, and Ferraris. After off-duty hours, we were living the lifestyle and doing what the guys back in the barracks were reading about in *Playboy* and *Penthouse* magazine's forum sections. Not having to move around hours before dawn was rejuvenating, coming from the rigors of basic training and AIT. The two week's leave did its job. Seeing colors other than green was an exciting change of pace. The buildings were painted green and so were the vehicles, machines, walls, and all our clothing, including socks, underwear, and T shirts. The landscape was green. I think that even the animals were green.

Days before my military leave concluded I traveled around my neighborhood to say goodbye and wish my family and friends well during this era a many of the black guys from the hood were sent straight to Vietnam and hardly returned home same. They had bouts of PTSD. And many times, they arrived back home in a casket. My family and folks cheered me on however, they had this strange look in their eyes. A look of despondency with a smile on their faces that wasn't good at hiding what they really were feeling. I visited Vanessa, my newest girlfriend a petite banana skinned beauty. She was a classmate from elementary and middle school. We attended the same high school. With her I had experienced a strange sensation that had consumed me almost like a sickness. The thought of her had disrupted my normal day to day activities to the point where I felt weak in the knees and hardly wanted to eat. The worst part of it was that I tossed and turned all night having a hard time to get to sleep un abled to stop thinking about her. The catalyst of all of this was during the middle of a game that she wanted to play called: doctor / patient. It was play acting where she is the doctor and when she finished her examination, she, cured the injured party with sex. This was the first time in my life where I was totally embarrassed. I thought that I slipped and had a bad accident by urinating inside of her. I was disturbed for a few minutes until Vanessa helped me to save face by assuring me that what I did was not pee. I found myself going over to visit her home from once a month to 3 times a week. These feeling about her had altered my ideals of pleasure where I no longer enjoyed reading technical manuals during most of my down time.

I kissed Vanessa, good-bye. I made no promises because I witnessed what happened to young ones in love due to the separation; they fell apart after only one month in Job Corps. I really could not understand all of that crying after receiving a Dear John letter. My family traveled and moved around so much that I never really got attached to anything or anybody. My philosophy was, when I get to Rome, do what the Romans do.

The very first time that I flew in an airplane, Uncle Sam flew me first class in a brand-new United Airline's 747 from metropolitan Detroit to LaGuardia Airport in New York. From there I took a shuttle to one of the tragic 9/11 Twin Towers. I sat in a midlevel lounge that had a panoramic view of the city. I waited for more than three hours in the plush, intimate and small but beautifully designed lounge with a well-stocked bar that had a black-and-white marble top counter that was surrounded by six matching barstools.

I had on my dress uniform as I mingled here and there with the few patrons sitting at the sparely spread tables. Most of the curious customers asked me how I liked the military so far. And they also asked me where I was going to be stationed at overseas. I was summoned to the heliport on the top of the tower to catch an olive-green Huey helicopter to Fort Dix, New Jersey. I still clearly remember being inoculated so many times in both arms, like a pin cushion, until I could not lift either one.

For three days I went through the army's template that prepared the troops for duty abroad. They really placed emphasis on what to lookout for, how to stay out of trouble, and, most importantly, how to be mindful of protecting yourself from the solider-trapping, dangerous disease-carrying females. I road in a C-41 cargo plane on the trip back to the New York airport for the flight overseas, and I loved every minute of it.

All was well until two hours into the nine- hour flight to Iceland. I took a window seat in the coach section on the Lufthansa Airline plane. The destination was in Frankfurt, Germany. I was relaxed and lost in thought while listening to the smoothly timed whirling sound of the powerful engines. But we ran into a huge thunderstorm roaring over the Atlantic Ocean. It was unavoidable and too large for the pilots to be able to maneuver around the turbulence.

Looking down at the dark ocean, I saw nothing but water. I thought about an escape tactic to no avail, mainly because there wasn't any land anywhere. For hours I watched the bright lightening ferociously pound the wings; only the thin glass window separated me from being fried as a result of the vicious light show. I started thinking about doomsday.

I gave up trying to think my way to safety, and I thought, "Oh well. At least I don't have far to go if it's time to go to heaven." I went to sleep, and I woke up as the brighter lights came on and the captain's voice said that we were about to land in Iceland where the plane would be cleaned and refueled to continue onward to Germany.

There was a four-hour layover, and I normally would have used that time to venture around and tour the city. However, any city with "ice" in its first name discouraged me from leaving the plane or airport. As I looked out of the picturesque windows, all I saw was ice-covered everything. And there were many times at the Greyhound bus station when I was left behind because I toured the surrounding area. This time I sat still and waited.

The plane finally landed in the Frankfurt airport on a Wednesday night. It was too late for me to get picked up by the army, so they put me in an extravagant hotel that overlooked the Rhine River. The lights reflecting off the water made for a gorgeous view, so much so that I stayed up until dawn with my face in the window, looking at the boats and ships traveling on the beautiful waterway.

I was shipped by train to Erlangen. Once there, a military jeep took me to the base. It was on a Thursday. I remembered that well because it was the only day that I had the chance to meet my roommates and a few other troops in the barracks. I was processed in, and once the brother's found out that I was from Detroit, the base tour was over. At around 7:00 p.m. on Friday, a brother from Chicago named Gabby escorted me in a jeep while he was on duty. He took me off base to a club located downtown Erlangen. The Player's Club was a small, intimate nightclub. And it was subterranean as were mostly all nightclubs. Those two world wars' bombings were the contributing factor for the bunker-style, lower gathering place.

Gabby and I descended the twelve steps, and I heard the song of Curtis Mayfield's song "Back to the World." This was a heavily played song that seemed to have so much meaning for the boys returning from Vietnam. The song abruptly had stopped them in whatever activities that they were engaged in and sent them into a hypnotic trance as they stared into space.

We took a left past the old pull-knob cigarette machine. Above it listed the club capacity, which was fifty. To the right and straight ahead were four booths on each side, which seated four patrons in each. Just ahead was a small table surrounded by four chairs on the right side of the ten-by-ten dance floor. The disk jockey's booth was directly behind the dance floor. To the right of the disk jockey was the eight-stooled classic bar.

Before we took one step inside of the club, I was introduced to a brother who showed me how they formally connected with a very sophisticated handshake called "The Dap." It took at least twenty seconds to complete with each brother, and they were thrilled that I learned this very complicated greeting on the first try. Whew! There were also four three-inches-squared tables that were lined perpendicularly with the small table that was placed next to the steps. Unlike the other brothers in the joint, the group in the back had extremely huge Afros that were the same size as activist Angela Davis's. They were toasting with each other, and all dressed like the character in the movie *Super Fly*.

They were ballers from New York, Chicago, Los Angeles, Miami, and Dallas. And at one time—with a population of nearly two million Detroit, a town that at one time was saturated with nightclubs and never slept—people entertained in their homes, and it was fashionable to build luxurious bars in basements. When the clubs closed the doors at 2:00 a.m. to prevent new party goers from entering, the partying moved on to the after-hours in private homes. It was perfect for night owls who went directly to work after their last drink.

The players didn't look like they belonged in the military. At night they loaded their hair with Murray's Edge wax and tied it down with a stocking cap. In the morning their hair was army-regulation size. They washed it out when it was time to go clubbing.

At 7:00 p.m. it was time to get down to business. This brotherhood was serious about pulling ladies. It was minutes taken, and listed five by laws, that they followed. Outsiders were not included: Allen Page from New York, Larry Little from Baltimore, and Gaby from Chicago, who I came with, was assigned to escort me to my first rotating mission to Munich. Once there I was shown the ins and out of the trade—how to speak, dress, walk, and drink and how to entertain the females.

I was a quick study and was supposed to rotate to Stuttgart for the next lessons. But I fell in love with the cosmopolitan city of Munich. At first sight. This was my home away from home. I was a solider that worked in the town of Erlangen. And I took the train whenever I was off duty to primarily reside in Munich. Whenever I was there, I told the ladies that I was an American exchange student.

I was given the nick name "The Mack" because my fashion style was not as flashy as the *Super Fly* brothers' style. I dressed more conservatively, like Max Julien's character in the movie *The Mack*. There were five bylaws followed by the brotherhood, but I added a sixth additional bylaw for myself. The charter bylaws that we were tested on were as follows:

- Rule #1: etiquette. One had to acquire reading material from the library to study the customs of the Europeans countries that surrounded Germany, Spain, as well as Asia. It impressed the Frauleins when you knew their ways of living. The newest fraternity member was assigned a mentor and guide to point things out along the way. We were tested after thirty days.

- Rule # 2: wardrobe or looking the part. A carload of brothers escorted me to the tailor that operated in the military exchange in the town of Fürth, Germany, where the Korean tailor had the finest material, fabric, and expertise to hook a brother up. The Italian tailor was in the large city of Nuremberg. He imported his material from his home country. You left there dressed to the nines.

- Rule # 3: treatment / attention. It was always a safe bet to treat the lady of the day like she was the queen of Egypt, pay attention to what she was saying, and comment on her appearance—her hair, nails, clothing, and ambitions. One of the stipulations in this rule was that a gentleman never tells.

- Rule # 4 A: the strike out. This is about when to stop working the club. When one won't, another one will. After you are rejected by three different women, go to the bar, sit, have a drink, and listen to the music. You were finished for the night. Even the homely and beat-up ladies will reject you when they notice that you just weren't wanted.

- Rule # 4 B: do not sleep with all of them. Always keep at least one popular female as a close and trusted friend. She will keep you informed about the other females' availability, habits, income, and the times when you should get with her. Does she drink heavily or not? And how much before she is ripe to go?

- Rule # 5: marriage = run. You are too young for that institution. Have fun with your life before you try on some shackles. Most of the European women wanted to get married to a solider after just one date.

- Rule # 6: this was something that I added to the bylaws for myself. This rule was a borrowed player move I witnessed from rock 'n' roll legend Elvis Presley. He used it many times. It was "if all else fails, sing." Sing to them or with them. It worked like a charm for me most times.

Over the duration of three months, I went through the whole spectrum of women from the fly girls to the homely farmer's daughter. Sometimes I woke up after drinking for three days because the circulation in my arms was cut off after being pinned down by a big one that, because of the drinks, appeared petite when I took her home.

It was no surprise when I was shot down by an elegant woman who would not give a man the time of day if they were not listed in a who's who book. But I always gave it a good college try. It was flabbergasting when the farmer's unappealing daughter slapped away my advances. That left me dumbfounded and sent me into self-diagnostic mode, looking down and thinking, "Maybe she didn't like my shoes or the way I dress.

Since I could be rejected just as easily by the homely lady, I chose to start dating, romancing, and dinning the best looking and most talented female in the clubs, and then I worked my way down, remembering player's rule number four A: the strike out rule. I struck gold when I discovered that I had a knack for dealing with and dating the types of women who would be called a diva. I have dated many of this type, from lounge singers and theater actress to exotic dancers. All shared this quality.

As I listened during their emotional roller-coaster rides that went from one extreme to the other, it did not bother or shake me one bit. I remained sturdy as a rock. It got to them when I told them what they really needed to hear instead of sugarcoating any advice. I would not let them miss rehearsal or slack off because they didn't feel like going.

WORLD-CLASS SPEED

My late wife used to say that maybe I was born in a sloth family because I took too long in the bathroom and moved around slowly in and out of the house. I often appeared to be detached from time concerns and nonchalant mostly because I moved my body around like a snail and drove slowly, not concerned about time or about rushing to get from point A to point B.

Many times, in issues of romance, I have been accused of catching onto women's telepathic suggestions that they think I can pick up on, just too slowly. Verbal communication still works better for me. But when I ran it was a different story. I surprised folks because of what I kept hidden, that I really was blessed with the speed of Mercury—the messenger of the gods in Roman mythology.

Not long after I arrived in Erlangen, someone from the military base's recreation department spotted me scampering around in a pick-up football game. In the army, all you needed to start a game was two people playing catch with each other Saturday mornings. They came to play, seemingly crawling out of the woodworks. Those good games mostly lasted four hours long.

I was invited to tour the sports complex, which sure reminded me of the same operation as the one back at Job Corps. The attendant asked me if I would like to participate in the 1972 summer Olympic games held in Munich, Germany. During the decades of the sixties and seventies, when you watched the Olympics games, you saw military personal from all branches of the services—navy, air force, marines, coast guards, and army—participate in a multitude of sports: skiing, archery, boxing, wrestling, among other events. He told me that he had a lot of the slots filled. Then he asked me what I thought about qualifying in the track-and-field events.

"Sure," I retorted. As always, in my qualifying events, I never had the opportunity to warm-up or get in some prior practice. Even now I still need to run for three-and-a-half miles before I can get out of second gear. I won the 100-meter dash and the 100-meter low hurdle. But a person has to have the best average in all three events to advance.

You had the opportunity to choose two events that you wished to participate in, but the third was a different story altogether. The officials had me high jump over a horizontal stick with a pole. Running with a pole? In the ghetto, no one ran with a long stick. All we needed was speed, the ability to jump over low and high hurdles, and to be able to leap over fences while making a break from the unit called the Big Four. They terrorized us young boys by pulling into the alley where we played football. They would threaten to beat us Black kids up the next time they saw us. The four of them slammed their car doors, making us jump as they got out. They were huge and scary. After that, every time we saw a dark black police car we ran.

I totally bombed out with the pole. The man that was always second behind me averaged higher and moved on. No gold medal for me that year. I was curious about how I would have placed in the track-and-field events in the actual Olympic games. So, my barrack roommate and close friend named Jerry, whom I also called my brother, travelled to Munich to attend the track-and-field events.

Once we arrived, we were surprised by the number of people there. Because the Oktoberfest was in full swing at the same time, miles of beer tents were set up everywhere. Drinking beer was game on for my brother and me. We thought that we were in heaven. It was a pleasant autumn moonlit, slightly breezy evening in Munich. As we tried to hit all the innumerable beer tents, our legs started getting gimpy, and we settled on a tent in the middle of the thousands of beer lovers to continue our trying out the different brands.

I sat on the end of the bench, and directly across from me, at the next table, I met a friend, a weightlifting coach from Israel. He introduced his self as Yaakov Springer. We both ate a Wiener Schnitzel and sauerkraut dinner.

He introduced me to his favorite drink called peppermint schnapps. We were yapping it up and having a great time while continuing to put down some beer. Yaakov shared some very interesting information with me, like explaining that once women turned eighteen in Israel, it was mandatory that they had to serve two years in the military.

I wondered what would happen if they did that here in the United States. The women here would revolt if they had to leave their family to go to war at eighteen. He told me that when you rode the bus, anytime someone boarded wearing a long overcoat, it scared all the passengers to death because so many times they were loaded with explosives underneath. A great evening to remember, for sure.

Jerry and I wobbled away from the beer tents and tried to find a place to sleep. There were no places to sleep within a hundred surrounding kilometers. The rooms were reserved years in advance, and private homes were renting spaces on their packed floors. A soldier's trick was to buy a ticket at the Bahnhof train station for a departure that left the next morning and then sleep a few hours on the benches. There were masses of people sleeping on the ground, in and all around the station.

The next day I was in shock! "Oh shhhh…," were the first words that came out of my mouth. I read in the paper at a newsstand that my beer-drinking buddy Yaakov Springer had been killed by a Palestinian terrorist group called Black September.

Off the record, I did find out exactly in what place I would have finished in the actual 100-meter sprint. My pre-Olympic trial timing was .14 seconds faster than Olympic gold-medal winner Valeriy Borzov who ran for the Soviet Union.

I was a lot faster than my Olympic timings. There were times when I ran so fast that I scared the living shoot out of my own self, burning rubber so fast that I didn't know if I was about to liftoff or enter another dimension. What made me say "oh, oh" was the fact that there were no brakes at that speed. Those other Olympic competitors had nearly four years to prepare for that moment. I had maybe only ten minutes to get ready. Give me the opportunity to warm up like they did, and I would have smoked the gold-medal winner like the triple-crown winner horse Secretariat did to the other horses at the Preakness Stakes.

For almost four years, I walked around with the knowledge that in world of athletic competition, hypothetically speaking, if I'd had the choice of long jump instead of the pole vault as my third event in the trials, I would have been the fastest man on the planet. I could have spoken out and made an issue about this, but, as always, I was content knowing the Lord, Jesus Christ. And I once more knew something that no other human was aware of.

BEST OF THE BEST II

Cerro del Oveja or
Hill of the Sheep

It occurred on the rugged Zugspitze Mountain in southern Germany. I was a young eighteen-year-old vehicle commander whose duties and assignments were way above my pay grade. The army sent me to school to command and obtain a license to drive eight types of military vehicles, anything from regular jeeps to small Sherman tanks. My listed title was specialist first class, 17K20 radar crewman. However, if you could perform well in other occupations in the service, you did other occupations.

We were being tested and graded on proficiency by Warrant officers who had the coolest assignments in the service. Looking at a couture map, both teams scouted the perimeter and chose a place to hide behind and peek at the enemy. The chosen hill had an eighty-two-degree angle. In a vehicle, it would seem like a rocky climb that was straight up. And should any jeep in front of the other make any mistakes, all the rear vehicles would slide backward like dominoes.

While setting up camp and enjoying the lush scenery, a huge flock of sheep came from out of nowhere, eating a hearty breakfast and grazing in the grass. They brushed up against us, and they felt soft and harmless. "Awe, just look at them! Aren't they cute?" We left the area to rejoin the wagon train. The thing about traveling with the wagon train in a combat support company was that this section moved around in the daytime delivering food, mail, showers, and medical needs. We radar operators worked at night and got no regular sleep because we had to convoy with the train. At times this no-rest inconvenience went on for thirty-six hours. After many days of doing this, the ground started looking like a foam fitted mattress.

We arrived at our mountain-test location at dusk and set up shop in the jeeps on the backside of a switchback. The parabolic reflector was set fifteen meters above, on the precipice of the front side. All was well at sunset; the night was pleasant, and we got a little relaxation as we prepared for the unexpected testing.

As if on cue, the weather changed, and it began to lightly rain—and rain, and rain some more, just as the examination started. The rain darkened the moonlit sky and turned into a thick, heavy monsoon, to the point where you could barely see your own hand in front of you. The rain totally soaked the switchback's narrow trail to the point where you had no footing whatsoever on the nearly straight up slope.

In addition to the slippery slope, the sheep had done number twos all over the mountain range, and we kept on falling in it up and down in the muddy-and-sheep-do-do trail all night. We were covered from head to toe in sheep manure. It was sticking out from under our steel pots helmets. Our faces were caked with it. Our fatigues were saturated in sheep droppings.

We scored first place in every situation that the testers threw at us. Our team was called a collection of misfits and screwballs by the most hard-nosed sergeants. The whole lot of the lower-ranking men we were not fit for military service. We malcontents, in 1973, became the darlings of the 3rd Armored Division.

Being an electrical-intelligence specialist—the title assigned to us at our duty station, a combat support company, which seemed insignificant but was totally critical, working under the 3rd Armored Division—meant working with the large powerful artillery unit and those big, extremely heavy tanks that rumbled, blew up, and mowed down everything in its path. My primarily function had us at an observation station perhaps six times a year. So, basically, my group killed most of our mandatory time fixing the same not broken vehicles at the drab base called Motor Pool.

Being whisked to the boondocks at 4:30 a.m. for a month or two sometimes was a great change of pace. Better yet, when it was time to do our job, we were sent to the communist borders of Czechoslovakia and East Berlin.

We scouted every inch on the west side of the Wall that separated East and West Berlin, both sides of Checkpoint Charlie. Knowing where the tower guards were located along with the foot patrol who paced in between. Our occupation title was now changed to "forward observer." I often wondered why I was sent to Fort Huachuca, Arizona. But it became very clear: the army never did let me get out of my point man role.

Instead of me running point in front of a company, platoon, or squad, I was now using my instincts around and awareness of feeling alarmed when something was not right in front of the whole grand military machine. We were trained to work with the navy and air force, who were always staged somewhere out of sight and far behind us.

My roommates/brothers—when you saw one, then you knew that the other three were somewhere close. We were the usual suspects when it came to getting out of extra duty. Most of the noncommissioned officers—the lifer sergeants that held the rank of E-5 Sergeant and E-6 Staff Sergeant—hated us for it. They were still working, while every day we were all gone off base at 5:00 p.m.

These were my brothers: Jerry N. was from the Boston area. He was an engineer by trade but was literally a genius. He was called "the nutty professor" and dressed in off-colored shirts and baggy pants that we called floods because the length fell two inches above his shoes. He was always busy inventing things out of any material like a Jacob's Ladder from scratch. He had an addiction to the One Arm Bandit. Then there was Miles P. From Hawaii, a beach bum surfer but a brilliant tactician who went into the Rip Van Winkle mode. He slept for months after he received a Dear John letter from his girl. Ralph M. was from California and was a Tom Cruz looka-like. He was the one stable roommate, a grounded, down-to-earth fellow who always saw things in black and white. We called him "Beetle Bailey" because he never ironed his fatigues or had any inspiration to acquire rank or motivation to make a career out of the service. He remained a private throughout his tour of duty, which was very hard to do because over time, you were automatically promoted to the next rank. And finally, there was me, a person with a great memory. But I choose to not remember many dates, times, and events on purpose because they just clog up the mind with too much information.

On base I was called "Sam the Sham" by the first lieutenant duty officer named Majkowski. I always remember him because he had the same last name as the Green Bay Packers' quarterback. He always shook his head and smiled when he called me that because I had to catch the train to Munich and was a master in getting out of extra duty—and I did it legally.

There was a sergeant assigned to each vehicle, which meant each one of the four of us was supposed to drive while the sergeant commanded the radio for communication with the other upper echelons. But in our case, we received a bad reputation throughout the base, and they wanted nothing to do with us—the lifers. Mostly those who were transferred in from Vietnam to complete their tours of duty seemed to openly harbor resentment against us.

On the other hand, we were popular with the enlisted personnel. They were involuntarily drafted, many from back home were given a choice of the army or jail. We were the entertainers. There were always two guitars in our room, and we all could play, some better than other. Even when we had no money, someone would come by to ask one of us to go with them to a jam session or to a college tearoom off campus. They called us hippies. The Acting Jacks even moved their room all the way down to the opposite side of the building so that it appeared that they were not associated with us.

There was one specific unwritten rule amongst the many that were not listed in the military rules and regulation handbook which suggested that once you had a year in your unit, you were supposed to become an Acting Jack, a sergeant, by name only. They've got many of the headache, the heavy workload, duty shifts, and privilege of a real sergeant, but not the pay. We rebels called it the sucking-up position because they volunteered for all that extra duty but were rarely sent to or made it to the NCO Academy.

I always told those who asked me why I didn't want to become an Acting Jack that, first I was a real sergeant in ROTC, and the enemy did not shoot at me with real bullets. To do that job, I wanted real pay. And besides, I always felt that I was born an officer and a gentleman. They also despised us because, when it was time to do our actual jobs, they went to train in the winter months in the tundra of the unforgiving, frigid weather conditions at the base area of Hohenfels, also at Grafenwoehr. Anyway, we were assigned to our occupation as radar operators at a military instillation located just outside of the delightful, easygoing town of Marktredwitz. The children growing up there rarely saw a Black man. And being the only Black person on the base in town, I was treated like royalty.

I was the beneficiary of some great dining and very exclusive, private dancing by a few of the most breath-taking ladies that I have ever seen. Those ladies, hands down, would give the touched-up girls in glamour magazines an unfair run for their money. The quaint town was in the northeast part of Germany, close to our primary observation post, which was on the Czechoslovakian border. And due to the nature of our work, we had to go on duty only once every three days.

And because we worked in the mountains, we had to learn how to ski. In the armory, along with weapons, were an assortment of various sized skies that we could check out on our off days. The bindings fit right on our military boots. We did all our flipping and falling on the slopes of the Fichtel Mountains. At first everyone in our unit fell all over the place trying to ski, but after a little while, we were hotdogging, going down hills and cross-country. My favorite was moonlit cross-country skiing with no breeze, gliding in light, pristine white snowfall with torches. My goodness, the thought of that is still thrilling. When the sergeants returning from Vietnam got wind of this, it really sent them over the top.

When it was time for our company to rotate to battalion duty, two of my roommates, along with myself, were sent to headquarters as backup drivers for a month. During this period, the army sent my mother the first silver award certificate for me driving on the infamous Autobahn for over 100,000 kilometers without an accident or incidents. Later my mother received my gold certificate for driving error free for over 250,000 kilometers. The next week they sent her the first of my five Letters of Commendation.

The driver from battalion headquarters who was from California, escorted us to designated areas showing the guard post and routes that we had to check daily because those terrorists were blowing up key military equipment and buildings even way back then. The driver had never driven in winter, let alone in the snow. I repeatedly had to tell him to slow down when engaging in the winding, icy mountain curves. He did not. Much sooner than later, he hit an ice patch, and the vehicle began to slide into the oncoming traffic lane, right toward a two-and-a-half -ton truck. I told everyone to hold onto something and brace for impact. Kaboom!

The jeep spun around six times and rested on the edge of a hundred-and-twenty meter drop off. There was not even an inch of space left before we all would have gone over the cliff. Besides the driver, all the passengers safely jumped out of the windows. I took a quick headcount and saw that the driver was lying knocked out in the oncoming traffic lane. I grabbed his jacket and slid him out of the way just in time as a car rounded the mountain, about to flatten the driver. I preformed what little first aid the situation called for. I elevated his head and took my jacket off in the freezing cold to keep him warm. When the medic arrived, they thanked me and said that I did a good Job.

Later in the same month, a second lieutenant fresh out of West Point oversaw the whole company for maneuvers, which was held in the world-renowned Black Forest. I love any forest, but this one was special to me because I worked there many times. It was mystifying to stand beneath the natural beauty of the dark green pine trees as they casted enchanting, dark shade throughout the day.

In any event, I was his driver. After about an hour of driving in circles and stopping to regroup miles off course, he looked so confused and I didn't want to overstep his authority, so I softly said, "Sir, I am trained in reading maps of all kinds: nautical, contour, and even star charts."

During my teenage years, I was posted in front of the TV for every space flight. The rocket on top of the slow-moving gentry creeping toward the launchpad gave me the jollies. For hours I researched and studied everything that I could if it pertained to flying. I read all the technical manuals in my sight. During the sixties and seventies and all the years until the infamous 911 tragedy that resulted in the closer of mostly all airplane flight schools, there was a slew of flight magazines in bookstores and libraries to get lost in. From my father's and uncle's garages, I already knew how to work on the fuselage and tune up the engines. I was learning to pilot a small Cessna and

Beechcraft. There was a time where I was comfortable and sharp enough to fly either one by instrument.

I asked him to give me the map and compass. Twenty minutes later we were pulling up to the hidden compound where we were supposed to be. From that point on, during actual war times, if the action did not require a team of radar operators, for the rest of my time during rotation, I was the only one on our team required to report to battalion headquarters. I was their messenger between the companies during radio silence, and I was also their whisky, beer, and mail runner.

I loved sleeping in the tent with candle's soft lighting and heat, along with the heavy-duty, big-time officers while the rest of the company slept on an air thin mattress on the ice-cold, snow-covered soil. When the month was over and we returned to our company's home base, even though I wasn't a sergeant or an Acting Jack, our executive officer made me a commander.

What really pissed off the sergeants during bivouac and war games was that I was given the standard operation procedures (SOP) booklet, and they weren't. Every morning at around 5:00 a.m., I had to authenticate the section of the book, the colors for the day, and the password to traverse forward through guard post and camps. That was sensitive, classified material way beyond my pay grade. Those haters looked furious as I walked by them.

Occupation examinations for combat readiness were approaching, and they were scheduled to take place at an unfamiliar location we had never been to before to test our competency in harsh environments. Due to the extreme weather conditions, it was among the most disliked and feared training areas. They called it the "The Top of the Rock." Because of the high altitude, its formal name was Wildflecken. But it easily could have been called Alaska junior in the wintertime.

The cold was bone-chilling, and no matter how many layers of clothing you had on, the blistering wind cut through your insulation like it did in the winter months in downtown Chicago. You felt as if you had nothing on at all. I really didn't know how in the heck the Germans fought those world wars in that kind of weather.

We caught a break, or so we thought, because it was early spring 1973, and it rained only during this season. It was daylight, and we packed up and left the moving wagon train to scout the site of the examination. We went over the contour map and chose two hidden mountain locations to cover the front and flanks of the perimeter.

Our first challenge was to negotiate the steep eighty-two-degree climb without destroying all the millions of dollars of equipment in our possession. Our superiors always told us, "If you break, it you buy it." With our salaries that meant that you were done in for life. Under great duress, we crept our way up to the top of the first hill.

The sergeant and Acting Jacks decided to break into two teams. Since I was a commander, I would be overseeing the site with my three roommates. This was not the appropriate procedure because one sergeant was supposed to sit in each of the four vehicles. I knew that to them we were contagious, and the sergeants acted like they didn't want us to rub off on them because they'd studied intensely for the testing, and we were goofing off, partying it up until the last minute. Also, if one part of the test was failed, they could always point their fingers at us.

It was around 9:00 a.m., and we saw a few sheep grazing on the hill, followed by the shepherd who had a whole flock behind him. They looked so cute while they surrounded our equipment and rubbed up against us. "Awe, that so nice," we were thinking.

After about two hours, they left, and so did we because it was time to rejoin the wagon train. We were active until dusk without sleep because we had to drive along with the constantly relocating food, shower, medical, and supplies trucks. It was sundown and time to go to work. When we reached the test area, the sergeants took their two jeeps and headed for their side of the mountain, and we took our two to our spot where the sheep roamed. I had the driver park the command vehicle ten meters down on the switchback and had the radar reflector dish camouflaged between uphill rocks as light rain began to fall. I calibrated the radar system, then used it to locate the power sources like generators, capacitors, and transformers. And I signaled in the azimuth and distance of the possible targets, which in actual war would be knocked out first.

The testing started around 8:00 p.m. We were covering one jeep that entered the perimeter, and it stuck out like a sore thumb. No matter whose turn it was on the monitor during the rotation, I would still have to leave the command vehicle to verify the targets and then go back down to call in what type of fire mission we needed to handle the enemy's movement. Do I call in the heavy artillery and mortars? Or do I alert the air force?

Collectively, our entire squad functioned like a quarterback having a pair of great receivers with hands like Lynn Swann and John Stallworth. Our pinpoint accuracy was always at a plus or minus ten meters on the first shot. The team from mortars and artillery laid waste to their targets. With the second volley, they fired for effect.

As the night thickened, so did the rain. It started pounding us as hard as hail rocks. Up next, three two-and-a-half sized trucks tried to sneak in. I gave this one to mortars. Unfortunately, the hill was slick with sheep manure. I fell on my butt, sliding down in the manure to call in the fire mission. I could not be tricked by approaching vehicles because I worked on them at home in my relatives' garages. I was accurate and more than prepared in distinguishing the different sound that compressors, gas, turbine, and diesel engines make.

It turned into a monsoon type of rainfall. Visibility was all but gone, and we could only laugh at our situation because we all fell down rolling in the sheep sh*t while going up and down the hill. It looked funny sticking out from our boots, helmets and rain jackets. We named it "sheep sh*t hill," taking nothing away from the team of sergeants working on our flank, who were also on top of their game.

At the break of dawn, the rain stopped as we drove back to rejoin the wagon train. The morning sun had dried the manure that was now caked on our faces and every stitch of clothing; it was baked onto our bodies. But after surviving that testing all night, we didn't care. Two weeks later we were singing "99 Bottles of Beer on the Wall" repeatedly to kill time on the long ride home.

A month later, while walking out to roll call, I elbowed Jerry and had him look at the bleachers set up on the parade field. That meant a big shot was unexpectedly attending roll call. They pulled up during the middle of roll call, and after the companies went through attendance, the radar squad was call in front of the lieutenant colonel who was the base commander. Aw sh*t, we thought they were about to lock us all up. I mentally went through the list of things that we may not have gotten away with.

Instead, he made a speech. He talked about how proud he was of the whole base. Then, one of the junior officers gives him a plaque. He talked about the proficient and skillful manner that radar ream demonstrated during the examination at Wildflecken. We were all shocked when he announced that we were the best. OK, who's sweating? The gesture was a little acknowledgement. Big deal we thought. So, what! we were the best in Germany. The base commander continued with, "This radar team is the best in Europe. Congratulations." We stood at attention, and it looked like our feet were on the ground, but we all were flying high. Our heads were floating high above the clouds.

FIVE AFTER SEVEN

Oh no! Not again. "Why does this keep happening to me?" My mind was rambling with thoughts about how I swore I would not do that again, but it happened once more. It was Monday morning, and I was late for roll call because I woke up five minutes after seven. That timeline was fine if I were back in the barracks and didn't eat breakfast—I woke up, washed, put on my uniform, tightened my bunk, and had just enough time to make roll call. However, that was not the case; again, I woke up off base in a hotel or in the apartment of one of those German girls.

They say karma comes back around to bite you when you are not looking. And this was a perfect example of how I really didn't get away from doing extra duty. Every time I got back to formation a few minutes late, I was put on two weeks restriction on base. The real mood killer was that I was put on two weeks of extra duty. In those two weeks, I preformed six months' worth of regular extra duty, cleaning out the latrines, mopping the whole second story, doing head count at the mess hall. And I was woken up at 2:00 a.m. to pull four hours of guard duty in the freezing predawn cold. The sergeants got their jollies off watching me slop water on the super long hallway floors.

How do I keep on getting into this predicament? It starts early Sunday evening when I dress nicely but not as flashy as I do on Friday or Saturday nights, when I am trying to pull a hammer (A vernacular black soldiers used to refer to a German female). I was only going out to Pappies' guesthouse located just outside the base to have a quite evening, drink a few beers, and return to the base to retire early, not even thinking about women. I thought about the preparing for the motor pools, working eight hours on something that is not broken because they had to give the radar unit something to do. Sunday was the day where you unwind from the Munich trip or heavy clubbing that started on Thursday, always on the second brew. Unexpectedly, two females that I knew from the club circuit, who at some point in time I was trying to get with, walk into the guesthouse and sit in the booth with me. Two beers turn into drinking peppermint schnapps with beer as a chaser while fattening the jukebox with coins. It turned into a good time. Sometimes, but not all the time, a military police friend from the base would walk in to join us halfway into the night.

The drinks start working on all of us, and the women separate into the booths and sit with each male as the touching, leg rubbing, and light kissing began. Going home with a female on that Sunday night was the farthest thing from my mind, but, like clockwork, as the place closed, we called a cab, which was always a Mercedes Benz. And, like clockwork, I woke at five minutes after seven, finally getting a good solid night's sleep, most likely due to getting only four hours of sleep from partying the whole weekend.

I wondered how in the heck a woman could sleep with all that weight on top of her. In any event, I tried to look and act cool while panicking because I would be put on report, would be restricted, and would have to perform a ton of extra duties for missing roll call once more. It was as if I were a character in the movie *Groundhog Day*.

A beautiful, sandy blond debutante who was very new to the game had just turned that legal age and started regularly coming to the clubs that surrounded the base. After about three months, we met early evening at the guesthouse located just outside of the base. She finally chose to take me to her home to relax. I was thinking I'd hit the jackpot. This one seemed to be marriage material. We made love.

It was Friday at 8:00 p.m. That was the time to get ready to go to the club. I was lying back in the bed with my fingers interlocked behind my neck, resting on a pillow. Sonya gets out of bed but tells me to stay there until she gets back from going to her mother's house. *OK*, I'm thinking, *no big deal*. She showered and got dressed. She passionately kissed me good-bye and walked out the front door. I heard keys turning. There was nothing unusual about that.

For a few moments, a powerful feeling of joy overcame me, so I was kicking back, watching German TV in which some of the frequent programming would have been rated triple X in America. I thought about the topless beaches where I've been, and the outdoor urinals installed on the side of bars and some guesthouses. I was contemplating a little as to how the Germany's was still suffering from Hitler's hangover: Say any word about him, and they would go into a flustered expression.

My jubilant, ephemeral feelings started wavering. It was getting too late to go to the club, but I thought I could perhaps still hit an afterhours spot that night. The time was midnight and worry and unease began to creep into my thoughts. I asked myself, *where is she?* Oh, oh. I checked the door, and what I hadn't noticed before was that the lock could be opened only with keys. I went to the windows, and they have iron bars on them, with no inside release latch. *Hot damn, I'm trapped. There is no getting out of here until she gets back tonight or, rather, this morning.*

Friday became Saturday. And Saturday, became Sunday. What in the heck! I was a caged animal with no phone. There were no cell phones back then. I had no way out. Where in the heck was that lady? Was she hurt? Has something happened to her? I didn't panic because it was Sunday. I had no chance to get some clubbing in. All I could do when she got back was get ready for duty Monday.

It was Monday morning and still no Sonya. I knew that back at the base they were in roll call because the time was 7:30 a.m. This means that I was officially absent without leave (AWOL). There was this sergeant who wanted to bust me, anyway, because he did not like how I kept getting out of extra duty, and he seemed to be at a desk after working hours all the time. I was thinking that I would receive a reduction in rank, and they were going to take away my check for a month or so.

At around 11:00 a.m., Sonya walked in the door with groceries and was joyful when she saw me. My madness turned into relief because I was no longer in love, and I was out of there. I asked her where she'd been. She kissed me then stated that she stayed at her mother's house, happily talking about me. "For three days!" I interjected. She knew that I was a solider, and I needed my weekend clubbing. And, most importantly, I had to report for duty. That was when the shoot really blew my mind; she said that she loved me very much, and she did not want any other women to ever speak to me again. *What?* She continued with, "You have to stay here with me, and you can't go back to the army." *Oh, hell!* Beauty can really fool you. I done messed up and went home with that psycho beech from the Bates Motel.

The mother of all screw ups occurred way out of the way from civilization, in the outback of Grafenwoehr. This one female who I met in the only nightclub in this small farm town was a sultry, raven-haired vixen with the allure of a black widow spider. And I fell into her web. It was a relaxing Sunday, and I was working at battalion headquarters during peace time, which was a great job. It was one day on, three days off for us four drivers. You could leave town if you wanted to, if you were back for your duty shift. But I was the only driver who slept in the tent with the officers during red alerts and war games such as the one called Reforger. There wasn't any shifting; I was on duty 24/7.

I go to the club with absolutely no intention of pulling any women. And then I met her. We had a memorable night of partying and arrived at that point where we were just looking at each other deep in the eyes, where words were no longer necessary. We head to her small studio apartment attached to the back of the club. What are the chances of this ever happening in the boondocks? I woke up again at five minutes after seven, only at headquarters, there was no roll call. You didn't have to report to pick up your assignment until 8:00 a.m. I breathed a sigh of relief, for only a few minutes. She wants to do it again because we have time. I protest, trying to keep her hands off me, thinking I really didn't like two weeks of extra duty. She wins. Uh oh! That time there weren't any local cabs, and I was nine kilometers from headquarters. I had to walk back. I double-timed it all the way there.

I arrived at ten minutes before nine. I was sent back to the barracks to sleep in a bay with twenty other soldiers and no creature comforts. As expected, I received the two weeks of restriction and almost lost a month's pay and rank. But the real knockout was that I had to do something that I had never done before. I was told by top (soldiers use this name that refers to the sergeant major) to report and do some disciplining correction work called KP at the Mess Hall. The head chef was a bearded, scruffy looking, hugely intimidating master chief. He wore a dirty, greasy apron and spoke as meanly as he looked.

He took me all the way to the back of the facilities to a truck-bed sized bin filled to the top with potatoes. He turned around and pointed toward two huge kettles which looked like fifty-five- gallon oil drums to me. He told me to keep cutting until they both were filled. With a nub of a cigar dangling from his lips, he walked back to the front of the mess hall.

Devastated, I was cutting for an hour, and the pots still looked empty as if I hadn't cut anything. I was miserable, and like they always say in jail, I was thinking hard that I would never do that again. I started at 10 a.m. When it was lunchtime, I was allowed thirty minutes and then had to return to the drudgery of cutting potatoes. It was 1:00 p.m., and I was going over everything that I'd done in my life, trying to figure out how I got to that point. I looked out of the small, rectangular, moss-covered rear window and saw two guys tossing a football around in the grass field in between the barracks.

In Alabama, there was this very big, happy white kid from Oklahoma who I briefly played football with on the army's Redstone Arsenal football team. After we stopped the other team on a fourth and goal, he came off the field yelling, "Football is better than sex." I don't know about that. I didn't smoke cigarettes, but sometimes after a hard-hitting game like that, I came to the sideline with an uncontrollable urge to look around to see if I could bum a square.

I took a short break from the kitchen and went out the backdoor to play catch with the guys throwing the football around. The next thing I knew, we had a full-blown football game going.

It was a hard-hitting game, just like the old-time Detroit Lions versus Pittsburgh Steelers game with Mike Lucci, Mel Farr, and Lem Barney against Jack Lambert, Jack Ham, and Mel Blount. After every play it seemed like they were carting another player off the playing field. In any event, spectators packed the sidelines, the spaces in between the buildings were filled with onlookers. Halfway through this leather-slapping game, the officers started coming to watch, so much so that they took up all the space of the westside end zone. We played for four hours, and the score was tied. Someone on the sideline yelled out that it was almost dinnertime, so the players decided that the last score would win the game.

I went back to quarterbacking and drove the team down to the twenty-five-yard line with short passes and runs the produced only three or four yards at a clip. That was because the opponents highly resistant zone defense only allowed yards in front of them. I saw that the corners were cheating and jumping the routes. I had the receiver run a hitch and go, and he caught the route jumping corner flatfooted, putting a lot of air under the ball, and I arched it into the end zone.

While the ball was still in the air, I turned my back to the play and walked to the sidelines with my hands held high to signal a touchdown. Then I heard the crowed erupt. The elated crowd happily dissipated, some to the barracks and some straight to the mess hall for dinner, taking with them the feeling that this was a defensive thriller existing in a place where dirt and grim were the rule of the day. The game gave the officers and weary soldiers a much-needed, entertaining change of pace. "Oh, sh*t!" I forgot to cut up the potatoes scheduled for dinner, and what's more, I left my post.

I tried to snatch the backdoor open; it was locked. And what was even more dangerous was that I was going to have to face that dragon master chief. Oh, boy! I was doomed as I tried to duck and blend in the line of the hungry warriors, attempting to sneak past him. I made it all the way through the chow line with only a few feet left until I reached the back room without observing him anywhere. Unfortunately, I froze solid, just like refrigerated dead meat, as he leaned on the doorframe, waiting for me, looking real mean and chewing on that stub of a cigar. I'd been caught red-handed. I was thinking that I was going to get court martialed, have my rank reduced to a private, lose all my benefits, such as a slash in my paycheck, and have my options of living off base taken away.

I was withering away like a melting candle. I shrunk down in size to three feet tall. *Lord, have mercy on me.* It really caught me off guard was when he smiled. *What?!* He continued with, "Great game. You are out of your KP obligation. You do not have to come back here anymore." Hallelujah! That was the first and only time that I had to pull KP while I served in the armed services.

Headquarters requested for me to return to my driving duties when our company rotated back to battalion. But I wasn't escorting military officers from place to place. After I obtained my international driver's license, I had the responsibility of escorting and bodyguarding Germany's war games umpires, German diplomats, and German civilian guards to sensitive checkpoint areas.

Watching war games and standing right next to an umpire gives a solider a unique perspective regarding how those destructive, lightning-quick heavy-armored vehicles can really be on top of you before you can blink an eye. Those German Panzer tanks can move fast through the tree lines, like a hot knife through butter.

I was the driver of the military vehicles with the flags on the front poles. Higher ups made me wear dress uniforms with bloused boots, a white ammunition belt around my waist, a blue-and-white rope around my right shoulder, and a white ascot around my neck, tucked inside of my jacket. No doubt about it, when a solider dresses like that, he or she automatically looks like they can kick ass. I continued to escort the German's high-ranking officials and civilian workers around until the end of my tour of duty.

PATSY AND HEIDI

I was working off another two-week extra duty and restriction to base. Low-ranking enlisted personnel dragged around all day long, half asleep and daydreaming about what could have been. It's like 97 percent of convicts doing time in the joint who think, "If only I hadn't look at the camera, I would not be here."

Once 5:00 p.m. approached, everyone seemed to wake up in the motor pool. After I ate dinner, if I wasn't doing the extra duty headcount at the mess hall or something just as boring, as a way to finance my off-duty cavalier lifestyle, I fixed and repaired soldier's broken electronic items, such as the then popular reel-to-reel recording devices, cassette players, guitar amplifiers and cords, turn tables, and the little, bad investment portable TVs with four-inch screens, which took eight expensive D batteries yet only functioned for an hour or at best two.

As something new, I started hanging out at the base's recreation facilities, such as the gym, bowling alley, and the NCO Club, for a month or two, instead of quickly donning civilian clothing and jetting off base. The real reason? It was because of the nightmare I'd experienced when I was locked up and caged for three days in the home of that pretty dingbat who would not let me leave. She kept on blocking the doorway when I was already late for formation. She told me that I had to quit the army and stay with her, all while she blocked my escape path to freedom. *Oh, sh*t! This lady is serious.* *"Keep cool, Lamarr! How do I get out of this catastrophe?"* What really was the dagger in the heart was when I tried to gently move her out of the doorway, and Sonya said that if I tried to leave, she was going to scream "rape" and tell my army superiors what I did.

A million and one scenarios ran through my mind in a few minutes. My thought was that if I got out of that situation, I would turn straight and would never leave the base again. It was my charm that got me in that situation. I was going to have to use charm to get me out. I turned on a smooth-as-ice player performance. I had my eyelids open halfway, giving her that come-to-bed look, and I said, "Come here, baby. You know that I love you more than anything in this whole world." All the while, I was wrapping my arms around her hourglass waist and kissing her gently ear-to-ear and on her the back of her neck.

I said, "I didn't like the army, anyway. I am going to get a couple of suitcases from the PX (The military exchange retail store), pack my things, and walk out of there for good when it gets dark."

"Really?" she joyfully replied.

"Sure, tomorrow I'll start looking for a job."

She kissed me and squeezed me so hard it felt like me eyeballs were popping out. She said, "See you tonight, lover."

"OK," I said. I walked at least five blocks away from her apartment, way out of view, just in case I was followed before I held a cab.

I was totally club shy and hesitant about even going off base when my two weeks restriction was over. The season was fall, and, as always, that was a time when I marveled at the pleasing hue of the falling foliage. So, on that night, right across from my bedroom window was the NCO Club.

We enlisted men were allowed to order food from there. Later, in my tour of duty, I was allowed to walk in and order my meals from the officers' club. So, I went and ordered a hamburger and fries from the bartender, a mid-thirties, attractive, cheerful Spanish lady named Judy. Her husband abandoned her and left for the States without her. She turned out to be a very good friend.

While chatting with her and enjoying my meal, at around 7:30 a.m. two ladies walked into the club with large bags. Judy escorted them to the back of the club where they could change clothes. They changed alright, into sexy lingerie. There were a few patriots sitting at the bar, but I was the only one sitting at a table.

The music came on, and one at a time, they started dancing right in front of me. Wow! They were very pleasant to look at. They reminded me of the girls on the front covers of the magazines that were occupying the shelves on the newsstand. When they finished their sets, they sat at a table all the way on the other side of the NCO Club. Others walked into the club in groups of twos and threes, starting around 9:00 p.m. At 10:00 p.m. the club was three quarters filled. On weekdays, the club closed at 11:00 p.m., but I departed when I heard the head bartender announce last call for alcohol.

Now, this was a very enlightening evening, so entertaining that I thought that I might start to hang out on base more often, sometimes on a Saturday. The meals in the mess hall weren't that great. You could tell by looking at the short chow lines. I decided to eat once more at the NCO club.

The scene was exactly like the last time I was there. The ladies arrived at 7:30 p.m., changed, danced in front of me, but this time, instead of sitting across the room after a set, they sat with me at the small, rectangular table with lit candles and two ashtrays. At the time, I had no idea that these two women would be the template for developing my future choices concerning my dating and romantic endeavors. I had barely turned eighteen years old, and because of those two, I started to get a feel for the kind of female personality that I best match up with. And it was primarily ladies that enjoyed and loved work in the discipline of the preforming arts.

Heidi was a mid-twenties, street smart, blithesome, cute, petite, shapely dirty-hair blond who was born in the Netherlands. The voluptuous Patsy was a big-boomers, pretty- happy-go-lucky, laugh-at-everything brunette, born somewhere near Greece. They both exhibited hypnotic flair as they gyrated in sync with one of their favorite tunes by the master Carlos Santana called "Samba Pa Ti." The other song was titled "The Coldest Days of My Life" by the Chi-Lites, a group that was based in Chicago, Illinois, the place where the group derived half of their name from What was unusual about this budding relationship was that they traveled in the same club circuit as I did.

We were all surprised when we met one Friday night in an NCO Club in Grafenwoehr. The next time it was in the city of Widen. But the meeting in an outside club in the city of Nuremburg was a sister- and little-brother bond sealer. To me they both fell under number 4 B from the player's handbook: Don't sleep with them all. Keep some as great friends.

There were these eight to ten city blocks in an area called "the wall." The wall was a legal district of blocks and blocks of nice-looking women posing on beds behind an eight-by-five glass window frame. Their price for pleasure was twenty marks per hour. At the time, that equaled six American dollars. On each end of the ten blocks were bars. That was where the higher-priced ladies and exotic dancers converged. It was the place where I again happened to meet Patsy and Heidi. That time around, they started guided me on what type of women to sleep with and who to avoid like the plague.

On the weekend I still took the train down to my home away from home, Munich. But the distance of my train rides became shorter because the city of Nuremberg was closer to where I was stationed, and I didn't have to travel far to enjoy some tantalizing clubbing. Forty years later Patsie and Heidi's dating lessons were still reliable. I continue to have the dancers break the house rules by leaving their place of employment to date and or spend the nights with me Those intense, flaming-hot relationships are short-lived, mostly due to jealousy. The dancers could frolic with males, but once you enter a relationship with them, they do not want their men frolicking with other women. Their reason was, as they always said, "It's my job." My success rate over my lifetime of pulling not just dancers but the best exotic dancers from out of a swinging club even at sixty-five years old, was 95 percent.

GARMISCH

Standing outside in the squad formation on that sun-shining, midspring day, we received our plaque that said we were the best, so we could hang it on a wall really, but it didn't resonate with us. What the base commander said next was that we would each receive a boost in pay and would also be given a three days and three nights paid for vacation with meal money and the choice of going either to Stuttgart or to the Edelweiss Lodge and Ski Resort in Garmisch, Germany, located a stone's throw away from the Austrian border.

Well, I'll be darned. That got the blood circulating. We were feeling it. My roommates and I chose skiing. The sergeants and Acting Jack wanted to hang out in the city of Stuttgart to see the architecture, clubs, and parks in the city. Something that we ordinarily did daily. Oh well. They didn't want to get caught hanging out with us inferior, guitar-carrying beatniks, anyway.

We were commissioned by the Department of Defense to be the only ones who were authorized to wear insignia that was a small patch that said "radar." It was to be worn only on our field jackets, above the left side of the pocket. Higher ups changed the color of our ID cards from green and white to brown and white. Everyone in the whole military machine knew that this color identification badge meant that we were a different class of soldier. We became the darlings of the 3rd Armored Division and caught the attention of the thinktanks working at the Pentagon, who moved our whole team's security clearance to S2.

The very next time we received a mission, a first lieutenant took the red eye straight from there. He was a walking computer. At the briefing he passed out yellow-jacket folders to the team. That folder was secured by red ribbon covering the words "Top Secret." It was then that it sunk in that we really did something special.

The bigwigs took us all over Germany to show us off. We had to go to all kinds of military ceremonies and tours, but the showing off that I did like was when we were escorted to a secret base to witness the demonstration of new and different prototype weapons. We saw the prototype firing of the machine gun that's currently used in Black Hawk helicopters. During our regular duty stations at the observation post on the border, we had to take an infantry, mortars, or mechanize reconnaissance squad along with us to show them how the best gets the job done.

We picked Monday as our third day to take the vacation because we normally busted out from the scene on Fridays, anyway. We arrived in town by train, then a cab took us to the American hotel where we unpacked and relaxed. And as usual, we put away a few brews so that we could hit the slopes of the Eastern Alps on top of Zugspitze Mountain bright and early the next day.

We shared two double bedrooms between the four of us; however, for a solider, sleeping in a chair or on the floor was the same thing a bed. We all woke up in one room the next day, bodies on top of the dresser and all over the place. Jerry couldn't make it out of the bathroom, so he slept in the tub with his hat still on his head. Ralph woke up in a chair, arms dangling on the sides, still holding tightly onto a half-drunk bottle of beer in his right hand. I was on the floor. Four beds, and no one slept in any.

It was a gorgeous Saturday morning. The glistening sun was shining clean, white light. Snow fell, blanketing the cobblestone streets and sidewalks of the alluring Bavarian-style buildings and storefronts. Every time I visited the charming village of Garmisch, it reminded me of the Jacob and Wilhelm Grimm's story *Hansel and Gretel*, which describes the gingerbread houses that could be eaten.

We walked through the quaint village until we investigated a store window that had displayed a bottle of Lambrusco wine sold for only two marks a liter. During this era, it was three marks to an American dollar. Man, that felt like heaven. It was a beautiful day, and we found cheap wine right on time. We bought a whole lot of bottles with our meal money and took them back to the hotel to sip on until it was time to head to the ski lodge. The problem was that all day we'd bent our wrists and elbows to our mouths, drinking the cheap wine like it was beer.

It started around dusk when Miles ran to the toilet and stuck his face in it to throw up. Then Ralph started and so on as we each took turns discharging our guts. We spent the whole night and most of the next day throwing up. We finally made it to the lodge Sunday night. But we were a sad looking bunch, too weak-kneed from barfing, and we had no spunk or energy to ski, let alone try to get a Fraulein's phone number. So, we basically moped around for a little until we decided to go back to the hotel to recover. Monday morning, we did unenthusiastically get a little skiing in. But the lodge was not the same on that day as it had been on the weekend because hardly anyone was there. Oh well! We packed up, checked out of our room early afternoon, and took the train back to our unit to get ready for the next day. All in all, it was a very memorable journey.

Something had changed with the women who were in my circle of friends as I neared the six-month countdown to the end of my enlistment. That was a time when all the soldiers who were getting out of the military soon yelled, as a rite of passage, "Short!" early in the mornings in the hallways, loudly echoing the words for all to hear. Everyone in the military knew that this meant that this person was leaving soon. And so many wished that it were them.

What was once fun in the dating game became routine. Because the Frauleins from Erlangen all the way down into Munich seemed to have a sixth sense about the time I had left overseas, instead of playing the game of dating for two or three outings before bringing the subject up, they cracked on you during the very first date, stating, "I know that you are about to leave. Take me with you." That really soured the milk when you are only looking for a good time. And rule number five from the player's handbook kept on cropping up, sounding the alarm, like when someone has the feeling that they were about to enter a bad investment.

My dilemma was that after a few years, I'd become quite fond of a few of the regular ladies that I had known from my teenage and young adult years while growing up abroad in a foreign country. I'd started to care about them.

In Munich there was this spot where I spent many nights sitting under the midnight sky to do my contemplations and lamentations. It was called Arc de Mercedes Benz. A hundred percent of the time, it was a certain Fraulein who was on my mind, and I'd be thinking about whether I should take her with me or let her go.

There were two unforgettable tunes in my heading during meditation, searching for answers. Out of all the memorable Beatles' songs, this one song played over and over during my serious meditation times. It was called "If I fell." I haven't the faintest idea why this song stayed with me when I'd only heard it once at a skating rink. All I remember was taking a bunch of little children skating one Saturday morning. But I didn't call it skating; I called it dodge-little-kids-on-wheels day. In any event, the disk jockey played that song only once, but for some unknown reason, it stuck with me and still goes through my head whenever I am trying to make a meaningful relationship decision.

On the other end of the spectrum, and the more persistent outcome, was that I was hurting while I stared at the Mercedes Benz emblem in the middle of the arch. I was melancholy because I thought that I had this one in the bag, and yet there I was, suffering from a broken heart again, when just a few days before I was on cloud nine.

This other song in my head was a repeat healer from the group called War. This tune was titled "Deliver the Word." The opening line, "if misery is your best friend," said it all in a nutshell. One way or another, those songs helped me batten down the hatches and weather through another stormy heartbreak. As the say in Rome, "Sometimes a cake is just a cake. And sometimes a friend is just a friend. That relationship was not to be."

The armed services are one occupation in which their employees required that they must be on call 24/7. There were jobs in the civilian world where an employee, in the still of the night, could be whisked away for months, to another time zone. These displacement cause havoc on matters of the heart especially when it has something to do with the reporting for duty and the sudden dispatching to another country in the middle of the night was an inherited occupational hazard in the life of a solider. When they arrived at their duty station from home, they would go bananas after receiving a Dear

John letter at the end of their tour of duty. Some went home basking in the glow of having a new bride. Not too long afterward, she had what she wanted—citizenship—and would leave the wounded warrior with nothing but lint in his pockets and financial ruin.

Many who had been recently discharged from the service had no choice but to reenlist because of that. And in just about all cases, those who had chosen to send their money back home to the States for savings, to be available to use when they returned, were extremely disappointed because 95 percent of the time the money was spent. Player's handbook rule number five was the real reason I did not bring one back home with me. When it was time, I packed my duffle bags, left the excess baggage behind, and caught the first smoking jet back to America.

HEAVENLY BROTHER

In the late seventies I began working off a government contract through a program called Civilian Employment Training Act. (CETA). They sent me to an organization called Focus: HOPE as a driver / maintenance worker. The second day, I was sent to work over at the expanding resources center located across the street from the food distribution warehouse. It was a picture-perfect late spring day. As I crossed the heavily trafficked highway, I met a man who, at first glance, wore faded jeans, mid ankle-length black biker's boots, a plaid shirt, and had a head full of long, dark hair. He was working on his big, fat, powerful 750 Harley Davidson motorcycle in front of the building.

He reminded me of the many young white friends that my younger brother and I used to hang out with back when there were no dividing street walls between the city boundary of Grosse Pointe and Detroit. He took a break from his task when I asked what he was doing. After wiping off one greasy hand on his hanky, he stuck it out and introduced his self as Bill Cunningham, founder and director of the Focus: HOPE organization. If I'd made a bet on the type of character he was, I would have gotten it wrong by a mile.

I knew a little about engines and told him check the gas line filter to see if that was the reason for the hard start. It was, and our relationship was an instant older-brother-little-brother bond. He took me everywhere with him. When you saw one of us, you knew that the other was somewhere close by. He took me to his church that he pastored, to his home, to special events.

What I was really excited about were the days when he took me to a radio or TV interview. I would sit behind the glass, on the top floors of the powerful WJR Studio, located on Woodward Street, next to the Wayne State University campus. It was a normal early morning routine. One day, when they were short-staffed and didn't have a purchasing agent, he said that Angel Eleanor J. to give me a check of one-hundred-twenty-five-thousand dollars made out to "cash" to deposit. I was a little nervous, thinking, "What if a bad person knew what I was carrying?" Until the organization hired a permanent procurement officer, I did the banking and paid for and purchased supplies and building materials for the renovations of the resource center.

Father Cunningham treated me like family. What really sealed the deal for me was when Eleanor gave me a two-hundred-fifty-thousand-dollar check to deposit. On the way to the bank, I was paranoid and repeatedly checked my mirrors on the van to see if I was being followed. I knew a few bad guys in the neighborhood who were into cashing any kind of check—welfare, Social Security, employment, and personal checks. To me this was huge. The crooks at that time were robbing armored cars for lesser money. Feeling suspicious, I kept on wondering if one of those guys got a tip about what I was carrying. Thankfully and uneventfully, I completed my task.

One of the most dominate traits that we shared between us was our love of wine. On the bottom floor of the resource center, which was covered in wood and sawdust from constantly undergoing refurbishment, was a table for the guess and visitors that was always stocked with an assortment of donuts, wine, and cheese. Many days I would walk inside the center at 8:00 a.m. or 9:00 a.m. and bump into a smiling Father Cunningham. The first thing that he would say was, "Have a glass of wine. I am about to have one." In those days, I usually suffered from a hangover because of partying every night. Rent was cheap in just about every city, and times were good enough to celebrate every day. I grabbed a wine glass and complied with the quickness.

There were two major events sponsored by the organization: one was an annual Focus: HOPE Concert held at the Music Hall located in Grand Circus Park, in downtown Detroit. And the second was the Focus: HOPE March. Preparing for those events was taxing and time consuming. It was just him and me at 3:00 a.m., drinking wine and talking brother stuff, all the while hammering away in the unventilated attic of the resource center, putting together posters for the enthusiastically involved marching public to carry.

With him I had to learn a whole bunch of related backstage chores at the Music Hall, to ensure the concert was always a success. Those were the days when I worked closely with the program director, Eleanor J. It was as if I were attached to her hip pocket. She and I used to meet often during my morning newspaper, coffee, and donuts runs at the place called Dutch Girl Donuts located on Woodward Ave. That was where, every day, she picked up a box of fresh pastry delights for whoever visited the resource center. At the Music Hall, I did whatever she told me to do, from passing out fliers to the public to helping to carry and plug in the music equipment. I even gave my opinion while listening during the sound checks.

I also moved the tables and chairs in and out downstairs for the after-party celebration, got the food there, and knocked on the singer's dressing-room door ahead of their performances. But the one thing that I really enjoyed while working at the Music Hall was when I had to work the curtains. I was a natural at opening and dropping the heavy drapes right on cue.

One of the most dispiriting situations that happened as I approached the end of my contracted work there. I was offered a job to remain onboard, but football practice while playing with the Jets was at 6:00 p.m. But the food distribution center worked until 7:30 p.m. It was never about making more money with me; I was already rich. So, working extra hours for more pay was not compatible with my after- hours hobby's.

What really saddened me about leaving was what was happening to Father Cunningham. As the organization grew, so did the public perception of how an administrator was supposed to look, dress, and act. The board decided that it was a bad idea for a powerful person such as Father Cunningham to run around in jeans with long hair while driving a Harley. The move was catastrophic. It was a pocketknife in his back. The bigger dagger came when they told him that he had to start wearing business suits and cut his hair.

I witnessed him change from a spirited, happy-go-lucky person into a sad puppet. He was no longer his vibrant self. The lines in his face were starting to deepen, with a permanent expression of unsatisfaction. This situation reminded of the biblical story of the hero Samson. He looked and acted the same way when they cut his hair. He lost all his power. As I attended his funeral not to long afterward, I truly believed that my spiritual brother, mentor, and friend not being able to be his self was too great of an internal struggle. To me it was the real catalyst of his early departure.

SOLAR SCARE

Some of the troubles that I had in my carefree day to day living in the cheap rent at the time motor city. It was a place that I called paradise. My anxiety began when I was told to stop hanging out with the one who the angels rebuked. This lady told me that she was a working girl. At the time, I was a little naive and was not aware of what she meant when she said that she was in the hospitality industry. When my thoughts cleared, I wound up being her bodyguard. They upstairs did not like it one bit.

I loved going to sleep because I constantly had an opportunity to fly around the earth, especially when I was young. I was thrilled when I learned how to land. Every now and then I began to fly in my same vintage biplane. It was a Sopwith Camel single-seat aircraft. One ominous night in my lucid dream, I was joined by another flyer who not only flew with me, but he gave me a lift past the stratosphere into outer space. In the beginning it was an informative, joyful flight. But the ride home was designed for punishment. We stopped just short of the twenty-five kilometers from Earth's Karman line. And the next day, I was permanently scared straight.

I had an old saying I'd use before I went out on the town: "What kind of Fraulein will I seek this night?" There was the good girl. There was the bad girl. Ninety percent of the time, I chose the bad girl to pursue as the lady of the evening. The good girl, who was necessary in my life, was the long car ride, the scenic route to romance. First you had to take the time to get to know her and the kinds of dreams, desires, and lifestyle she chose to maintain. Is she classy, or does she pretend to be? What kind of talent does she possess? Is she strong willed or a sheep? Does she complement your personality? Is she adventurous? Can you take her home to mother?

If you chose right, in the long run, the path to stability is worth the months of wining and dining before you have the night of unmatched passion. So, there's a lot to be said about what are you looking for. You could not take the bad girl home to mother, but you didn't have to do all of that calculating with that one. It was a much shorter distance to home plate. All you had to do was wine, dine, and show her a good time. That's why the bad girl won that back-and-forth deliberation just about all the time.

I was a wholesome teenager, sucking up all the knowledge I could, when I was shipped to Europe. I didn't drink, smoke, or indulge in any kind of mind-altering drugs. I was a pure athlete. It was a time when I roamed this world but was not susceptible to the ways of it. The culture shock I experienced when I got back to America was mindboggling. I didn't blend right in with the native young ladies in the hood. For a long while, they referred to me as "white boy." My education, mannerisms, and cosmopolitan ethics made me stand out like a wide-eyed Maryland farm boy whose highlight of the year was attending a Ritchie Bros. tractor and farm equipment auction and visiting Time Square in New York for the first time.

Growing up in Europe, the women that were my age were completely different. In Germany, until they were eighteen, the children had to go to school on Saturdays. Like it or not, they were more educated and goal oriented. At most they had one child out of wedlock or none. When I woke up after a date night, there were no bare-footed little ones asking me to fix them breakfast. Here, the little ones roused the unknown males to avoid shaking their knocked-out mothers because they would scream at them with a barrage of curse words if woken. At the clubs in America, the women lied and said that they had no children.

Because the Europe is connected to so many other countries, the women were accustomed to taking a train ride to England, France, or Spain. The thing about it was that you could talk about any of those country's history, and the women could recite the history of that culture, all the way back to the first century, with ease.

Meanwhile, the glaring difference back in America was that almost all those pretty neighborhood girls had never even traveled to the west side of their own city, let alone to a different country. Many were sweet as cheery pie but deadly as a serpent. Handsome looking females who dressed elegantly but carried shaving razors and switchblades somewhere on their bodies. After sex, there were just too many moments when there was nothing to talk about. Talking just about money and what you can do with it sours a relationship real fast. It could be three weeks before you found out the truth. And it always happened on a Sunday when the grandmother brough the kids back to their mother, saying, "I've had enough. These are your children." What really blew my mind is that in most cases, they didn't have one kid or two at twenty years old—they had four. My goodness!

One Sunday, after finally going home with this one young lady who I'd seen for weeks on the bar circuit, I found it interesting when she explained that many of the females at the clubs wore clothing with the price tag still on it for that night. The next day, they took the item back for a refund at the department store, only to get another dress for the next weekend, to do the same thing all over again.

In any event, it was Sunday. It was early in the morning. We were lying on the floor, cuddled up underneath a wool blanket. We were too hot-natured to make it to the bedroom. Suddenly, I hear keys tinkling at the front door. It opens, and four sleepy kids, followed by an older, towering dark-skinned man enter. Oh, sh*t. It's the spouse. This lying jezebel.

It was too late. Our clothes were scattered all over the front room. There was no way for me to get a weapon or reach my clothing to look decent before that man pursued a raging crime of passion. Trying to look cool, I could only watch with my hands cupped behind my neck. The real bad part about the situation was that the lady and I were completely buck naked. I finally knew what they meant by being caught with your pants down.

It was bad. I had never been a fight in my birthday suit. *I was thinking, If I ever get out of this, I will never do this again.* I was relieved because the man didn't say or do anything. After all the kids were inside, he stared at me for a long minute, turned, and walked back out of the door. Once I had to jump out of an upstairs back-bedroom window in my underwear with my shoes and clothing in my hand to escape the fury of a mad spouse tearing up the house as soon as he walked through the threshold of the front door. At the club she said that she was not married.

After my tour of duty, I wasted my time enrolling in and graduating from a myriad of technical- and business-related schools such business administration, electronics, construction, and building—skills that I already possessed but not on paper. Passing those classes lead to nowhere in the job market. Why? Because I found out the difference between accredited classes and nonaccredited degrees. Unless you knew someone important job wise, in those days, the labor market paid no attention to nonaccredited degrees.

So, I enrolled in an accredited degree program at Wayne State University in 1981. I pursued a minor degree in computer science. which was a nightmare for me because handling twelve credits was a handful by itself, especially if you had two part time jobs and had to get to football practice on time.

During this era, to program the computers, we students worked with batch cards, and most of the time, you had the time of your life typing individual cards one by one to write out the algorithm. The major problem was that any little mistake such as a wrong punctuation mark, a comma or period in the wrong place, or a bad math formula, and you were doomed to spend the whole entire week, nights and weekends, punching out batch cards while going over the computer sheet line by line, finding and correcting the seemingly small blunder that threw the whole program off.

The remote printing locations also sucked up all your time should you press the wrong button and send the job to a closed building. That was what made me get out of the occupation of computer science. I spent a whole lifetime in the basement of the science building, looking for where I went wrong, so much so that I was regularly the last one, like at the bar, being put out at the end of the night.

During the third semester, learning to write computer programs with those batch cards became way too time consuming and problematic for me because I was trying to obtain only a minor degree in this field. I questioned everything in and out of sight and was as curious as the proverbial cat at the age of twelve. My adventures and misadventures were primarily in the sport of football and the never-before-revealed encounters with those who resided in the spiritual world.

Because I was commanded to stop doing what I was doing, I chose to get engaged to a cheerful, petite, stunningly beautiful Black young lady named Tracy. For reasons explained later in my story, I had to hide my number one lady, the top girlfriend on my list of potential mates the ones who I was intimate with. The young lady that I considered as marriage material i.

My fiancée was the kind of person whose personality was such that every person or animal that she encountered loved her. I didn't break the player's handbook rule number five on purpose; it was an advocate who told me that perhaps it was best that I stop sleeping around and get married.

We used to go out a lot to jazz clubs. The Watts Club Mozambique was once a spot for jazz lovers until the male dancers moved in. Dummy George's a place where singer Marlena "Go Away Little Boy," Shaw. Was a regular featured artist. And there was the night club called Black Orchid, located on Livernois street, where one night I felt that Chicago's own singer Terry Callier was trying to make a move on her as we sat directly in his eyesight, in front of the stage, while he sang his heart out and focused directly on her, singing "What Color is Love".

She loved walking around the Detroit Zoo, talking to animals who smiled as she spoke to them. Tragedies struck her family in unfathomable ways. It was the nightmarish cancer that was beginning to ravish her immediate family. First it was Tracy's father, then a sister and an aunt. This all happened in a six-month period. The very bad news for us was when she was hit with the symptoms.

It was a devastating, spirit-crushing yearlong battle before she had to be placed in a Hospice. I knew of such a place because my fellow coworker and best friend at the time who I called Odie, placed his father in one. It was not good at all. His dad left after being there for only a few days, instead of the weeks they said he had left.

It happened on the same weekend after she was placed in the facilities. I was asleep in my bed when I felt the weight of something heavy moving around on top of me kissing me. It was so heavy that I started opening my eyes to see what was weighing me down. Tracy got her last kiss in. She was smiling. I sensed that for the first time in a year, she was pain free as her body ascended upward and then disappeared. There was no mistaking that she left her family and me at that very moment. In genuine mourning with a crushed spirit, I got dressed and made some calls around to her family's home, and unlike before, no one answered. I drove to her mother's home only to feel sadness and hear crying through the front door.

I became unglued and shaken. I could not even bring myself to push the doorbell. I turned around blinded by grief, and with watery eyes, I drove home and tried to drink the stabbing heart pain away. There was no doubt about it—I witnessed her leaving her Earth home. She was gone. For me, that was just a taste of the unthinkable events in my life, which was paled in comparison to that which had yet to come. The more that I knew, the more I was subjected to trials and tribulations emulating from the spiritual ream.

It was on a Friday evening when I was put out of the science building. I was residing in Highland Park, which was about five miles from campus. Home was a straight shot up Woodward Avenue. The late autumn night was gorgeous. A zephyr of the sort with temperatures hovering near the bottom sixties. I was frustrated because this evening I could not repair the 250 batch cards that I carried in a small box cradled under my right arm. My car was in the shop. It was a nice night, so I decided to walk home.

I made it past Claremont Street north on Woodward Avenue when in the distance, something shiny caught my attention. The closer I got, I noticed that the object rested in the middle of a shadow silhouette the shape of a woman. Walking closer the object, I noticed the glittering was from a diamond bracelet on the left wrist on a good-looking lady—correction, a fabulous-looking lady. When I reached her, there was another correction—this lady was the shoot, fine as hell. She was petite with curves all over. She had waist-length black hair. Underneath her short black-and-white rabbit jacket, she wore an elegant silky, red dress. She looked like she was dressed to go to a ball.

While no longer concerned over my work, curious I stopped in my tracks. In my mind I wondered what in the heck was she doing out here at that time of night. She introduced herself as Debbi. And she was a working girl. I wasn't naïve, but at first, I didn't catch the ramifications of her words. I was thinking that she perhaps worked in a fancy hotel or something. We talked for a little while, then she suggested that we have a drink at the bar across the street.

Once there, I met a lady who managed the joint she was called the nick name "Big Momma," She sat with us for a few drinks, then she told me that she was the madame of that area. She controlled all the ladies of the night in that sector. They brought most the money that they made to her. She, in turn, looked out for them in a few ways; most importantly, she got them out of jail. She left us to mingle with other bar customers. I still hadn't put two and two together about Debbi. Time passed, and the drinks had her in a touchy-feely mood. I was sitting on the barstool facing away from the counter, and now this gorgeous work of art was standing in between my legs with her head resting on my chest, explaining her problems.

It came in the darkness of the night, stealth-like, with the destructive appearance of a dark cloud of locusts approaching on the horizon. They called it crack cocaine. It was slowly eating away at the player's game. One by one, the girls were betraying their pimps in favor of the new kind of pimp. The Johns started becoming sneaky, tricky, costumers who didn't pay and ran away, sometimes violently, after they got a hit of crack. Drink-induced tears began forming in the corners of Debbi eyes as she explained that she needed someone to watch her while she worked. Oh! I got it. She meant she was "working in the hospitality industry."

I was still doing bodyguard work for certain people who needed an escort. I worked for a realty company, picking up late rent from difficult tenants. Fortunately, I never had any trouble collecting. They always gave up the money in a hurry once I knocked on their doors. I loved my work. To be honest, I was secretly always looking forward for some action. I never charged anyone a cent because money was never a motivator for me. So, I volunteered to look out for her during the first of the month and some weekends.

There weren't any problems in our arrangement mainly because Debbi only dealt with white guys from up north, factory workers and such. She said that the reason that she didn't fool with Black guys was because they were cheap. The white guys took one hit of crack and spent all their money, so much so that they would offer their vehicles for pawn to keep the night with her going. They rarely had sex with her. Instead, they watched her undress and pose while they took a hit and did their thing.

Someone upstairs really did not approve of what I was doing. My helicopter guardians repeatedly warned me to stop doing what I was doing. It was dangerous duty, but I was having the time of my life hanging out with her girlfriends and with some of the real pimps that were a carbon copies of those portrayed in movies and on TV. I loved partying all night with them and then coming outdoors only to be suddenly blinded by the rays of the brilliant morning sun.

It was another of one of those three-days-and-little-sleep weekends when I'd had enough and went home to bed around 4:00 a.m. At some point in my dream, as always, I started flying around slightly above the clouds over an area where I have flown many times before. When I was bumped into on my aft starboard side—the bottom of my right foot, for civilians. I looked down only to see a teenage male angel pushing my right foot. Never and never since had any person or thing joined me in flight. He asked me if I wanted to see the rest of the solar system. I answered, "Sure. Why not?" So off we went.

We scooted past the moon, and out of the corner of my right eye, I glanced at the bumpy, rusty-looking Mars. Wow! Not even a second later, my heart popped out of my chest. I gasped for air as I viewed the sheer size of Jupiter. Compared to Earth's golf-ball size, I was looking at a basketball. We were still flying when one-tenth of a second later, I saw the rings of Saturn. We stopped. For a long while, all things considered, I just marveled at the majestic way those remarkable, wonderful colored rings surrounded the planet.

After the beauty of Saturn and Uranus, Neptune's rings were sort of average, something like a kid brother who was not grown yet. We paused at Pluto. I scrutinized it for a second. I looked back towards the sun. Then I looked back at Pluto. It looked like it belonged there with the rest. I called it a planet.

We traveled farther away from the solar system to see what else was out there. It was nothing but total thick darkness after a long flight of seeing nothing. The next galaxy was only a blurry pin light very far away. A few minutes later, we passed a rouge planet stumbling around like a lost, wayward child. But the farther we traveled, there was nothing out there. The distant, faint speck of light I could tell was just too far away. It was time to turn around and go home. And so, we did. We shot passed the planets and stopped abruptly just outside of Earth's Karman line, which is about twenty-five mile outside of the atmosphere.

I didn't question my copilot at first because the scenery out there was awesome. It was like that joyous feeling that goes with you when you leave the amusement park. The trance was broken as it started to become cold. In fact, I was shivering. I turned toward my tour guide companion and said, "It's too cold. It is time to wake up." He answered, "You are not asleep. You are not sleep. He told you to stop doing what you are doing."

Only a few minutes passed, but it seemed like hours as I endured an unbearable coldness, colder than the numbing sensation of touching and getting stuck on a block of dry ice. As I was blacking out, I was shanking so bad that I was vibrating. My teeth chattered to the point of my jaw breaking. In my dimming vision was this pretty blue marble called home. I could clearly see the Great Wall of China, the boot shape of Italy, and the Great Lakes that surrounded the upper and lower peninsulas of Michigan. So near and yet so far.

I was so frozen that I began to go into shock from the blistering cold. Then! I woke up in my bed still shanking from my lucid dream, or so I thought. I got out of bed to look at the thermostat. It registered a very hot eighty-seven degrees in the apartment. *Then why am I still shaking?*

I went to the bathroom and looked in the mirror. I was shocked as I saw black spots on the tip of my nose and on my right cheek bone. I nearly jumped out of my skin when I looked down at my hands. The tips of my fingers were black. Thinking back, I gasped when suddenly I remembered where I'd seen black spots on a human body before.

COACH GEORGE ALLEN

Legendary football coach and local St. Clair Shores Michigan native George Allen was the second representative from a professional football organization who had contacted me to give me the opportunity to join their team for the upcoming season.

The next pickup games that the alley boys played in after my younger brothers shut out the New York Jets draft pick, always had two scouts present at, no matter where we played. I don't know how they knew where we would show up, given that sometimes we did not know where we would play until game time. A car often pulled up at the field. It was a black, secretive-looking Crown Victoria automobile with totally blacked-out windows, the kind where you can see outside but could not see inside the car unless the windows were rolled down. And sometimes they were.

The man wore Vince Lombardi–style glasses, but the face looked familiar from TV. And if I didn't know any better, I would have sworn that he was Russ Thomas, the Detroit Lions general manager. *Naw! What would he be doing at a pickup game?* I was sitting in a neighborhood bar in the early spring of 1984. It was a small place with a capacity of about sixty with a standard juke box that played the background music. With dim lighting, the joint had a tranquilizing, intimate atmosphere.

A middle-aged gentleman walked in and sat down beside me at the bar as I was relaxing with a glass of wine. He broke my tranquility by asking me if I wanted to play professional football. I shrugged my shoulders and answered, "Perhaps." My mind was not on football that night. He continued with, "If you did, how much money would you want for the year?" I answered, "I'll accept no less than a million dollars a year." I knew the value of football talent. I would have felt cheated, like if I had been picked up at a garage sale, if I accepted a football contract that paid me less than a million dollars a year. He did not answer me. He downed his drink, shook my hand, and left.

I didn't think that he was serious because football players weren't making that kind of money for a year's work. Only the top, elite Pro Bowl players made that kind of money. However, I knew that I was a sudden-impact type of play maker who came from out of nowhere.

At the time I wore number twenty while playing for the Great Lakes Raiders semipro football team. Soon after the meeting at the bar, I had the pleasure of spending time with the Lions legend and Hall of Fame corner-back Dick "Night Train" Lane at a Wayne State symposium. He sat with me, and we talked for a nice little while that evening, and at the end of our meeting, he gave me a few pointers on playing the safety position.

I met the strange man at the bar again. He never introduced himself, never said where he was from or who he worked for. He only happily said that I could make perhaps six million dollars a year with incentives games played and performance bonuses. I had picked up this stupid idea, and I don't know where it came from, but on spring break from college I thought you were supposed to go on a drinking binge. I indulged heavily in this unspoken act for a week. I drank Hennessy, like a lush, starting after break-fast every day until night came, then I continued sitting with a glass in my hand in after-hours joints.

He told me that I would have to first sign a free-agent contract as a walk on. And after I played in six games, they would tear it up and renegotiate the terms. So far so good. But unfortunately, he had to mess things up by saying, "And would you play for the Detroit Lions?" I was 90 percent drunk and was not mindful of my choice of words. I answered, "Hell no. We don't play football like that." The sharp alley boys didn't, and neither did my Great Lakes Raiders teammates who didn't even get paid to play, but they didn't make that many mental errors by jumping offside on a fourth and four. None of us dropped balls constantly, missed tackles, or exhibited a total lack of effort on the playing field.

I told him that they do not care about winning because year after year they did nothing about the line of scrimmage. In my liquor-induced retort I told him about the blocking that the Cowboys gave their running back Emmitt Smith. I told him that my grandmother could gain a hundred yards behind the Dallas Cowboys offensive line. And I also told. him how Detroit Lions, running back Barry Sanders got hit the moment he touched the ball.

I went on a rampage and continued by saying that I didn't know what they called it, but that was not professional football that they were playing and that the run and shoot offense was maybe good enough to get a team to the first round of the playoffs, but basically that was it. But that was the farthest they could go because the deeper a team advanced into the playoffs, the better the talent and position of the other teams got across the board. Scoring real fast looked good for the fans, but it left the defense on the field way too long.

Playing sandlot and semipro football is one thing; playing on the big stage and getting paid was another. When good people play on bad teams (not me), they tend to duplicate the same bad habits and start uncharacteristically dropping balls or getting called for holding when the offense just made a first down from fourth and fifteen. My guys did not believe in accepting losing and playing terribly to be normal.

I didn't care what others thought about me turning down that kind of money. I analyzed that organization over the years, and I learned that because of the way that they did business and how they handle their players, the oddsmaker in Las Vegas gave the team longshot odds to appear in the Super bowl. In the real-world, the Detroit football team had absolutely zero chance of winning a championship.

I did not understand the logic of how they drafted their new players. How in the heck do you pick a player from the draft order that the expert numbered in a lottery order? The team would already have six above-average linebackers on their current roster. And yet, at draft time, just because another linebacker fell to them as the best player available in their slot, even when the team had a serious need for an offensive lineman, they would draft the linebacker. My road dogs and I played precision football. They played in some ugly games. I refused to sign with them.

I watched them play that year, and six games into the season, there was no way I could have lived with myself. Apart from watching Tampa Bay for years demonstrating how not to play for sixty minutes, I never learned how a team could have played football as bad as that. I knew my game awareness for a winning formula, my psychic abilities, and my tolerance for the sport. The teams had some talented, young players; however, at times they were overwhelmed in crucial moments and doubled down with ill-timed, undisciplined bungling, and they exhibited a jinx-like (bad luck), knack for playing the refs. Never given the benefit of the doubt, they were besieged with phantom penalties, blatant non-calls, and head-scratching rule changes that canceled a normal touch down.

This was discouraging and just too bizarre for me to stomach on a continual basis. It seemed like it happened only when this team played on Sunday and a usually reliable officiating crew had an off day. The conclusion that I reached from observing was that the team was caught in a constant rebuilding loop. Starting from scratch every three or four years is not a winning formula, and that surely wasn't for me.

Suspiciously, shortly after my declining, all my letters that I had received from other NFL teams and the United States Football League stopped coming to the house. Correspondence I called we are un abled to use your services at this time but maybe later letters that I received from the Seattle Seahawks and Oakland Raiders, the Washington Federals, the New Jersey Generals, and the San Antonio Gunslingers evaporated. But the real mysterious change was that every two weeks I would receive a thick Sears catalogue–sized pouch from the late coach Sam Wyche. He would be asking me to send him one thousand dollars so that I could come to his football camp and then learn how to play football. Even his packages abruptly stopped coming. I'm not sure what happened to my correspondences from other teams, but I surely don't believe in that much of a coincidence.

Coach George Allen, Hall of Fame coach of teams in the National Football League, as well of teams from the United States Football League, gave me my second shot at professional football when he coached the Arizona Rattlers. I had no idea that he was born in the Detroit area. He was noted for preferring veteran players over younger ones. Coach Allen got wind of a time that I ran on the Special Olympic track at Wayne State University field when I was going through the preseason timings for the Detroit Titans, the only semipro team that let me walk on as a quarterback from the start.

As a forever backup quarterback, during practice I never had any problem working with any teams' receivers and running backs going through the passing tree segment, after which the head coach tested me by explaining a very elaborate play. Then he asked me to repeat it back to him. I did, and he said, "I have my quarterback." Unfortunately, the league folded the same week that the Titans' season started. After all my prior contacts magically disappeared, Coach Allen was also one of the few coaches who did not follow football protocol. He believed in giving wayward players a second chance. Another thing that he did that was contrary to the rest of the league was that he didn't discharge or dismiss a ballplayer once they reached the age of thirty. He preferred veterans over younger players. And unlike other coaches, he knew that everybody hadn't hit their prime once they reached that age.

There were many late bloomers such as me who didn't get trapped in a mindset that told them they could no longer do things with their bodies once they hit some arbitrary timeline. Manly the reasons why many of the over thirty crowd couldn't do great sporting activities requiring physical strength anymore was because they never had it in them in the first place. Some nonathletic brainiacs decided that thirty was the finishing line for a football player, that was until the masses woke up and realized that sixty was the new forty. However, that goes along with the life- long project of continuing to be exercising the spirit, mind, and body making a habit of practicing moderation with food and drinks.

In any event, Coach Allen got wind of a 4.22 forty-yard timing that I ran twice during assessments for the only team that let me quarterback from the very beginning. I received a letter from him, telling me that I was invited to attend the tryouts in Arizona. The problem was that I had no money and only one week to get there. So, the hustle was on.

It was the end of the month in the neighborhood, which meant that just about everyone in my circle of family and friends was broke, nix for the people that I socialized with every day. Who brags when they are partying with you, gulping down drinks that they didn't chip in to buy, and saying,

"Don't worry? You know me. I always got your back. If you need anything, come and see me." For me, I always take drink talk with a grain of salt. Asking for help is something that I rarely if ever did.

However, I had a long road ahead with a short time to make it happen, and I needed the assistance to come up with the fare for the flight, hotel, and food. Just as I suspected, every one of the big talkers had an excuse as to why they could not help. Spending the week soliciting funds for getting to Arizona was time consuming and exhausting. My father was the only help that I received in getting there. From that hustling, I was spent by the time that I boarded the last flight in the Detroit Metro Airport to Phoenix.

It was the tail end of winter. I had on a sweater, jacket, and long johns, and I was still freezing from the blast of cold air that comes with wide open airports during the winter months. The plane touched down in Phoenix around 10:00 p.m., and to make matters worse, there were no cabs outside. I waited for an hour or so to no avail. I had to walk from the airport to find the first hotel in sight. It was after midnight. When I finally found a little dump that had to do, I had only a few hours to unwind from the turbulence of getting there and the flight. I had to be at the field at 8:00 a.m. I was unable to fall asleep right away because I was worried about bed bugs in the creepy, jail-sized room. It was around 3:00 a.m. when I did.

As always, I made it to the field on time. When I arrived there, it wasn't what I expected because I'd never seen that many players on one field before. There were around 300 hundred young men running around, doing different drills for all the assistant coaches who had whistles around their necks and stop watches in their hands. This gathering was unique in that this was the United States Football League. The very next year, the National Football League stolen Coach Allen's idea about bringing all the rookie players in at one time and giving them different skill tests to perform. The NFL moved this event to Indianapolis, Indiana, the very next year and called the same thing "Combine."

The very relevant conditions that I did not factor when readying myself for the tryout were jet lag and the scorching heat. What was lost in the mix was that I lived in Arizona during my Advanced Individual Training for the army. I was aware of the weather conditions there, but I somehow forgot about them. When I left Detroit, the temperature was around a freezing forty-five degrees. The temperature when I arrived at the field was 110 degrees. I was burning up a soon as I got off the bus.

The Arizona Rattlers wanted me to try out for the defensive back position. So, they had me workout with that set of skilled players before we did our timings for the forty. When it was my time to run, Coach Allen and a few of the other coaches stopped what they were doing to come over and witness the ultra-speedy back burn up the track. The sun was West Coast bright. Before I ran, I looked at the arrow on the wet-bulb temperature board that now pointed at a burning hot 125 degrees.

Ready to run and dehydrated I got down in a three-point stance to take off. I made it twenty yards before something zapped all the energy out of my body. I didn't just break out in sweat; I broke out in a waterfall. I was completely exhausted and drenched and in uncomfortable clothes that were sticking to me by the time I had reached the finish line with a pedestrian five second timing, a time that I hadn't done since before I was a teenager. It was a terrible speed for a defense back.

You get two tries, and my second was even worst. I was dripping wet, like I'd been in the rinse cycle of the washing machine. I could barely make it to the finish line. All the coaches knew something was wrong with me. The whole sequence of events from getting funds to get there, walking from the airport, and not considering the heat, all took a toll on my body. I wasn't acclimated. I was devastated, resting on one knee, and I managed to stand up as Coach Allen approached me. He saw that I was in very bad shape when he put his arm around my shoulder, and what really surprised me was that out of all the hundreds of players there, he called me by name.

He looked me in the eyes and said, "Willie, you really stunk up the place." He smiled when he said that. I knew that this was a lighthearted moment, and he was joking, or perhaps he wasn't. To keep my confidence up, he told me to water up and go participate in the other drill for defensive backs. And there was always next time. What I really took from all of that was the fact that he called me by name. To me that was very special, coming from the iconic football Hall-of-Fame coach.

THE BODYGUARD:
"WHAT THE U.S. ARMY HID"

I didn't get picked out of a crowd to obtain the luxury of sleeping on a cot by the front entrance in the officer's tent by chance. My fellow comrades slept on the snow-covered, frozen-solid ground in an unlit, unheated pup tent, but it was because of my ability to relay messages and find other companies camping on the side of tricky roads in the dense forest that the officers kept me with them. It was also because of my marksmanship skills.

On the day that I officially ended the overseas part of my tour of duty, I sat down at a desk in the office of a discharge center in Furth, Germany. The civilian female clerk was assigned to assist me in going over my files to make sure everything was included before I flew back to America. She meticulous went over my discharge folder line by line, and suddenly her jaw dropped open. She gasped for air as she stood up with my file in her hand and told me that she would be right back.

What now? I was thinking. She went toward the back of the building where, on the upper level of the back wall, there was a small ten-by-ten office. It had twelve iron steps attached to it that reached the doorway. *Here we go again*, was the thought on my mind. Because I really wanted to go home, the worst-case scenario just had to creep in. I had three years left on my contract that said that the army could call me back to active duty when it was necessary. I figured that she saw some orders in my file. It was known among soldiers that in the military nothing was written in stone orders could be changed in a batting of an eye. A solider maybe shipped to Alaska in the winter, in the middle of the night on the orders of a high ranking official

I saw her talking to a higher up through the only four-by-three window-pane. They seemed to be having some kind heavy discussion while looking at my folder. I was really getting nervous thinking that I was not going home as the second lieutenant with the regulation haircut—dressed in brown khaki with all the awards and trimmings pinned on his chest—began shaking his head with the file in his hand as he descended the stairs. *This can't be good news*, I thought as I floated into a bad state of mind where everything started moving in slow motion. The officer sat down in the clerk's chair, pulled it to the table, laid down my file, looked me in the eye, and said, "Mr. McClain, you can't put your marks-man-ship scores of (Expert M16 semi- automatic rifle, M45 handgun, 25MM machine gun, M79 Grenade launcher, 50MM machine gun) in your permanent file. You need to think about this. If you, do you will be the target of every militia organization around the world. Seeing this, they all will try to recruit you in a heartbeat." I knew that he was correct. I also knew that he had my best interest at heart.

I only needed half a second to decide to leave the box in line twenty-six—where decorations, medals, badges, and commendation were listed—and line twenty-seven—a box to mention remarks—on my DD214 official discharge form from the service almost empty and pretty much dumbed down. I had to if I wanted any semblance of what is called peace of mind.

What made me think that they were about to order me back to active duty was that the reenlistment recruiter in our company knew that I fell in love with the city of Berlin, almost like I did with Munich, after the few times that we radar, operators inspected the Wall that separated the eastern and western sectors of the city. When we had an opportunity, we walked about the town afterward. So, he offered me a six thousand dollars signing bonus, which back then, was a boat load of money and is still unheard of for an enlisted man. And I would also have been given orders to report to Berlin for my next duty station.

What he offered was a tremendous prize for a youngster, still just twenty years old. But here comes the letdown. He stated that I would be given all those goodies on one condition, and it was a doozy. He said that once I signed the contract, I would never be able to return to the United States for any reason. *What!* I don't drink absolutions or ultimatums down very well.

It doesn't taste right, and they just don't sit well in my stomach. *Let me get away from this crazy man.* I loved the military life and still watch the Star Trek franchise on TV because it was military. And I really wanted to stay. However, I believe in keeping a plan B up your sleeve, leaving the backdoor unlocked and having an option and or an escape route in all matters, just in case I change my mind. Telling me that I could never go home again was a career killer.

The very first time that I had to decline a million-dollar contract because my escape route was cut off and the backdoor was locked occurred only a few months after I broke up with my Gypsy woman. That one stays with me for a lifetime because it involved a real-life princess. I wore a red silk shirt with a tailor-made, three-piece black suede suit along with black suede shoes. I was dressed sharper than Teflon Don on a Sunday dinner date.

I was sitting at the bar, staring at a picture on the wall in a guesthouse located in northeast Germany. A slight breeze rushed in brushed across my face as the front door opened, causing me to turn back and look at who was coming through the entrance. This beautiful young lady walks in, followed by three generations of men in her company. They sat at a table in a curtained room that was off on the side of the main floor. She seemed preoccupied. The uncle came over and invited me to have a beer and sit at the table. Beer! I'm all in.

We yap it up for a few before the conversation became business-like when they showed me pictures of the two homes that the young lady owned. They later said that they could be mine. They enlighten me on the legalized businesses that they own, and all three men—her grandfather, uncle, and brother—emptied out their pockets to show me the thousands of dollars they carried around without a concern. I stopped counting at the twenty-five thousand dollars that was between them. What hit me like a sledgehammer was the fact they offered me finance employment in the family business and the two houses where one was located on the East Coast and the other on the West. All of that along with more than a million- dollar dowery if I married the princess. Wow! I didn't know what to say. I was leaning toward saying yes on the spot throughout the negotiation. She was so pretty that player's club rule number five flew out of the window. That wasn't what changed my mind. It wasn't the money. From the age of fifteen, I was already rich.

What stopped me from marrying the Italian princess was that at the end of the arrangement, I thought about when I wanted to retire. I asked if it was true that once you get in, you could never get out. The grandfather and uncle answered, "Yes, it's true." The grandfather reiterated, "You can never get out." These guys were tough, even the Lord God gives you a choice. But not this gang. This along with my marksmanship skills and player's club rule number five was the deciding factor and real reason why I had put the brakes on in my marriage to the princess.

Why did I sleep on the cot near the entrance of the officer's tent? And what was all the commotion about leaving information off the existing document on lines number 26 and 27? Here is the reason: Only expert M16 was listed on my discharged. What was not put on was the rest of my marksmen evaluation, which went as follows: expert M45 sidearm, expert M79 grenade launcher, and expert M25mm machine gun. The armory sergeant who kept the marksmen records was curious and wanted to know how I would perform on the big caliber 50mm machine gun. So, he scheduled a test for the next time we had to spend months in rugged Hohenfels training center.

The day came, and they escorted me to the firing range. It takes two people to operate this powerful weapon, a shooter and a loader who also has the job of knowing when it's time to change the melting gun barrel and what types of gloves to use when changing the barrel. The first thing that I had to do and was tested on was taking the weapon completely apart and then putting it back together—a cinch for me. Then, I had to know what kind of ammo to use when loading gun, what to do if it jammed, and when to changing the sizzling hot barrel. I had no problems up to that point.

The other fellow who operated the big machine gun with me fired first. The target was an old, rusted Opel midsize automobile, stationed 100 meters down the firing range. He put some holes in the still intact car. When it was my turn, I ripped that car apart. At my finish, I blew off all the tires. There was nothing left of the car but the smoldering iron frame. We policed up the spent rounds and headed back to the instructor's booth to pick up our score cards. He handed my card to me upside down. When I turned it over it was stamped "Expert?"

What also was omitted from line twenty-seven "remarks" was that I was a commander at eighteen years old. My mother received five Letters of Commendation from the Department of Defense. And in my company, I was awarded the title of "Soldier of the Month" five times. She also received those. Every time I got restricted to base for waking up five minutes after seven offs bases, I had nothing better to do than to shine all my boots, have all of my uniforms cleaned and pressed, and make formation on time. And I got off the base by voluntarily going on roving patrol with the military police to check on the guesthouses and bars where the troops normally hung out. I won that title five times, every time that I threw my hat in the ring.

I was one of the very few enlisted men who was allowed the privilege of ordering food from the kitchen of the officers' club. Those guys ate the finest cuisine. I walked into the joint one night, not knowing that they were dancing, celebrating, and partying their tails off. It was the officers' ball. The place was hooked up, colorful balloons everywhere. Man, oh man, they all were dressed sharp. I believe that some young men join the service just to wear military dress uniforms because I could have easily been one of them. Seeing them together made me think that there aren't any other formal outfits that one can ware on this planet that stand out and match an officers' dress. It makes the distinguished wearer stand out and look like a freshly polished and glowing crystal chandelier.

I was a little nervous, walking cautiously down the aisle through a partying crowd. They were smiling with a drink in each person's hand. A few heads turned and looked at the out-of-place solider attempting to reach the back of the joint where the kitchen was located. I turned my head to the left and looked at some of the most handsome table setups that I have ever seen. The place was jumping. I spotted an officer that I knew from battalion sitting at a table. I thought, *Do I really belong in here?* He smiled, tilted his champagne glass toward me, and said, "Salute." From that point on, I relaxed. I was posted on that back wall, mesmerized at the sight until my food was ready. I always enjoy looking at a good time.

You automatically received a secret clearance when you graduated from Fort Huachuca intelligence school in Arizona. They said that for my own good, on my discharge, they left off the fact that when we tested out as the best for excellence in 1973, the whole radar section was awarded a S2 top secret military clearance. We received two missions from S1 before the conflict in Vietnam rebooted, throwing the whole military machine for a loop.

The first was a scouting mission; we were briefed by a first lieutenant who took the red-eye flight from Washington. And that was a first briefing where we each received a manila folder secured by a red colored circular strip with large font letters stamped on it spelling "Top Secret." The second mission that we received from the top brass in D.C. showed exactly what they thought about us collectively.

It was 4: 15 a.m. The alert siren sounded on base. It was a red alert, which meant that everybody had to hit the bricks. In the middle of the night, the countries of Egypt and Israel had serious fighting words. There was nothing unusual about rousing everyone out of bed at that hour, so we packed up our gear and thought we were headed to travel with the wagon train. However, that morning was highly out of the ordinary. They took our radar equipment away. The battalion went in one direction, and our group had to report to the base airport and wait for orders.

Still, that was nothing too unusual. "Hurry up and wait" was the soldier's motto. And so, it went. As dawn early light began to illuminate the tarmac, we could hear the whirling helicopter blades whipping against the wind. They became more and more audible until we saw a big, fat, menacing-looking Huey began to land near us. Still, that was nothing out of the ordinary. Because we had repelled down off steep cliffs and mountains, we'd learned how to jump out of helicopters with our bulky equipment on our backs before.

The aircraft landed, and the captain disembarked the chopper to brief us on this sudden mission. The first thing we noticed was that how sharp he was in his flight uniform. It fitted him so well that it looked like it was tailor made. It made all our crew wanted to join the air force right then and there. It was a stealth mission, and S1 did not want to alert the whole

United States Marine Corps, so they wanted to send us to ground zero for a recognizance mission instead.

No problem so far. He briefed us and told us that our equipment would be dropped out of the back of a cargo plane before we got there. And then he started talking sideways about how and when to cut a parachute. We all stood at ease, looking bewildered as he explained how to land and roll once we hit the ground. "Wait, what!" came from all of us as he explained how high we would be jumping from out of the back of a cargo plane once we reached our destination.

The problem was that we'd never even had the chance to jump off one of those high towers that they practice on, let alone fall from the sky. This was a new one for us, and we looked at each other, shrugged our shoulders, poked our lips out, and said in unison, "OK." Most of us figured, what the hell, we are going to die from something, anyway. We might as well do that. S1 thought that we could do anything and be great at it.

At the time, hiding my expertise from militia organizations around the world seemed like a good idea. However, thinking back, it was complicated. On the one hand, sure it prevented me from being recruited by some unscrupulous individuals. But on the other hand, my discharge was so diluted and watered down that it looked so plain when I tried to obtain civil employment. It just wasn't a good reference source. When employers look at a discharge, and if it has award-winning expert written all over it, they will create a high-paying job just for you. For instance, I was sent to school and trained to drive eight different vehicles, anything from a jeep to a small tank, whatever mode of transportation that officers at battalion wanted to be escorted in that day. I've maintained a legal chauffeur driver's license ever since then.

I did bodyguard work on numerous occasions. I work well with intelligent people, and I can shoot straight. Those skills might not be relevant for employment in a metal stamping plant, but a Fortune 500 executive might have looked at my fully loaded DD214 discharge, and hypothetically she or he could have thought that perhaps they could use an award-winning driver to escort them around, one who was honest, smart, dressed nicely, and didn't like wasting bullets by missing the target. I really believed that leaving too many achievements off my discharge prevented a lot of profit-able, out-of-the-box employment opportunities.

Off the record, if there were any words that I would use to describe how I feel about my marksmen skills, they would be "nothing special" because chiefly anybody can shoot guns. Growing up, mostly all the young boys in the rural areas of the country, and many of the ghetto's city dwellers, were taught, as a rite of passage, how to drive the family car before they were fourteen years old. It was just about the same age when they received their first rifle. I had a Winchester plus the holster and pistol, the same one that the man called Paladin in the TV series *Have Gun—Will Travel*. But mine was a quality replica. It fired plastic bullets from the chamber, but they still hit their targets. But I was prouder of the dead-center accuracy that I had with my archery skills. From scratch we made our own bow and arrows, which I preferred to use. Every Saturday morning after we boys shot two games of marbles, like clockwork, my uncle Robert would come out of the house to the backyard where we were playing and show us how to throw knives at targets from any angle—trees, fences, houses, in the ground. We were even good at that.

CHILDREN OF THE NIGHT

I was looking down at my fingertips and suddenly remembering where I'd seen charcoal black spots on people's face and hands after my dream about flying through solar system made me gasp for air. That was the first monumental occurrence in my life since dealing with celestial beings that compelled me to reexamine my existence in detail. What was perplexed me was how in the world I got frostbite after waking up shaking and freezing from a dream. Now, I became apprehensive and timed every time that I looked at my hands to whenever I did something that the angels told me not to do. I started thinking that perhaps these guys were serious about my place in the universe.

I had to speak with Debbi, my hospitality working girlfriend who I had listed as a four-star female in my small pocket-size personal black book that I kept since my military days. My relationship with her fell under rule number four B from the player's handbook. Because of that dream (or reality) that got to me, I had to tell her that I could no longer cover her back.

I was introduced to symptoms of gangrene, frostbite and black fingers and toes during a time spent in brutally cold midwinter Minnesota-like temperatures. We were whisked away to a military war exercise that was in combination with other nation's militaries called Reforger. It was located at Camp Wildflecken. We were taken once more at 4 a.m. A few of the soldiers who had mastered the art of sleeping while standing in formation scampered around, lifeless like a robot going through the motions and packing war gear by memory, still half-asleep.

Unlike before, this was a two-month assignment spending time in the frozen tundra, far away from civilization. One by one, after only the third week there, troops started reporting to the medical tent, complaining about dark spots on their face and hands. Their feet turned a greyish, ugly color and smelled bad. During the next week, those symptoms ballooned into epidemic proportions throughout whole battalion, mainly with the ground troopers and tankers. Radar operators had no relevance and didn't factor in with these types of tank exercises. So, they sent me to help out with the overwhelmed medic to learn how to treat the cases of hypothermia-, first-, second-, and third-degree trench foot, gangrene, and frostbite. These, I recalled, were the same kind of black spots on my face and hands after that solar-scare dream. Or was it a lucid dream?

I was more intrigued about hanging out with Debbi and her cohort than worrying about their clients. I was on the path in college of obtaining a minor degree in psychology. As a required step, I started with observation, taking notes in my mind on what the catalyst was that made them get into a life of the world's oldest profession. And what made them tick? Almost all of them, at a very early age, were forced into an incestuous relationship by a close family member. What was stunning was the fact that sex in the bedroom did not fire up the oven anymore. They all had an affinity for the spontaneous thrill of possibly being caught, thriving on the cusp of danger and excitement that came with open-air, public sex.

I witnessed the pimping game in the city being destroyed by the stealth introduction of crack cocaine. No longer did they have total control of their ladies. The crack took away that bond. The money didn't get back to them. Little by little, the incoming funds became smaller, to the point of nonexistence. Beatings did not work on the girls anymore. They took the lumps on their heads and still held onto the costly eight ball of crack hidden inside their vaginal cavity.

The pimps didn't fare too well with the crack, either. They stopped snorting the powder coke through their noses. I saw them smoking non-chalantly, like it was legal, in the back of the many after-hours clubs that used to saturate the city. They thought that they were not like their girls and could leisurely smoked the coke without consequences. But they were dead wrong. In three months', time, I saw some major players lose their Cadillacs. With no money coming in from the girls and no other skills or talents compatible with regular employment, some pawned or sold their vehicles for crack. There was nothing sadder then seeing a played-out pimp talk about what he used to do, now driving around in a rust-colored Pinto with the license plate taped on the driver's side back window and an out-of-place spare tire on the passenger side of the front wheel.

Debbi was an attractive, petite lady with a nice personality, who had the language, charisma, and style of a thousand-dollar-per-date-night call girl. She came from an upper middle-class family. She dressed extravagantly. There was this one month where I was baffled after I took her to Dittrich Furs in Detroit to repair a genuine waist-length fur jacket that she bought from them. What tossed me into a state of mental uncertainty was the fact that she displayed all the signs of being a regular customer. She knew where to park, and only a person who knew the ins and outs of the fancy store operations and could take care of business that fast, coming back to the car in less than ten minutes.

She never talked bad about anyone and always looked at the bright side of any situation. She was simply a good person that many of the clients that she dated would have gladly married and taken home to mother. She had a beautiful, wholesome, caring nature. She was a person that truly did not belong on the streets.

A week had gone by, and the black marks has yet to disappear. In fact, they did not go away for almost two-and-a-half months. Thoughts of how I got those marks made me extremely leery. So, I went to tell my good friend that I could no longer watch her back. I never tried to explain the strange phenomenon that happened so many times to or around anyone, mostly because they already pegged me, thinking that they knew me. And some-how, they thought I should be like them. But I was not. They were under the influence of a condition called the Mandela Effect. This occurs when so many people remember experiences that don't match reality. And every time I did try to give others the details of my life, they just shot right over their heads. They always had this bewildered stare and twisted their heads side to side like dogs do when they can't make sense of what their master is saying.

In a matter of months, the once-thriving, festive streets around the bars and business where she hung, had a creepy, ominous feeling that something wasn't right. The usual darkness outside was as if the night was covered by a transparent coating of glossy varnish. I could sense the covered-up trouble brewing even before I spoke to her. She had a defiant attitude by nature. A few weeks prior, she was a witness to a robbery and murder. She was at a drug-den house party when all hell broke loose. They busted in shooting, taking out the door man and the homeowner that night in a house located in an area across seven-mile road. She wanted justice for her fallen friends that she'd grown up with in the hood. There was only a week or so to go before she could eagerly testify. There was one huge, glaring problem that all her close family friends and I explained to her as to why it was a bad idea: the shooter who was a two-time felon, and that incident was his third strike. Residing in certain large cities, walking the street was far more dangerous than walking in a few hot-spot terrains in the military. Those young boys were not playing in this town. The nightly news showed the tragic scenes of a deadly drive-by shootings. They were part of the gang that lived right in her neighborhood. To them, a life was not worth ten dollars.

They were mostly fatherless, self-governed young boys that were ruthless and extremely violent. They shot, robbed, and firebombed the houses of newbie dealers who tried to invade their territory. I know first-hand because I went inside of the burned-up homes just to see what they did it to a few of my close relatives. Once I was approached by a twelve-year-old kid on a bike who packed a 22 automatic. He had a big wad of paper money and bragged about the large bag of nickel-and-dime crack that he had to sell. I clearly remembered the incident because I was thinking, *here is this little punk kid with a pocket full of money. And I am grown man with only eight dollars in my pockets.*

Debbi was the only living witness who was at the tragic robbery. She did not care. She never made it to court. A week later, about the time that I normally would have been with her, I just happened to read the early edition of the *Detroit News* and almost passed out from shock! "Girl scheduled to testify. Body found riddled with machine-gun bullets on a street across Seven Mile and Woodward." I believe they even spelled her name right in the newspaper.

MILLIONAIRE BALLPLAYERS

People around me just didn't know what to think about me because I had a nonchalant attitude about money. I never cared about other people's money or what others possessed. I was always glad for them or anyone coming up. I was never impressed if it wasn't mine. I became a millionaire at the tender young age of fifteen. My fictional mentor was *The Great Gatsby*, penned by F. Scott Fitzgerald. This book was required reading in one of my English literature classes. My nonfictional guide was the reclusive, allusive, multitalented Howard Hughes. Growing up left-handed in a right-handed world, one had to be ambidextrous and multitalented. I could bat a baseball, shoot any firearm, or play the guitar with either hand.

Our garage was loaded with a variety of sports equipment: baseball bats and gloves, basketballs, volleyballs and nets, a tennis table with paddles, roller skates, ice skates, a golf bag loaded with clubs and irons, swimming fins, snorkels, goggles, many bowling balls, and some footballs. But twice a year, we had to move everything to the upper-storage space to make room for telephone books. Thousands of white pages and the gigantic yellow pages filled the garage all the way to the top. My mother, father, and I had only four locations to cover twice a year: St. Clair Shores, Grosse Pointe and Grosse Pointe Shores, and Indian Village on the east side of Detroit.

For four years, I had been in just about every rich and well-to-do person's home, delivering the phone books. I kind of didn't like the Van Dyke side of Indian Village because the apartment buildings many did not have elevators. Those long walks to get to the front door of some of those homes weren't a joke. Anyway, for the first two years we only had to put the heavy books on the front steps, but by the third year, the clients wanted the books brought all the way into the back pantry. Or most of the time there was a small brown desk that had a long center draw with three large rectangular drawers on the left or right side. The desk had a folding middle door that locked the workspace tight when pulled down. In this arrangement, the telephone was always near the desk.

The maids or butlers or whoever answered the door had me take the books to the desk. And they started giving me sandwiches and a two- to twenty-dollar tip. And, more importantly, they gave me advice on how they made their fortunes. The male homeowners usually sat at the desk, figuring out a budget. Ninety-five percent of those rich guys smoked on a pipe and told me the same thing about what it was like to be rich.

There were three main conditions that stood out in all cases: first, your conduct had to exhibit graciousness. Your personality has to say upper echelon, even when you're dressed in jeans and say nothing. You had to act like you were rich in bad times as well as the good; second, remember, it's only money. They all said that there were many roads to Rome. In different ways, you can always make more; and third, never keep your money in your home. It was always kept in another secured location.

I adopted their philosophy at fifteen years of age. Since that time, my behavior and thoughts were prosperous and of privilege. And even when I was homeless and sleeping in my car, I still dressed nice and lived the life of Riley. I always thought that my loot at the time was just sequestered from me some place else. If anyone asked me why I never questioned the cost of anything that I bought, I would tell them every time that I just like what I like. I wasn't concerned about money because I was already rich.

I wouldn't do anything uncharacteristic for money. Why? Because I have the Lord in my pocket. The following is an actual event that occurred in the city by the Bay. I had to get the heck out of San Diego quickly for a hell of a reason. I was laid off from my decent ship-building job. Tuesday was my appointment day at the unemployment office in San Diego. The official name of the place was the Employment Development Department (EDD). I spent hours sparring on the phone sparring with the nerve-racking computer software system that had a name called Marvin. I was assured by Marvin that in three weeks my bi-weekly unemployment check will be delivered to the general delivery section of the post office in San Francisco.

So, it was time, and I went to the General Delivery post office to get my…Oh, no! It's not there. That wasn't uncommon, though, because everyone on EDD's phone was screaming at Marvin. The computer had sent my check to Sacramento. But in another three weeks, it would be there. For the record, six weeks broke in San Fran is comparable to serving six weeks on Alcatraz Island. It's a major crime.

No matter, the Lord calls me one of His favorite sons. He says, "Do not worry about where you sleep or what you eat. Do you not see the birds? Do they worry about such things?" Alright, my Lord. Broke and tanked out, I thought about the *MAD Magazine* character Alfred E. Neuman's favorite saying, "What, Me Worry?" I did have an apartment-size Cadillac to sleep in. And unlike the homeless masses, I had a heater that worked during the cold nights of June. As I bedded down for the evening near Golden Gate Park, I never had any doubts about what my Father God could do. I had a peaceful and restful sleep.

The next day I woke and got to the restroom first, always after the maintenance people finished their cleaning duties, and did my morning wash and whatever else. Afterwards, I scraped up some change, then I headed to the gas station located on Fell Street to get my morning coffee, doughnut, and the *Chronicle* to start my day. I turned the corner and looked at the electric vehicle charging station, and there lay a weird-looking twenty-dollar bill. I thought that it was play money because I had not seen that new design before. Were those shady counterfeiters at it again? That twenty was smelling fresh and new, like it had just fallen off a treasury truck. Could this be real? So, I took the copy machine money inside the gas station. The clerk gives it a thorough once-over with every test that he had at his disposal. He said, "The money is real." I tried to spend all of it in case he changed his mind.

The very next morning, I travelled in a different direction. Standing on the corner of Oak and Baker Street, I looked down. Lo and behold, there was another twenty-dollar bill, exactly like the one that I had found the prior morning. Brand new, clean, and smelling like newly printed money, I had it checked out. And that one was good also. The following day, I ventured toward Ashbury and Hayes Street. I found another new twenty. So, I think that I had a good friend looking out for me. He or she must have been philanthropist or one of those do-good folks who don't want to be recognized for their contribution.

On the fourth morning, I headed to the record store on Haight Street. Right on the corner before Golden Gate Park, six people, three young ladies and three college-aged men, walked ahead of me as I headed up Cole Street. I looked ahead of them, and I saw a shape on the ground that almost looked like money. *Those folks are going to see it, and my lucky streak will be over,* I thought. They stopped and formed a circle as they talked. The shape laid directly on two of the six heals of their shoes. They never looked down. They finished their discussion and moved on. I was relieved as I walked to the spot and picked up the brand-new twenty.

From that day onward, I found a fresh-smelling newly printed twenty-dollar bill every other morning, no matter what direction I traveled. Over the fifty-day duration until Marvin finally sent my check to the correct address, I found a new twenty-dollar bill twenty-five times. I knew where it came from. I didn't tell anyone in San Fran how I was making it during this time. I had made a few friends there, but if I'd told anyone about the money that I was gifted daily, the

Panhandle would have once again been synonymous with the 1848 Sutter's Mill Gold Rush. People would have been sleeping underneath my car and following me around all day, searching for what I called my "manna's from heaven."

Prior to the September 1983 purchase of the United States Football League team called the New Jersey Generals—by then real-estate magnate, later president of the United States Donald Trump—the top-heavy portion of the National Football League's players such as quarterbacks, running backs, and receivers were the beneficiaries of millions of dollars a year. The rest of the players such as linemen and or defensive backs received no more than lower six-figure pay days. Most had to supplement their income by working an off-season job.

Back then the football season was no longer the six months a year. However, when the Generals signed Georgia's running back Herschel Walker to a ship load of money, the shutoff valve on the water spigot broke wide open, flooding the football world. Players, the ones almost considered as non-essential, were suddenly getting seven-figure big, fat paychecks. Just like Curtis Flood did for free agency in baseball.

That was it for me also. Back then I never thought much about football salaries. Because $300,000 a year to sign a free agent contract was not much money for me to be concerned about. I was already rich. I loved the sport and would have played for free.

I received a maybe letter from the same football club when they signed Herschel Walker. I thought, *hey, wait a minute.* In practice I would have to tackle that solid M1A2 Abrams tank barreling toward you down the playing field. All for my formal football coaches would tell anyone that I would blow up that fellow with a tremendously hard hit, just as powerful as an Armor-Piercing Grenade. I knew my talent's worth. And at that junction, I would not play for any team for any less than a million dollars a year.

It was a few weeks before the 1987 National Football League draft. Once more, at the field of one of our scheduled pickup games, that stealthy, black Crown Victoria town car with the man who looked just like the Lions' general manager Russ Thomas (who I called "mister business" and as usual wore Vince Lombardi eyeglasses) showed up on our sideline of the field. I called him that because to me his only concern was making money, not winning football. We could never close that schism between our philosophies.

The Detroit Lions was a wreck, and it was mind-blowing to me when the organization goes to New York for the annual pro football draft needing a quarterback, desperate for improvement in the defensive back field, or needing a run-blocking lineman. The organization could have already had eight quality linebackers already on the roster, but Mr. Thomas' philosophy was taking the best man available because the football experts said so. They would come out of the draft having picked another lineman. I just couldn't agree with that kind of thinking.

We had two regular twelve-year-old ballplayers that my teammates and I were coaching. One kid showed up at one of our game one day, and we told him that he had to have someone his age to play across from him. The next game he showed up with his twelve-year-old cousin. I found out that if you teach them winning, error-free understanding, the fundamentals of the sport, it is instilled in them to always believe that they can win when the chips are down. Then they have the fortitude and resolve to make it so.

We had a nine-on-nine pickup game. The scouts were there. In fact, the scouts continued to show up whenever we have a game, ever since my brothers shut down that New York Jet's draft pick. That day, right before the game starts, the Lions third-round draft pick Jerry Ball showed up to play with us.

For the record, no one has ever hit me that hard in all my football years combined. It was on one memorable play. I was at quarterback. Throughout at least four series, I slightly lifted the back heal of my right foot eight times to put in motion the twelve-year-old to see what kind of defense they were in. If someone followed him, then they were playing man to man. The young boy did not complain as an awful lot of new players do just because he did not get the ball, as we all did. We carried out our assignment. On the ninth heal lifting, as he passed me, I gave him the ball. He gashed them for a thirty-yard run. On passing downs, Mr. Ball kept getting closer and closer to decking me. On the very next play, he reached his target. It was a pass play. Because of my peripheral vision, I never had to turn my head while looking downfield.

Out of the corner of my left eye, I saw my receiver breaking free thirty-yards downfield. I needed to get the ball to the forty-five-yard line where he should be. I was a pure Purdue Boilermakers tutelage pocket passer. I threw to a spot. In front of me I saw this frighteningly huge freight train thundering toward me. It was only a forty-five-yard pass, but launching from the middle of the field, I had to put a lot of air under the ball for it to reach at least sixty-five-yards down field. I had to put some power behind the throw and had no choice but to step into the throw.

Kaboom! Jerry hit me so hard that I flew backward, upside down for quite some time. So long that I had time to think, *damn, I've been traveling in the air for so long that the FAA is going to ask me where my flight plan was.* That was one of the prettiest passes that I have ever thrown. When I finally hit the ground and looked up, I was so fond of the twelve-year-old who caught and held onto the long pass. I was especially fond of the other twelve-year-old that we were teaching because he made a beautiful tackle on the spot for no further yards.

I never knew what those Lions were doing because, right after quarterback Andre Ware was drafted, he played catch with me at a park outside of Detroit. The difference between the two of us that I noticed was that on his deep passes, I had to step up to catch the ball. On my deep passes, he had to drop back to catch the ball.

It takes one to know one. I thought that Mr. Ware was an excellent draft pick. Being a quarterback, I saw that he had a lot of rust from college on him. He needed time to adjust to reading plays and to the sheer speed of playing and getting hit no longer by growing college boys. The brutal hits were now being administered by powerful grown men.

Personally, I would have paid no attention to public opinion. Regardless, I would have sat him for a year, rather than throwing him into the Lions' den. Starting him too early destroyed his ego and confidence. The negative newspaper clippings did not help in developing his maturity in the game at all. Sitting him would have given him time to learn how to understand and grasp the calculus-like intricacies while managing and winning more than a few pro football games.

FIGHT OF THE MILLENNIUM: WHAT I HID

The brunch with Lucifer. If there is one thing that I can guarantee, it is that not one man, women, or any of the other ten favorite Children of the Lord that were born on this planet have had the nightmarish experience that I had in the year of 1991 of looking at the original architect of "Pure Terror." We were only separated by less than one foot, locking eyes.

In the earlier months of that year, at Christian Faith Center, 8691 Echo Drive, in La Mesa, California, through Baptism I experienced a refreshing cleansing of my body and soul. I was born again by pastor Doctor Jerry Bernard. So many angels continued to show up in and out of my life since I was twelve that I sometimes felt like I was a character in the often-told fable about the Dutch boy with his finger plugging a hole in a dam while the cracks multiply all over and around him. The way that they made such a fuss about me, I thought that something special was going to happen to me after the pastor lifted my drenched head out of the water. Nothing happened, but maybe three weeks later something did transpire.

She was in her late thirties and was five feet tall with dirty-blond hair that was pulled to the back and tied in a ponytail. You could tell that she used to be kind of cute in her youth. She wore clothing that reminded me of the fashion styles that females donned in the late sixties. The jeans were from that era and so was the different-colored plaid shirt with blue, white, and red square patterns. The tennis shoes that she wore were also from that sixty's timeline.

I had recognized her as the lone female member of the trio of my earthly guardian angels. She intimidated me because she was no nonsense. Before this meeting, there was a time when she yelled at the other person who was trying to talk to me. She did the same to me, but she had this very mean expression on her face and had her fist balled up, like she wanted to sock me in the head. I had never seen an angel like that before. In the books and in the movies, they always appear to be benevolent, gentle, and kind. The others that I sometimes walked with or talked to were harmless. Not this one.

I was coming home from working the afternoon shift at a temporary inspector job that needed someone with a special skill to check and record delicate electrical parts by laser. I drove home toward the east side by way of Mack Avenue. At one of the corners near the railroad tracks, a person approached me in the dark that had the silhouette outline of a woman. Perhaps the tall height made me somewhat skeptical. As the person stuck their head inside the window on passenger side of the car, I asked curiously, "Are you a woman?" They answered, "I'm a woman." At that exact moment, a fog appeared no more than three feet in front of my car. There was nothing unusual about fog appearing from out of nowhere in Michigan. They tell you to wait a few minutes, and the weather will change. I've seen it rain heavily on one side of the street before and not a drop on the other. It was a very white, pristine, beautiful, thick fog that you could not see through.

In it was a scarcely seen car that was directly front and center to mine. The female angel got out of the passenger side and yelled for the other person, "Get away from him." He or she fled the scene. She yelled at me, telling me that I had better not do anything like that. She said, "In fact, you just wait here until I get back." She was the first female in my entire life that scared me. I did not know what in the heck was going on, but I had no intention of waiting for her to return. As she turned her back to leave, all the power suddenly died in my car. I thought about my space flight as I nervously checked the battery and lines for a bad connection, but there was nothing wrong. If ever there was a time that I came close to having a panic attack, it was that night in the fog. I had a cold sweat on the brow of my forehead as I repeatedly turned the ignition for the car to start. Have mercy. I really did not want to be there when that lady returned.

I saw the same no-nonsense angel again in the empty church parking lot. She had the same clothes on, but that time there was a turquoise, rainy-looking mist that surrounded her. I was a little afraid of this one because anyone who can cut off all the power in my car got my undivided attention. I have always done tune ups on my own cars. My tune up jobs guaranteed that a car would start right up, even at twenty-five degrees below zero. She said that after my rebirth, I was not allowed to do what regular humans do. I was of this world but, not in it. "

The spirit put the vise-grips pliers like clamps on my sex life. I was given three commandments to abide by in this order:

- Number 1: I should stop doing what I was doing and find a wife.

- Number 2: I was prohibited from having sex with a married woman, no matter if she is separated.

- Number 3: I was strictly forbidden to participate in any form or fashion of homosexual activity.

Commandments number 1: and number 3: were basically theme and variations of the same subject, hanging out with hoodlums and jumping into bed on numerous occasions with two women were actions not becoming as a child of God. It wasn't always guilt by association, sometimes it was guilt by participation. On the side on my own I sold small amounts of buds.

A knock on my bedroom window had disturbed my rare night sleep. The knocker was a friend who was a regular visitor that wanted to get the party started. Suddenly, it had don on me that my flock of family, friends associate, and I had been parting every day without a break for more the 365 days straight.

A week earlier an angel, who was a clean cut young white male in his late teens wore dungaree pants, a blue tee shirt, and white tennis shoes, as always appeared from out of nowhere. The angel spoke to me about an admonition from the Lord. Telling me to cease the excessive sleeping with different women's and to halt the continuing partying. I was unaware that

I had a problem because of the easy access and availability of the visiting ladies, my characteristic trait for moderation in everything including sex I didn't know that I metamorphosed into a fully blown sex addict.

One Friday, five of my growing up friends who had good jobs working in the automobile factories brought three off duty fire fighters over to my apartment for drinks. There were always two or three visiting ladies from the hood who regularly came over to chill with my music and I. this same Friday night when the fire fighters came over, five young ladies from the neighborhood stopped by. I felt that perhaps the ladies saw a bunch of nice-looking car and vans parked in front of my apartment and decided to check out the scene. In any event, since that day more and more factory workers, firemen and ladies with jobs stopped in and joined in the continuing festivities. Neighbors called the police concerning the overflowing cars and vans parked in empty lots and in front of my apartment building on the weekends. A police sergeant with a lot of strips on his sleeves walks in while the partying was in full swing the officer tells me about complaints from neighbors saying that where I lived was a residential neighborhood. The sergeant walks in every room examined the crowd turns around and as he walks out the apartment, he tells the quieted crowed that became that way because of the officer presence to "continue on," we know that you guys are just partying," then he leaves. A cook regularly came by daily to prepare a hearty meal inside of large kettle size pot and pans making sure that no one was ever hungry. The women when they were tired of smashed jumped into my king size brass bed never asking me. Sometimes two females wanted to have fun and asked me to join them. I didn't resist or complained. The women always told me that the reasons why they continue to come to my place was because they loved the people who came there, the comfort, amiability, and most important out of 365 days of partying there was not one fight between anyone which was uncommon for a black gathering 1 out of 12 just must show off wanting the attention only on them. Out of all those parting days nothing was ever stolen from their purse. The women said that they felt safe while they were in my home. I never thought about looking for love because many of the sleep over ladies made sure that I was happy.

As a Christian, my worldly exploits gave the heavens a headache.

Married women were 80 percent of my dating life. They were the real reason why I did not get married. They were ruthless.

Rosemary was an attractive thirty-something married next-door neighbor. Growing up in the city, the young ladies next door around my age were always unmarried friends with benefits. Her husband worked at one of the Big Three auto plants. The moment that he punched out with his buddies and friends from the job, he loved to sit on his front porch and drink Old Grand Dad whisky until he passed out. Many days he would call my brothers and me over to drink beer with him on the porch.

His hospitable wife took a liking to me and started calling me at 5:00 a.m. when he went to work. She would let the phone ring only twice to signal that she had unlocked the backdoor. In the breezeless, quiet darkness of the predawn hours, the time when all of the nocturnal and hoodlum creatures retired for the morning, stealthily in my pajamas I would jump with ease the four-foot chain-link fence and enter the house where she waited, dressed in a very sexy nightgown with two glasses of champagne in hand.

Dreamily, I was escorted to the upstairs bedroom. We sipped and chatted for a few minutes, mostly talking about how her husband neglected her, after which she loved it rhythmical and slow. In the beginning of the fling, the phone only rang twice a week. The next thing I knew, the rings sounded every weekday morning. Exit stage left I was worn down after months of this, mainly because I had to be at the office at 9:00 a.m.

What made me end this affair suddenly, grab a U-Haul, and move from my mom's house was that Rosemary started introducing me to her family and showing me off to her girlfriends as her new man. The smoldering behavior that sent me to find a truck was when she told me that she was leaving her husband for me.

Once I went to a wedding reception at a place called Dummy George's, a nightclub located on the west side of Detroit. I attended this occasion with my then-current girlfriend, who happen to be the bride's sister. That lady, who'd just gotten married in the afternoon, chased me around the club for more than two hours, trying to get me to take her to my home to have sex. But that's only the half of it. It happened more frequently than not.

On many jobs, while on the clock, at the homes of newly wedded women who had just gotten married the previous Saturday afternoon, they would ask me to sleep with them after work on Monday night. I liked them all but could not fathom trusting this type of bad girl well enough to marry her. Those kinds of warning signs had to be flashing in front of their husband's face.

Well, I thought, *I don't need a king-size bed anymore.* Women didn't care if you had another lady in your bed. When the pluck hit them real hard, they just climbed in my bed and went to sleep. So, after baptism, I went from having it all in the dating game. Frolicking, dinning, and dancing, with ladies in public and private settings females that were alluring, carefree and naughty. To sitting numb in a strip joint twiddling my thumbs wondering why should I contain my persuasiveness in social interaction? And how soon will I lose my ability to charm? I was used to dating good-looking bad girls. Although I had always kept one good girl on the side. I called her "Going Home" on my dating play list, just to keep sane.

So now I was in the extremely difficult situation of finding a lady that I could take home to mother. When you got to know some of the church ladies that were primed for courtship, 80 percent of the time they had ways like excessive spending, becoming frigid after marriage, lying, obsessive gambling, and habits that were just as bad as those heathens that they talked about.

About two weeks after my sex life was censored by the angel, I received another visitor from the other realm. This one initiated a fight. Because of my outer appearance, I looked like I was a frail, 165-pound weakling. But I was dense and deceptively light, like the matter of a black hole in space. At amusement parks, carnivals, and venues of the past, such as the animal circus or side fairs, I always cleaned up whenever I participated in many attractions that were held there. One was at the shooting gallery—the trick was to shoot the edge of the aluminum bottles, just like in bowling when you convert the seven-and-ten-pin split. The other one was at the guess-your-weight scale. For one dollar, the host would try to guess my weight within a plus or minus of ten pounds. And every time, their eyes would pop when I stepped on the scale because they always say that my weight was between 165 and 175 pounds. This was the same line of thought when my opponents, mostly bullies, tried to size me up. My average football weight was 215 pounds. The world-boxing commission considered this weight to belong in the heavy-weight division.

They always handed me a prize after their eyes went back into their sockets as soon as they found out that they were off the mark by forty pounds. After, I always turned around and gave it to the very first girl that passed by the shooting gallery or the weight machine. I never took home any prize that I won.

Since my very first fight after kindergarten class, I have gotten into an astonishing twenty-six street fights, plus or minus two. I have never lost in a straight fight, not against two on one and not against three on one. To me, I still considered them to be fair fights. What my current opponents forgot to relay to the next man up was that, to them, I looked deceptively slow and aloof, but, on the bottom line, I had a three-to-one punch ratio. Every time I got hit once, they got tagged three times. I was too stupid to run away from a bear or even run away from the numerous times that I faced a five-on-one bully or gang fight. Every time I stood tall; it was they who stood down.

At the onset of a skirmish, for some reason, I would become extremely calm and icy focused. I gave them a look that said, two-and-a-half or three of you are going to be reformed. And never think that five was enough to keep them from getting their tails whipped. I was good at how I adjusted to others' fighting styles. I believe that deep down I was addicted to it; that's probably the reason I did a whole lot of free bodyguard work. I never worried about money. Or perhaps I was just crazy and probably needed my head examined. Or both?

The angel was correct in telling me to find wife. I had become strung out, sleeping with a smorgasbord of some of the most beautiful women in the galaxy. Just one was never enough. When I vacationed in lower Baja, I traveled deep into the heart of the country where the downhome hospitality with real families is superb. I learned to bypass those tourist-trap border towns. Me being good-time Charlie, singing, dancing, dressing nice, lighting candles, and whispering softly in their ears under the glittering midnight stars worked just fine every time.

The hard part in becoming a born-again Christian, besides women, was that I had to give up fighting, do what Jesus would do; turn the other cheek and walk away. My adversaries had multiplied. They stepped up their routines of picking on and harassing me. On my insides, I was burning up because my personality had changed. I looked and felt meek.

For years I had to walk around in scorching flames because they raised the temperature inside of me up to 2,000 degrees Kelvin. I was solider. I was used to hurrying up to wait. Back then it wasn't any problem for me to sit still behind some bushes for four hour and wait for a person to walk by. Once I sat with a couple of friends for eighteen hours in a car, waiting for a shady dealer to come out of his house. But! Now I'm a Christian, and the enemies took this and ran away with misconception

In the span of one hour on that ominous Monday morning—which started out as another wonderful day weather wise in San Diego, especially when I looked into the eyes of a hypnotic angel, —turned sour when I looked into the eyes of the father of lies. I woke up late that day. Usually, I was out the door before the 9:00 a.m. showers to get my coffee, donuts, and a newspaper. I was preoccupied with the thoughts of why my world was falling apart not long after I got baptized. As I walked up and down the hills in San Diego on Market Street toward downtown and the coffee store, there was this house on the top of one hill. Outside the gate stood three young people. On the far side of the sidewalk near the curb was a nice young lady whose back was turned toward me.

She stood almost in my way so I had no choice but to look at her to see if see would move. She did not. I looked at her bushy eyebrows, her eyes, her face, back to her eyebrows, and my mind went, *Wow!* That youngster was the prettiest girl that I'd ever seen. I really wanted to tell her that. Years later, I saw a movie titled *Wild Things*. Perhaps actress Denise Richards had a twin sister with the same facial features and eyebrows that were unique. I walked uphill, still wondering why all these people were bothering me, especially since I was just minding my own business. I didn't see her on the way home, but she was memorable. I thought about her as I climbed the cement-covered, iron-rail steps to the second-floor apartment.

I entered my nephew's bedroom to drink my coffee and read the sports section of the newspaper. I took a small sip from a white Styrofoam cup when my sister-in-law's female neighbor walks into the bedroom door, and she sits one foot in front of me, and her appearance changed. HOLY SH* T! It had crimson-red eyes. It had a three-inch twisted, slightly downward nose. The chin was elongated and hooked downward. Its skin looked like burned red leather, which reminded me more of a shell than a skin covering. It had two yellowish-brown horns, which were half an inch and were protruding equally from both sides of its head.

I was not asleep. It was no dream or illusion. I was not hallucinating or imagining things. This was the real McCoy. This was no human. This was the terrifying creature. It had about a four-inch tail that curved toward the front, and on the end of it was the shape of a small triangle. I quickly did a self-diagnostic to see if I had any holes in my suit of armor. I was secured. Because of that, I knew that it was not allowed to touch me. "So, this is what the angels were preparing me for with their nonrelevant visits and conversations." When the crucial frightening moment arrived, I was without consternation. The minutes seemed like hours as we stared at each other eye-to-eye. I dared not to move my eye from his so that I would not show any kind of weakness.

I thought about those packs of twenty loose dogs that gather every night for a game of frightening the residents walking home late night in the neighborhood. One night I saw them chasing a man to the top of a car for a good while. They did this because they smelled fear. And now, it was my turn. It was a dreary, damp, moonlit evening when I decided to walk home from the club after hanging out with a group called Chapter 8. I walked into an empty, shell-looking area where there was only grass for a hundred yards in either direction. Awe sh*t! The pack spotted me. I wondered if they would leave me alone. Nope, they started forming into the V pattern those birds make when they fly south for the winter. They started creeping toward me. There were no cars to jump on or trees to climb. *Man! I better pull a rabbit out of the hat. Or I am dead meat.*

I thought about this story in the Bible when a character tore off his clothes and acted like a madman to get out of trouble. I started screaming "ahhhhh" very loudly and waving my arms high in the air as I ran toward the pack of dogs, who then stopped and started looking at each other going, *What in the hell?* One by one, the dogs at the end ran away first. And then the dogs in front looked back for their support and saw that their buddies had split. As I got closer, still screaming and waving, the leaders turned and headed for the hills to join their fleeing buddies who were getting away from this crazy man.

The creature said, "You are not afraid of me." Without moving my eyes from his I said, "No." I knew that the Lord had my back. The beast continued to stare at me, and it seemed like time had frozen. As I continued to show no fear, it finally said to me, "I'm going to get you." I volunteered to say nothing. I looked at what was attached to its stubby, thin arms. These were not fingers and thumbs. They were hoofs. A shade darker than the yellow-brown horns. They were divided into three on each of what were supposed to be arms. I had seen those exact same hoofs on animal before. I did not answer. After a few of the longest minutes in my life, the creature left.

While sitting, I had looked back in my head at the spot where I was sitting and thought about any middle-aged women sitting in my place. The image was so powerful, and next to meeting the real slim shady, it could never be forgotten, the sheer terror of the moment. She could have also represented society. I saw her have massive cardiac arrest from seeing what was in front of me, talking.

I turned around and got on my knees to pray feverishly to my Father, that no man or woman would have to experience what I did. I did not wish that kind of visitation on my worst enemy. That morning was the ultimate of horror. No one else on Earth needed to subject to a brunch with Satan. However, he was not finished with me. He sent a legion of his best demons to try to convert me into joining it, night and day. I often felt like I was back in high school in that preseason football camp in the middle of that circle, surrounded by 120 ballplayers sent one-by-one at full speed to knock me on the ground.

It was just too much, and there were so many times that I had to flee from San Diego. It constantly set up traps to get me into compromising positions, trying to blackmail me with underage girls or set me up with prostitutes so that I could be taken to jail. They were heavily spreading fabricated story and lies about me, saying that I slept people who I'd never seen before or that I did things for money that I had no interest in. People believe what they want to believe without proof because just as a lying person thinks that everyone lies, those who have sold their souls thinks that everyone else has sold their soul too or can easily be converted. It fits their superiority complex as they discard the glaring truth that they see the man has done none of what they say, year after year.

The spirit told me that the demons had a contract on me. It was with the unscrupulous money-hungry humans that has no knowledge of what and who is behind it all. My point man sensors continue to serve me well as Lucifer continued to send his demons to try to trick and taunt me by following me around and sputtering foul, ugly, unheard-of words about me. Words that I paid no attention to because I knew that if I continue to wear the entire suit of armor, the Lord is with me.

Make no mistake about it, I told everybody who would listen that the devil is real. Pastor Franklin, before he moved his church to an area of University Avenue, preached at a small, intimate, two step to the small ten-by-six pulpit. The seating area had the largest of the seats in the middle, and on each side of the aisle the seating was half the size. The building was located on Logan Street, near the corner of 30th Street, a few blocks from the famous 32nd Street Naval Station.

He would give any members of church all the time that they needed to testify about things that the Lord had done for them. I would first sing a hymn and then give a short Bible study about that thing that came from Hell. I constantly reminded the church that Satan was real. I would go to Bible study classes and say the same thing. I always preached that it was real. Until now, I hid the fact that I knew how and why I say that on this earth exists a real demonic entity.

THE SONGBIRDS

I grew up in the presence of greatness in its infancy stage. These are some of the names of the female singers that I consistently rubbed shoulder within my youth: Gladys Knight, Martha Reeves, Kim Weston, Diana Ross, Mary Wells, Valerie Simpson, Tammi Montgomery, Kim Weston, and later Althea Rene. Back then, the whole town was an incubator for talent, and it started in elementary school when they would do plays on stage.

The gyms and auditoriums of the middle and high schools where the talent shows were held is where most of the singers were discovered. And yet, the groups that went on stage before and after the famous singers were just as irresistible. They could have also moved on to the Apollo Theater in New York. However, due to luck of the draw, they unfortunately were passed over by Smokey Robinson and his posse.

I was struck with an epiphany the very next day after hanging out with the formal heavyweight boxing champion of the world. I was sitting at a cabaret-style table, entertaining five females in the nightclub located on the service drive of the John C. Lodge Freeway, which is located on the west side of Detroit. Formal boxing champion Leon Spinks walks in with five females draped all over him and his tan, full-length mink coat. He recently lost by a TKO to Larry Holmes. I was wondering what in the heck he was doing there. Even when you lose in a big prize fight, you still need a Brink armored truck to move your money around.

We sat on different sides of the club. On his side he had money to burn as he showered his flock of females with it. Of course, I gave them the once-over and somehow a thought popped into my mind: they reminded me of the Golddiggers from the Dean Martin variety show. The ladies at my table had a great time. As the only male at the table, I was dancing, singing, drinking, and clowning with them. We spent very little change, but being an ex-solider, I never cared how much a good time cost. The main reason was because you might hit the sack at 2:30 a.m. from a great night out, but two hours later the alarm may sound for an alert that snatches you away from civilization for a month or two. With a pocket full of loot, you had nowhere to spend it. While spreading out your bed roll on the cold, damp ground, you'd think, *damn, I should have gone out last night.*

Anyway, the next morning, a bright light turned on in my head. I figured out that by some chance, I was always amid Hall of Fame singers, movie, and sports stars for a reason. A radiant, early middle-aged lady came to our church on Euclid Avenue in San Diego. She was from Los Angeles and was beginning her embarkment toward Evangelism. The first Sunday she kept walking past me to get my attention, at least five times. What made me think that she was going out of her way to meet me was that the lobby and restrooms were located completely on the other side of the sanctuary. I figured that it was because I was singing my tail off back then.

The following Sunday, she sat down next to me. She told me her name was Denise Matthews. It didn't ring any bells for me, but my first impression when I saw her was that she looked familiar. She was exceptionally beautiful, but that was not unusual in Southern California. Her appearance was just like your regular next-door neighbor's. Every male in the church tried to squeeze into the small space that we had on the pew or onto the next bench behind me. I didn't know why, but I did know that I didn't like it at all. I was more than satisfied in the relationship that I had with my hidden girlfriend named Nida, so I wasn't thinking about making a move on her. I found out later that Denise was also known as singer and movie star named Vanity.

Every time that I reminisce about those days, I can clearly see Denise's face and still feel her soft, magnificent figure sitting next to me in church. She was not married at the time. During those long winter nights, when I was all alone, I'd think about some company and the ones that got or I gave away. It seemed like everybody that I rubbed shoulders with, young or old, became an important celebrity or super star. The day after hanging with Mr. Spinks, I reckoned that *Heck, I must be one of them.* It was the only logical conclusion that made sense.

The singers lived on the same city blocks, went to the same grocery stores, dressed and went to the same schools as those regular, young neighbors. They were gifted, but to us teenagers, in our era, they were just singers that were lucky enough to get paid. And how overly excited could you possibly get about a homegirl that you regularly see throughout the year?

The Motown Picnics were no more and there weren't any more reviews or New Year's Eve gatherings. The company moved its primary studio from West Grand Boulevard to Los Angeles. However, they moved a local chapter of their office to Woodward Avenue. During a time, I was an aspiring singer-songwriter, A few doors down the street from Motown, was a marvelous Grinnell's Music Store. The reasons why I had visited Motown so much was because it seemed like every week, I had to buy two or three Guitar High E Strings from them. Always before I purchased my strings, I would bang on an assortment of some of the most beautiful pianos and finest crafted guitars that you will ever see.

At the new Motown office, I used to go inside of the building so much that I walked past the security guard at the front entrance who sat right across from Specs Howard's School of Broadcasting. They thought that I worked there. In middle school and in high school, there was a group of us student that sung top-ten tunes at every class break. For some unknown reason, we harmonized around street corner mailboxes at dusk. My best friends from junior high and high school—Sam and Kelvin McCord, who later, I believe, joined the jazz band The Yellowjackets—and I all started out as three of the original members of singer band Al Hudson and the Soul Partners.

I wanted to know the money side of this entertaining industry. In order to learn all of the angles of the craft, I talked to the office workers, the music producers, the band members, the engineers, and a few of the singers that I could catch who were delighted to talk about their tours and the madness of traveling to small towns and sleeping in rundown hotels.

The big groups like The Jackson Five, The Spinners, and the Four Tops were smuggled in at 3:00 a.m. and 4:00 a.m. to do their recordings. A lot of their recording sessions were mastered at the United Sound Systems

Recording Studios, located on 2nd and Antoinette. The singers were traveling home on wheels and departed long before sunrise. The public never saw them. The more I talked to the whispering office workers concerning Mr. Gordy appearing in circuit court so much, the more the idea of me becoming a singer-songwriter soured.

This was a baffling business, more so than the boxing industry. When I learned that I would receive only twelve cents an album for my songs—and what's more, the singer or producers would buy your song outright from a hungry, cash-strapped artist and then put their names on songs like they had written them—I realized that being a ghostwriter or getting just twelve cents didn't jive with me. I could make more money collecting returnable bottles and cans.

The real stinging part of the business was that as I bumped into the producers and regular office workers, and they all had a nice car and homes. They were sending their kids to college. They dressed very nicely and had stable relationships. And, most importantly, they had regular working hours and were not stressed out like the singers who sold a prolific number of gold records with their number one hits. And in the same breath, they all were crying broke. Or they had money but didn't have one stable relationship. The person or persons who handled their finances lived way better than the hard-working, ten-concerts-in-eight-days singers. Alone with the consistent stress of producing another hit to stay on top, they were subjected to the nightmares of drug and alcohol abuse. What I learned from a coworker friend of mine named Aaron Riser, the brother of producer Paul Riser, put the nail in the coffin when it came to my singer-songwriter career. I liked the idea of going home at night way too much, rather than living off stimulants.

I never had any problem with sitting at the bar, chatting with a songbird who just stepped off stage after completing a set. My older sister Maria and I worked not too far from each other. She worked at a midtown hospital, and I worked at the eastside satellite office for Wayne State University's military veterans' program.

The veteran's educational opportunity program (V.E.O.P.) is a full-service organization for veterans pertinent in smoothing the transferring of recent and long ago discharged military veterans into an accredit college by assisting with class scheduling, financial aid, and tutoring needs. This essential linkage from the military to college is the brainchild of the director whose name was Paul Rease. He is a great mentor and father-figure to me. After work, my sister and I loved hanging out in Kennedy Square and the cocktail lounges located inside of the elegant hotels that used to surround Grand Circus Park located in downtown Detroit. One Friday we visited the lounge in the hotel which was on the southside of the park to put away a few rums and cokes for her, but I was going through a drinking phase when I only wanted Tom Collins. There was this alluring, petite, attractive Black female singer belting out some silky top-ten tunes. I spoke to her as she passed by our table. By her third set and our third set of drinks, she joined us at the rectangular lounge table with the lit candle in the middle and two ashtrays so you could smoke 'em if you got 'em.

Before her second to last set, I felt something rubbing against my right leg underneath the table. I almost jumped out of my seat, but you've got to be cool in front of the ladies. So, I calmly shifted my chair back to see what kind of rodent or bug was touching me. The songstress had her shoe off, and her stocking-covered feet slid underneath my pant leg, rubbing it up and down. Rita and I kicked it for half a year or so. But, like most relationship such as that one, it's always two magnetic personalities who, like trains, are just passing each other in the night. The same thing happened if she happened to be a ballet dancer, played an instrument, and/or if she was one of the bad girls who I blew an awful lot of money on that was already earmarked for such an occasion. We clicked and then slowly drifted away from each other.

Back in the days when the nightclubs in the city were really booming, I regularly sat and spoke with singer Marlena ("Go Away Little Boy") Shaw. We hardly ever talked about her music or the business. The last time that I chatted with her we talked about her plumbing problem where she lived. She was always relaxed around me. I could tell because she took her shoes off and flopped back in her seat.

Other than that epiphany that I experienced after hanging out with boxer Leon Spinks, it seemed like I was kind of a good-luck charm to almost all the up-and-coming young female singer that I had a casual acquaintance with, they blew up and became notable or Hall-of-Fame singers. My passion for spinning tracks didn't stop as I got older. I continued to spin records at social gatherings, parties, and mostly I played hot tracks in after-hours joints. For most of my life, I kept up with what was happening in the music business by reading magazines such as *Downbeat, hit Parade* and *Rolling Stone*. However, there were two sources of music information that I followed religiously and rarely missed to stay current. One was radio icon award-winner, the legendary Casey Kasem and his American Top 40. And my main source to stay in the know was *Billboard* magazine.

I knew my music. I had an instant report with any disc jockey in any club all over the world. We would carry on as if we'd known each other all our lives. Back in Detroit, there was a time when radio stations, mostly on the weekends but sometimes during the week, would set up remote satellite live broadcastings in used-car lots, furniture stores, block parties, grand openings, and disco nightclubs. Radio stations were enjoyably vibrant throughout the communities. The disc jockeys were easily accessible to the public.

My primary listening stations were WJLB, WGPR, and the jazz station WJZZ. As always, I knew most of the disc jockeys off the air waves. I was friends with almost all WGPR's track spinners before they hit the big time: Tiger Dan from the Blue Chateau, Foody, and Fat Cat from the local bars where they commanded nice-sized crowds. I was WJLB's Bushman's maintenance man when he lived in a upscale downtown apartment building. His son's babysitter lived in the same building as I did, and she was a special love interest until those creepy people who were possessed by darkness came around.

The professional tune spinners didn't always play the top-ten hits at the clubs. We had contacts to purchase underground and avant-garde music from new and off-the-charts bands. That were not listed in any of the major music magazines These men and a few ladies were the dancing jocks who I knew and hung out with when I wanted a guaranteed rocking-good time. However, on the days that I relaxed, dressed more formal because, I didn't take my church clothing off, or drink like a lush, I hung out with the record spinners over at radio station WJZZ the jazz station. This was the station that the winding-down-for-the-weekend crowd listened to on a Sunday. I tuned in nightly at around 9:00 p.m. There was this velvety voiced, silky-smooth female that came on the airwave's late night, who pleasantly put me to sleep. Until I met her! I was no stranger to the station because I used to call a few of the jocks, mostly Calvin U., to talk or request a certain record constantly.

The station was always live, remotely broadcasting at the many of the nightclubs in and around Motor City. The Labor Day weekend Montreal Jazz Fest in Harts Plaza downtown Detroit was the event where the station's disk spinners and the many top-notch jazz musicians came to play from all over the world.

We were under a cloudless sky and glittering stars that reminded me of glowing dots that winked and shimmered on the smooth ink black sky. The smell of shish kabobs, pretzels, and the foul smell of old spilled beer was piquant in the evening air, coming with slight warm breeze moving off the Detroit River. Sitting with a jubilant, festive crowds, listening to melodious world-class music was the kind of a memorable night that stayed in the front of your mental Rolodex.

She was intelligent, beautiful, and as pleasant as she sounded when see lured me sleep every night, my kind of women. I started courting her on the spot. Her name was Vanice J. Now instead of talking to the other DJs at the station, I called and talked to her almost every night. I brought her flowers to the station and attended the events where she'd MC at night. I serenaded her to the point where I felt that in our relationship, I had a good lead past third base.

There was a young singer out of Detroit who made the one-hit-wonder list name Spyder "Stand by Me" Turner. His sister and I were sometimes lovers and always good friends as we got older. It was at the grand opening of a nightclub called River Town where Vanice was the MC. My brothers Zachary, Cliff, and I sat in the booth right next to the turntables, where she faultlessly entertained the thrilled well-dressed patrons. The guest musician was Joe LoDuca, the same artist that wrote the theme music for the television series *Hercules* that stared Kevin Sorbo.

My brother Cliff did his "it's my birthday thing," and instead of giving him a shot on the house, the manager was in a partying mood and gave him a whole bottle of champagne. He promptly starts drinking like it was beer. The ladies in the next both over and I told him that you can't drink it that fast. He shrugged us off and continued to down it in big gulps. He had to go to the men's bathroom which was located downstairs, and he never made it back up. Joe LoDuca was in the middle of the atrium at the time, playing some breeze jazz on one of his four guitars. The other three were on an upright stand to the left of his shoulder, and at the end of the guitar trio was a chair where he sat down when he finished a set.

It was funny because upstairs we were partying big time, and after a long while, we started asking where Cliff was. We finally looked down where Mr. LoDuca was jamming, and that's where we saw Cliff—head back, knocked out in the artist's chair. No one bothered him or skipped a beat. The partying continued full steam ahead. The way that he was sharply dressed, he looked like he belonged in the guitar setting.

The courtship with Vanice was going as well as any. Because we were entertaining, we usually chatted with the folks in the establishments, only having time to sneak a blinking to each other. It was smooth sailing until pro football came calling for me to relocate to different towns. I became consumed with playing for a winning organization. And due to using all my resourceful talents just to survive in another far away town, which was taxing every night, I was drained and didn't even have money to call her. The relationship unfortunate faded to black.

One of my all-time favorite nights out on the town was at the Cabaret Lounge. It was on a pleasant autumn evening, in the air was that fall aroma that comes from cooler temperatures and trees dropping colorful leaves. The small, intimate club was a smaller version of the larger and popular 20 Grand nightclub located on the westside of Detroit. My brother and I frequented the club often because it was within walking distance from our home.

We were there so much that we knew the owner who was called "Big Red." My younger brother, Cliff, did his "it's my birthday" con every time that he went there, which was a lot. Big Red, who was towering and built like a trim offensive lineman, knew Cliff was full of it, but he made him burst out with a jolly Santa laugh, so much so that he gave him a free drink every time.

Another night, when I was short of cash, I walked to the club alone. I was friends with the group that regularly played there, Chapter 8. That was also where the songstress Anita Baker launched her illustrious career. Many of the local singers, one hit wonders, and bands came there—Special Delivery, One Way, and The Dramatics often dropped by.

On that evening, the group that entertained was named Enchantment. They took their second break, and they all headed for the bathroom. It was time for me to check in also, so I followed them in the john. They had one guy blocked the bathroom door so that no one could get in or out. They lit up two joints and passed them around. I was finishing my beer relief. I turned around, and one member passed me a doobie. He told me that no one could leave until they hit it. I complied. Feeling good, one of the band members started singing their number one hit, leading with "Hello sunshine / It's mighty good to see you doing fine." We all chimed in. I had no problem singing background to any top-ten hit. I could sing with anyone back then. That was some bomb smoke as we blew the light out with that song.

It was time to get back to the stage, so the doorman unblocked the door to let us out. But we couldn't get out of the bathroom because the hallway packed like sardines with patrons. The club was half-empty when we went to the head, but the 10:30 p.m. crowds came in while we were singing. When we finally got out, we saw that no one was in their seats. Everybody in the club was standing in the hallway, listening to us.

It was a gorgeous summer evening in the backyard belonging to the coach of my semipro football team the Great Lakes Raiders. As always, I was gathering with the big linemen. When I was with them, I used to suck in air and hold it in my stomach to balloon it outward so that it appeared that I had a gut like them. In one hand, we each had a filled, clear plastic twelve-ounce cup. We were posted right next to the fresh kegs of beer that tasted especially great after you'd won a football game.

I happened to be near the turntable spinning the heavy beat disco sound of this new artist who blasted onto the club scene. The song that was playing was called "Bad Girl," a fixture in my life. I picked up the album to read the jacket. I saw a face that startled me. Why? Because it looked like I had seen that face before. People always say that everyone has a twin. I thought that this lady was a doppelganger of someone that I knew, but I just couldn't place my finger on. For years, every time I picked up one of her albums covers, I went into a reminiscent search of where I'd seen that face before.

It was in the year of 2015. I sat in a doctor's office for the usual two-hour wait and picked up a very old, perhaps ten years back, issue of a music magazine. As always, I proceeded to read every book or magazine within hand. I read the biography of a late popular singer and was flabbergasted. They say that the world is small. I didn't know just how small. I knew for certain that I saw this face before. She was my very first number four B lady from the player's brotherhood. "Don't sleep with them all. Keep some of them as your best friends." She was the one in Munich, Germany, who introduced me to my first European girlfriend who hailed from Turkey. She was one of the characters in the circle of friends that we hung out with and was also from the stage production of the musical *Hair*. She left Germany about the same time that I did and changed her name from LaDonna Gaines to Donna Summers.

BEST OF
THE BEST
III

THE WALK ON

R oll Call. The 2004 San Diego Chargers. Two men Missing.
This was the year where I was afforded an extremely rare opportunity to join a championship-bound professional football team for the third time as a walk on. It was a perfect situation for me as a football player to finally retire from the game as a winner. And it was also an opportunity that millions of high school, college, and minor league football players dream of, but the door never opened for them, not even once.

I was satisfied with playing in a football pickup game here and there with my nephews, high school players, and neighborhood kids. Football scouts were at the fields, digging tunnels under stadium bleachers, looking for the next five-star recruit. Even if you had never played the sport, a layman could recognize the difference between my game speed and polished play-making abilities and those of the overwhelmed up-and-coming adolescent future stars.

Shortly after my fourth sandlot game, at the bottom of the hill on Market Street and 47th, there is a donut shop where each morning I got my coffee, two freshly baked donuts, and the *San Diego Union* newspaper. On that day, five football scouts were sitting in a booth next to the window facing 47th Street. I glanced at them for a hot second, knowing who they were because they all looked the same.

Their attire always looked like they'd rather be at the golf course, teeing off. Almost all wore the classic Harrington jacket, the polo shirt, a traditional or argyle golf jumper, and you saw them in classic plaid or black and navy-blue tones. They also wore a baseball hat on their heads and sneakers. They reminded me of an excellent golfer from the Detroit area name Calvin

Peete from the way that they dressed. I could feel them scrutinize, assess, and evaluate from the back of my head. One of them enthusiastically said, "He can run, and he can tackle. I've seen him play before."

Perhaps two days later, it was morning and time to go to the bottom of the hill to see my favorite Vietnamese counter lady with the beautiful countenance and easy-on-the-eyes appearance. Oh yea, and she smiled every day as she dished out the coffee and donuts. That time when I opened the door to the shop, only two scouts were sitting in the same booth as before. Standing at the counter, looking down at the three level racks filled with an assortment of mouthwatering pastries, she was there on the other side, waiting with a radiant smile, happily knowing by now that I was expected at the crack of dawn.

Unexpectedly, one of the scouts asked me in a business-like tone, "Do you know a man named A.J. Smith?" Out of the blue, some forgotten twenty-seven years after I'd last seen that pure energy cloud that had mysteriously appeared during my stint as a Job Crops athletic director, it reappeared. It happened again in Pasadena, California, right after the conclusion of a thrilling, nail-biting January 1, 1998, Rose Bowl football game.

The contest was between the gladiators of the number-seven ranked Washington State Cougars and the number-one ranking University of Michigan Wolverines. What's at stake a National Championship? In the ABC TV broadcasting booth were the announcers Keith Jackson, a Washington State alum, and Bob Griese, the former quarterback of the Miami Dolphins, the only undefeated National Football League team. On the field, Griese's son Brian was at the helm of the undefeated Michigan Wolverines.

My brothers and I viewed the game from one of our favorite watering holes, Radio Bar located on Harper Street on the eastside of Detroit. With drinks in hand, we watched the game, standing up the entire time like we always did on the sidelines when attending an actual football game between any team—PAL league, high school, college, or pro football. We just loved that stuff. At the end of the game, which resulted in a twenty-one to sixteen victory for the Wolverines, the electrified spectators stormed the Rose Bowl playing field in celebration.

I was astonished and taken aback as once more I saw this massive whisper cloud of vapor and pure energy, which hovered directly above their heads. Why could I see this when no one else could? It baffled me for a few minutes. However, my life has seen a series of strange happenings since I was twelve years old. By then I was used to it, and there was no need for me to question that one either. I created the conditions for it to happen before. But that time I was mulling over the fact that this apparition occurred following the aftermath of a championship football game. *So, is this how I can recreate the condition?* I wondered.

On 1998 New Year's Day, exactly twenty-four days later, in the Super Bowl game between the Green Bay Packers and the Denver Broncos—a thirty-one to twenty-four win—held at Qualcomm Stadium in San Diego. I was shocked at the conclusion of the game because, there again, I saw this surreal energy cloud radiating from the jubilant sardine-packed spectators that had squeezed into the event. *What is the spirit trying to tell me?* I asked myself.

In any event, I have the spirit of the Lord on the right side of me and the unwelcome evil spirit of Satan on my left. And now, in the middle of me, I began to go on a lifetime task and adventure like Don Quixote chasing windmills. I became obsessed, attempting to chase after and catch a cloud. Oh well. I wasn't the only one doing it. I felt a whole lot better after I saw Captain Kirk chase around a cloud in *Star Trek*. The title was also called "Obsession." I knew that was fictional, but mine was not.

I started examining all thirty-two football teams from the owners all the way down to strength and conditioning coordinators. I even peeked to see what kind of water boy or girl did this task for their teams. I broke this down to each division and then to who would wind up winning the interdivision conference play. I matched player against player and team defense against team offense in each respective division.

Long before the return of the cloud, I analyzed the rosters of all thirty-two football teams at the beginning of the season. I was pretty much accurate in determining which teams would reach the Super Bowl, each year for over twenty-year period. My analysis was correct in choosing eighteen out of twenty winners. The New York Giants were the only team to blemish my prefect record twice.

The dead center prediction that I was fond of was my pick of a pro football team that I called "Cinderella." My Cinderella team was a team that no one in the football world took notice of. And, to qualify, you had to choose the team to reach the Super Bowl before the season started. Twice, in 1981 and 1988, I saw that the Cincinnati Bengals made all the right moves to reach the Super Bowl. Before the season started, I paid attention to what they were doing during the off season. They had solidified their backups and third stringers, a key component necessary for maintaining attrition as a means of winning and surviving a long, excruciating, battle-weary football season.

The 2004 San Diego Chargers were my Cinderella team that was picked before the season started. They were three deep in all phases of the game: the offense, the defense, and special teams. For instance, the running back quartet, which consisted of grade A plus LaDainian Tomlinson, grade A minus Michael Turner, and receiving a respectable A was the fullback, Lorenzo Neal. It was pretty much like this on every unit that donned the playing field, but my analysis had two variables that were not factored in at the time. And because of what I did not do, it had changed the dynamic of my predication and unfortunately altered the outcome throughout the Charger's season.

As I watched the team preform game after game, I had this nagging feeling, like pins stuck in the back of my neck, that something was missing, something relevant to the success of the Chargers' Gridiron march to the Super Bowl. And sure enough, that came to pass

because two key players were missing.

The spirit led me to the water by showing me the way to manufacture the environment conducive to producing my windmills, which was uncloaked, somehow, by playing in a championship football game. How could I do this when I retired from the semiprofessional game at the advance age of forty-six? The only ones who would still let me play on their team were my old coaches who knew that I still had a enough juice to contribute.

I was an extremely late bloomer who had not reached my prime until fifty-five years old. Even at that age, like at cat, I still could run faster backward then most youngsters who ran at full speed forward. A spirit in a memorable dream told me that Satchel Paige did it in baseball and quarterback George Blanda did it in football, but that I was much faster and stronger than both.

To the normal eye, I looked deceptively fragile and weak, but I was leg pressing 700 pounds, fifty times, three times a week. During the football season, I settled on working out with just pressing 640 pounds, three times a week. I often played left tackle on offense because I could, so I figured that 320 pounds times two meant that I could move two big, old, six feet six inches tall, 320-pound linemen easily out of my way, which I usually did.

On defense I held down the strong side defensive end position also because I could. I never let anyone come off the line of scrimmage clean. Not any running back or receiver or tight ends got past me without me hitting them or bumping them off the route. They usually exercised the wiser course of valor and stayed completely away from me like they did when I played free safety. When the opposing team found out about how I played in the defensive back field, they just didn't throw in my area. If we needed a big play, I would line up directly in front of the tight end and, using the power of my 700-pounds leg strength, bull rush any hapless, bewildered six feet five, 285 pounds tight end straight into the belly of the quarterback

I had accomplished the one impossible mandate in my lifetime of having a champion-caliber team to take a good look at me. And remarkably, like the spirit stated, I beat the astronomical odds of having the team dismiss the concern about the age gap between me and the younger players.

Elite speed and empirical talent at any age cannot be categorized. Speed is inherited. It's a valuable commodity which cannot be taught and is priceless to a football coach. They came from out of the woodwork. Unscrupulous individuals somehow got wind of my soon-to-be good fortune. Some sports lawyers from the Houston, Texas, area contacted me concerning representation for talks with the management of the San Diego Chargers. The two different firms believed that I was going to sign a free agent contract. I knew my worth in the league. I was an old, slightly used 200 mph Lamborghini, mixed in with brand spanking new 184 mph Chevrolet Corvettes.

I played seventeen different positions and could start in twelve. I was invited to the semipros' All-Star game so many times that I lost count or just didn't attend. What was unusual about this was that most times I wasn't given an assignment until I got there. All things considered, I was big time, and I knew it. I had the wheels to run with the big dogs. And perhaps I could teach a few of those young players a thing or two about the art of hitting. I was patient and stood on the sideline, aware that sooner than later I was going to start. This was how I wound up playing the entire game without a break.

I was not even paying attention when I replaced an injured player. I ended up starting on the offense, starting on the defense, on the kick-off team, on the kick-return team, on the punt team, on the punt-return team. Every time I tried to return to the bench after replacing a player, the coaches would say "Hey! What are you doing? Get back out there." I was never worried about money, but I was extremely confident that the organization would tear up the free agent contract after witnessing some error-free, wicked hitting and plays ending with me always on or near the fringe of the football. I knew that if I played my cards right and kept my conduct clean, that at some point in time, sooner rather than later, I would be in line for a one or more years of an incentive-loaded contract.

Twenty yards on either side of the line of scrimmage I was a menacing Dick Butkus disciple. Past twenty yards on either side of the line of scrimmage, I turned on my warp speed engines and morphed into the Oakland Raiders assassin Jack Tatum. Because the coaches could pencil me into a spot on the roster and no longer had to worry about that position, they could turn their focus and attention on other areas of the game. Management would feel giddy when they figured out that they had stolen something by paying me just $5 million.

All the way back from junior varsity football throughout my twenty-three years of off and on playing semipro ball, I was on the playing field just about every down. And I never had an off-side penalty or false start or late hit. And I always understood the situation concerning down and distance and never missed a game because of an on the field injury or take too many bad angles on a tackle. And what was one of the most important parts of the game, I didn't turn the ball over.

We, the guys that grew up playing in the alley, just did not fumble. We caused them. Nevertheless, when we watched a football game on TV and saw a hit that caused the ball to be dislodged, we all would yell "FUMBLE!" It was kind of cool when we looked around at each other and in unison say, "What's a fumble?"

Those shyster lawyers were unaware that I was a formal product of military intelligence, thinking and digging for useful relevant information is what we did long ago, growing up during the Cold War era. We watched TV shows like *The Man from U.N.C.L.E.*, *I Spy*, *Our Man Flint*, *The Avengers*, *Get Smart*, and we never missed a *007* movie at the theater. We had a spy club where every member had to learn Morse code, change all alphabet into numbers, and sneak into places where we didn't belong to see if we could. And first and foremost, we could find out information on anyone's past or present.

I could backtrack and find out about anyone or just about anything. If a person wanted to manage my money, I also would go deep into their personal lives. I had acquaintances in low places who were skilled in finding behind-the-scenes and hidden information. I could start by digging for information in old records at city hall, looking through the land and deeds records. And for legal reference, I plowed through a Martindale Hubble.

When I searched for the questionable business dealings between a certain law firm and their current clients, I decided that I would represent myself as a free agent after I discovered that the National Football League players, they represented all had seven-figure contracts. While the firm was busting out at the seam's finances-wise, the players were marred in Chapter 11 bankruptcy procedures. They were the exact same conditions that musicians seemed to forever endure—ripped off by the money watchers.

NIDA

The most damaging aspect of my battle with the schemes of the living devil was the multiple casualties in my love life. I had to hide all my relationships that were close to my heart. I did not want that creature anywhere near the lady that I truly loved because every time that it found out who my girlfriend was, he would use her to betray me, contaminate the relationship, try to get me in a sexually compromising situation, or use her to get near me so that it could try to use shame to control me. It could not penetrate pure love. If it wasn't real love, if the lady that I fancied loved money fame or power, then they were a prime candidate for the demon's junior varsity team of lies and corruption. They were given an abundance of what they loved most money, drugs, and shopping sprees, to sell me out.

Once, this young lady and I decided to become a couple. In less than an hour, she turned on me. She left out of the door with no money. She came back with a hand full of money and told me that I should try a ménage à trois—an open three-way relationship with another man. All of them were unaware that I was forbidden and would easily sacrifice my life before I went against the Lord's commandment. I knew when she opened her mouth who and what was behind the curtain.

Lucifer is not allowed to physically touch me, and I can't touch it. Like matter colliding with antimatter, our spiritual warfare lies in the area of powers and principalities. In his arsenal is his one-half of the world's population of disciples that leisurely and routinely participate in the capital vices of greed, envy, pride, lust, glutton, sloth, and wrath. It appears on the surface that I am overwhelmed in combat. Behind the scenes, standing by is an immeasurable battalion of angels who can travel great distances to troubled spots in a heartbeat. It is my earthly military skills that also keep me in a stalemate, making the creature yell at me in the ugliest, sickening, horrendous voice that is not meant for human ears. It is an irritating, high-pitched, squeaky voice that some women have. It's also like the disturbing sound that a person makes when writing on a blackboard and the chalk breaks and their fingernails scratch the board.

This fighting began sometime in the year of 1982. I was not aware of what was behind it all until the face-to-face meeting in 1991. I was under heavy persecution and trials that reached a critical junction in San Francisco when it sent a demon that had threaten to kill me if I didn't join him. I had to reach way back to fifth century BC, recalling the Chinese military strategy and teachings of Sun Tzu.

In the thirteen chapters of his treatise, only a few were relevant in my unique situation. I had no say, so in the very first lesson that said, "Choose your own battles," I was under a consistent barrage of attack. Frankly, I would have chosen lesson number six that stated, "The best way to win is to not fight at all," but it was unavoidable, and I was up to my neck in it. Lesson number three was the most significant teaching that applied to my situation. It went, "Know the enemy and know yourself." I learned everything that I could about the dark prince back when I lived in Rochester County, New York.

For a short time, I was sitting at a table that had a couple of books on it. One of the hardcover books was crimson red, and I picked it up. The title read, *The Devil Bible*. I questioned myself, wondering why that book was placed there. It seemed like it was placed there because someone knew that I would read it. Of course, I read it, and it was enlightening. It basically said, "There are no such thing as rules or regulations. Do what you want when you want. There is no such thing as a God. Your existence has no meaning, so you might as well have fun."

Satan split families and friends by instigating angry divisions and will go down the family line until he finds one that is susceptible to hypnotic impressions. He will catch them at their weakest moral level, using his power of illusions, in which he is also a master. And he can trick a person to drive through a red traffic light into oncoming traffic, thinking that it was green. His primary mission is to steal, kill, and destroy.

I know for a fact that no society can exist without laws, rules, or regulations. Otherwise, it would be completely pandemonium. The population would be in a constant state of anarchy. There could be no progress if everyone did what they wanted, whenever they felt like it while stepping on each other's toes.

I moved back to San Diego. That same year, I was placed at a table after standing for hours in the free-food line. Heck, a three-course meal is the same three-course meal on any table. I had money but nowhere to cook. Prior to being served, I happened to look down in front of me, and the red cover paperback book was there. I thought that someone really wanted me to learn how the devil thinks. I took it with me and read it once more.

During one of those moments when I sat still and quietly listened, the spirit talked, giving me knowledge. The spirit told me that the devil that visited me had a name. In the spiritual realm, it is called Gadreel, and its true appearance is in the form of a creature. I have seen three different versions of this creature that I was conscience of. My Father told me that I was born number five of his eleven favorite Earth children. However, in this holy family I had too many of the ways of the world. I was the lone Black Sheep.

In the other half of Sun Tuz's lesson number two—know yourself—I knew that I had a dark, vindictive nature. I was sneaky, harbored a calculating ruthlessness, and waited for my opportunity for vengeance when my opponent had forgotten.

It was the beginning of fall, and I had nothing on my mind. I was sitting on my front porch, enjoying the no breeze sweater-wearing weather. A wave of disturbing wind touched me before I saw them turn the corner of my block. Oh no! The same five guys had gotten into a scrape with my uncle recently. Collectively, they had never been on my street before. I asked myself, *why this time?* I felt that trouble was coming to my house. My young siblings and a few of their friend were in the house, watching cartoons. My parents were visiting relatives in Cincinnati and told me that I was the man of the house before they drove away. I had no weapon. Before they saw me, I jumped over the side rail and went to the back of the house into the garage where I kept my bag of tricks.

They stopped at our house just as I thought and started kicking on the storm door and banging on the window near where the kids were watching television, shouting for my uncle to come outside. This terrified the children. From the rear of the house, I hear them screaming and running frenetically throughout the house. While in the garage, I saw the gas can that I kept some gas in to cut the neighbors grass, who were regular customers. In the winter I shoveled their snow. I found an empty pint-size green Twin Pine milk bottle, and I filled it three quarters of the way with the gas. I found a rag and dipped it only halfway into some kerosene. I stuck the dry half of the rag into the milk bottle. There were always a box of the old inch-and-a-half matches with the striker on the side of the box. These matches will ignite when struck on a hard, rugged surface, and when lit, they will burn in a hard rainstorm.

I punched a lot of holes in the top of the gas can which was still three quarter filled so that it would sprinkle good when I shook it. I took the gas can, milk bottle, and matches, then climbed up the back of my house, ducking as I made my way to the front of the house by way of the roof. I lay flat on the roof, looking at the troublemakers. I saw them, but they could not see me directly above them. The kids cried louder as they continued to shout and pound loudly on the door and windows, to the point where I felt that the storm door was about to give. I tried to rationalize away my action. I knew the commandment "Thou shall not kill." But I thought that it did not say anything about me setting villains on fire. Just as I took a matchstick out of the box and crouched halfway up with the milk bottle and gas can in my other hand, I knew that I was going to jail. But I was going to get them. And I also knew that once you start down that path and enter the system, for a Black man there was very little recourse when you got out. Very few people during that era hired a Black jailbird. You had few choices to feed your family, other than working for gangster like Al Capone who was always looking to hiring a few bad men.

Just as I touched the striker on the matchbox to light the wick on the gas bottle and sprinkle gas all over them, a soft, pleading voice said, "Stop."

Simultaneously, the hoodlums stopped kicking on the door and stop banging on the windows. They turned around walked off the porch and left the scene. Whew! That was close. They didn't have a clue that the spirit saved them. The effect of their cause nearly had them headed to the burn ward at the hospital, if they had even survived at all.

A tactic from *The Art of War* was to continue to be useful in avoiding my being bullied into joining the real dark side. In my day-to-day skirmishes, I was always a solider, a mindset that I only sharpened when I joined the U.S. Army. But I basically learned how to function as a trooper from ROTC. But in this conflict, that was not enough. In my waking hours, during my circumspection walks, I had to be always mindful of the trickery euphemism meant to fool me into dropping my apprehension towards the father of lies. I needed the horned discipline of a battle-hardened warrior. This trait I learned autodidactically from reading and taking in the lessons from Carlos Castaneda's *Journey to Ixtlan*. I read this book over and over so many times until I could repeat in my sleep all the lesson of Don Juan Matus, the Yaqui Indian and a man of knowledge.

The demon could not use the vices such as greed, fame, envy, pride, wrath, or money against me because I never cared about what other people had. I congratulated them on the material items, what they had obtained, because I was mindful that all of man's comfort comes from the Lord. The creature continued to try to render me vulnerable by diverting or wiping out all of my finances and destroying my living arraignments to the point where I was homeless. And then it would dangle a pyrite carrot in front of me, hoping that I would bite. Satan verbally screeched at me with foul, ugly words when I don't take the bait.

I reverted into a warrior, disciplined and not needing anything to survive. When I'm in that mode, I'm peacefully content with nothing. And, if necessary, I have no problem going for days without food, water, money, or sleep. Sometimes, the devil uses one of my few real sources of kryptonite against me. My Achilles heel was pretty women. They could reek of unseen deception, and I would feel it like a gentle wind. And my point man sensors rung like the jarring sound of an air raid siren suddenly breaking the sleeping night calm.

And yet, once more I had ignored the warnings, letting my lower muscle run amok, refusing to listen to my upper mind. I knew beforehand that I was getting into trouble, so much so that when the peace officers stopped me in my car and that often occurred whenever I gave a ride to a young lady who had flagged me down. The officers knew who the young ladies were, I didn't. In any event, sometimes I wound up on the docket of a criminal court thinking, *those bad girls were so pleasantly good.*

Personally, I could never even the odds in this encounter, but I could shorten the playing field by reducing the number of females seeking ways to infiltrate my living arrangement whose real intentions were that they were hellbent on collecting the devil's contract that the Spirit said it had on me.

When I stopped drinking cheap whiskey, I stopped waking up with strange bedfellows. Although this was a serendipitous find when I realized that I could not handle the potency. Every now and then, I would hang out with the old timers in social clubs that were spread on corners throughout the neighborhoods. I would buy and drink the corn whiskey or the cheap, get-a-whole-gallon-for-seven-dollars drink. I saw a pattern of me sleeping with forgettable dates that I normally wouldn't dream of touching if we were the only two people left on Earth.

One night after hitting the pluck, I went home with this nice-looking, curvy, early middle-aged lady. At her home, under the soft glow of candle-light, we put away a few sips of cheap whiskey. It was time, and she told me to go to the bedroom, get undressed, and get under the covers. I do this, smiling over my latest conquest, with my hands cupped behind my neck, resting on a pillow.

I watched as she slowly undressed. She took off a padded bra. There was nothing too unusual about her being flat-chested. She removed her girdle and hips pads, and her buttock disappeared. It was strange, but nothing that couldn't be fixed when the lights go out. She took off her wig. Oh boy! She was balding, and her hair was in knots. She did not take care of her hair. I was drunk, and it was too late in the night to go traveling home. I was thinking about how I was going to slip out of there before dawn

I slept on my side, facing away from her. I woke way before dawn, like players do to get out before she noticed that I was not there. My eyes shook off the night and began to focus. I saw this jar on the nightstand on my side of the bed. I could not believe what I was seeing as my vision became clearer. Damn, teeth inside of the jar. Why did she put them on my side of the bed? She was way too young for that. Had I hit rock bottom? I hurried up and put on my pants, shirt, and shoes. The rest of my clothing I carried in my hand and exited out the back door. After that night, I was reformed. I never slept with a Sea Hag, and I never touched cheap whiskey again.

I lived in four of the five boroughs of New York City between 1994 and 1996. Staten Island was the lone place I didn't reside. Even there, I attracted an unusual amount of unwanted attention. So, for me to have a peaceful love life, I had to hide my relationship. I was extremely fond of two ladies, both who were Puerto Rican. One lived in Harlem, and the other lived in the Bronx. When I was followed, which was most of the time, I had to sneak around to see them.

As a matter of fact, I hid all my number-one ladies from the demons. I lived primarily in Queens. I took the J train to the city and transferred to the A train all the way to 125th Street. In that hub, I could lose anyone in the masses. Then I took the D or B train all the way to 161st Street, the Yankee Stadium exit. From there I walked backed down to 156th Street, to my girlfriend Rosa R.'s home. Sometimes I walked all the way from Queens to the Bronx, making sure I was not followed. It's not paranoia when troublesome spirits try to recruit you into becoming a member of their dark cult.

In the year of 1978, I lived in San Francisco for the first time, mainly because I loved the whole scenic Bay Area and the weather. Except it was sometimes too cold during the month of June. One pleasant evening I was walking down a bustling street that seemed to have a few small churches spread sparsely on a particular block. Two very attractive young ladies were at the doorway, stopping pedestrians and asking them to come inside. They flagged me down and cheerfully explained their mission. Well, I'm a sucker for beauty, and I was just about to go inside of the Peoples Temple.

I asked one final question. I said, "What do I have to do to join?" During these years, I was draped in gold and diamonds. Their answer stunned me. I said, "Thanks but no thanks" and double-timed away from there. They had committed a major sin when they said, "You have to take off all of your jewelry and gleefully give all of your money and possessions to the church." Some weeks later, 918 members of the Temple were dead from a mass murder-suicide in Jonestown, Guyana.

My casualty list grew when it came to holding onto soul-soothing love. I tried my best to keep the fight away from those beautiful ladies that were my heart. As hard as I might, I could not sustain explaining why I constantly had to leave or, more appropriately, flee the city. There are some cities where evil spirits are more prevalent and seem to engulf a sizeable portion of the population.

On some sides they are infested with rats, roaches, and demons. When you visit areas with a heavy prison population, you can just about bet that this area is one of Satan's favorite playgrounds. The devil spends time relishing with his flock in the prison yards. I consistently tried to cultivate a normal intimate relationship with a member of the opposite sex by shaking off trailing unclean spirits, going through alleys, crossing underneath the overpass of freeways, running fast for a long distance and then walking because they could not keep up, and doubling back on different modes of transportation. It was done all in the name of keeping those trouble-seeking moochers away from my immediate family and those who I truly I loved. They were everywhere—on the streets, on the busses, in the gyms, next door, in the churches, crawling from underneath rocks always trying to weasel their way into my love life. It was unfortunate because of the circumstances and because of the sacrifices that I considered wise to make in order to keep it that way.

In Michigan and in California I lost more than the law allowed of my share of complimentary relationships: Priscilla, Yvette, Tina Marie, Vicky, Elaine, Eudora, Teresa., and Ana were primarily the number ones in my heart. And I did the best I could to keep the demons in the dark, not knowing who they were. When they got too close, I had to shy away from my sweethearts.

Time away from a loved one makes the heart long. Too much time away makes the heart wonder. And yet there was no more devastating loss in my whole love life than there was in my relationship with my spiritual soulmate Nida. I met her in the late eighties at her family's business, a gas station in

San Diego. It was the year of meeting a companion and of perfect bliss. Both of our families had relocated from Detroit, Michigan, at a time when no one that I met was from California. Even in the city of Los Angeles it seemed like there were very few native-born residents. Most of the population had migrated from another state.

We clicked instantly from the moment we met. As we shared stories from the neighborhood Back East, it felt like we were on the same wavelength as the electron's protons and neutrons of an atom combine to function as one.

She was Italian and around five feet two inches in height. Her almond-shaped, hazel-brown eyes complemented her raven black hair. In my mind, I thought that she was probably some kin to the Greek goddess Aphrodite.

My very first girlfriend was named Janice, and she was petite and could easily have graced the cover any glamor magazine. From then on, every girlfriend that was close to my heart looked like they came from the exact same mold that the first Black Academy Award winner came from. I believe that I never got over leaving my first love. However, I knew that I would be a nomadic traveler from the start, which I was. And I knew that I would be in situations that were not meant for family life, and my assumptions were correct.

Nida was drop-dead gorgeous—angelic, blithesome, and radiant, like a twenty-two-year-old Elisabeth Taylor. When I introduced her to every Mexican friend that I grew up with, they were mesmerized, speechless, and could only say, "Wow!"

I hid her from Satan and his flock of misguided demon. To meet with her, I cut through alleys, cut through fields, parked my car blocks away, and then walked back to see her. I jumped over backyard fences, and sometimes I had to run past a shocked pit bull who didn't have time to react. I doubled back on public transportation. I was not going to let those unclean spirits get near her. But it was costly.

After I was baptized and that guardian angel who intimidated me or, more to the point, scared me, when they next saw me, they told me that it was best that I get married. I decided to marry Nida, but Satan had other ideas. The creature did not want me to marry because this made the heaven happy, and the manufactured lies would have no relevance. So, the creature poured it on by throwing up roadblocks and detours in my life—creating job losses and legal issues Back East that had me leave California.

Once I arrived in another town, my finances were always lost or diverted, even if the funds were sent first class by family members, creating hardships and homeless situations. This was done in the hope that it would force me into bad relationships that were motivated by unscrupulous, greedy people trying to collect on his contract. I often felt like I was in the exact same situation that had King David fleeing from King Saul.

There was nothing I could do to challenge the rumors that I would sleep with any age girl or any male or female. Liars never trust anyone wholeheartedly because they think that everyone lies as they do. Gossip, if it's not challenged, proliferates when it hits the street and on goes on as fact. Before you know it, the rumors go full circle, and by the time it gets back to you, people are telling you a story about yourself that never happened.

No one's perfect except the Lord as everyone has at one time or another, had a few misgivings in their lives that they do not wish to talk about. Perhaps I involved myself in situations very close to going down a dark path. But close only counted in the game of horseshoes. I could not squelch the rumors. I could only sit back and watch, always content with the knowledge that the Lord, and not man, knows the truth.

They said that I was crazy because the few people who knew about my marriage to the princess all said that they would have married her. How long? Just how long before one of her relatives found out that I was an excellent shot and would need a special favor? Her family was notorious for asking for favors. Is there anyone who believed that human target practice would have stopped with just one favor?

The demons said that I was gay because I did not act like them or sleep with the kind of women they did. Of course, I did not act like them. I grew up into an adult overseas in a foreign country. There were absolutely no Black females in the town where I lived. The ones who were there were mixed, and we called them "war babies."

I ski, skate, climb mountains, play chess, love classical music, am an all-star in numerous sports, love to dance, and hang out with rich folks in cosmopolitan cities who just immediately take a liking to me. Rich people and gangsters relax and feel comfortable around you when they gather that you are not after their money.

I was adventurous and a risk taker. I loved being debriefed after completing another successful military mission. Our whole radar team was extremely disappointed when the mission to jump out of a plane without any practice was scrapped at the last minute. As a team, we were confident and as good as the Pentagon thought we were.

How can a relationship such as that thrive when the other person had never even traveled to the westside of her own city and frequently played mind and power games, all while trying to change me when I had a nearly impossible task of trying to find my own self and be aware of my imperfections?

I believe that people are the Lord's children. It is too stressful trying to change someone else's kids. So, I take people at face value. When entering a new relationship and after sleeping then having breakfast together and we don't talk about visiting an art institution or spend the entire day marveling at the exhibitions because it is a place that they had not visited since a fourth-grade field trip. But after sex, she's talking about visiting a social worker. There is nothing wrong with doing what it takes to survive. Not trying to change the status quo generation after generation is a stagnation trap. On the other hand, raising children is an enormous job. I figured that being a welfare queen is still an occupation. It pays nearly the same as some fast-food joints. I avoided any baby daddy drama like it was a plague.

Those ladies who were my heartthrobs inspired me and brought out the best in me. They did not try to control or change me. They were individuals with high self-esteem, and they believed in equality. The good-looking hood rats had the opposite effect. Those Jezebels usually had experienced some childhood trauma like an incestuous encounter or rape that sent their lives off the rails. They were narcissists and naturally sought ways of destroying every unsuspecting male that fell into their web.

When I was hanging out with Debbi, some of her friends told me a different version of the same story as to why they did this on purpose. Nothing that was impossible, however. I was spiritual, they were not. There is no real compatibility and an awful lot of give instead of taking in a relationship like that.

My Mexican homeboys called me Shallow Hal. Not because like them big but because I did not sleep with all the young ladies that they tried to pass to me. They could sleep with anything that had a virginal. Because of that morning when I saw the teeth in a jar, my player's field was shortened. My selection of females became extremely limited and reduced to a selected few.

I was one of those people who identified with the similarities of their belongings. I loved quality. I'd rather have one good thing than a whole lot of middle-of-the-road items. The manufacturer who makes my car got it right when they said, "The best or nothing." Years ago, I let this homeless young man off the street live with me. I gave him a chance to get himself together. Virtually anyone could hitch hike from the tip of Maine to the lower part of California, problem free, especially from truck drivers going that way. There was a time when you could really trust people.

One day he brings home this huge woman that hardly fit through the doorway. There wasn't any space between the frame on either side of her. He takes her to the back bedroom. Moments later he asked me to join them. I declined. I tried others, but I always ran back to petite ladies with quickness because that just wasn't for me. I just like what I liked. This lady had to be at least 400 pounds. She was somehow disappointed that I did not participate in whatever. As she dressed and continued to head to the front door, she let me know her torrid feelings. While slapping her massive thigh, she said out loud, "He must be gay if he doesn't like all of this!" I was flabbergasted. I had nothing against her. I believe in to each his or her own. And I really do not care what others do in their bedrooms. I have never been a follower. I will not jump off a cliff just because the leader will. I wouldn't sleep with anyone just because they did or could.

My complete lack of interest, I believe, was subconsciously embedded from events that occurred a long time ago. I remember when my mother and father had separated, and he started dating a nice lady nearly the same size. I started harboring ill feelings about her visits because the next morning, after spending the night, my father, as he was leaving to work, would wake me after I'd just gotten to bed after the bar closed at 5:00 a.m. and tell me that I must repair his bed.

Each time they destroyed the bed. The box spring, rails, and planks were busted into fragmented puzzle pieces. I had to come up with jury-rig solution time and time again until I had to put cinder-block bricks underneath for him to sleep in it.

My biggest dilemma was that I worked for the Focus: HOPE organization and had to be there at 7:00 a.m. Losing sleep and having to find ways to repair the bed always made me late. As a prompt individual, I hated being late. One could set their watches by my arrival time. I have terminated a few serious relationships if they continued to make me late for anything.

Back home that was it for assisting the young men who were down on their luck. I fulfilled my quota for community service. After what he brought to my home, I never let any troubled young man, or any man live with me again. The gossip reached a flash point. The embellishment and rumor combustion were primarily initiated from there.

There was no letting up from the instigators that belonged to the dark angel. They had no win and nothing to show for all those years. Their capacity to persuade was a money pit that was totally inefficient primarily because they had nothing to sell. I had absolutely zero interest in what they concocted from someone's vivid imagination. They believed that by telling the same lie for ten or twenty years that perhaps someday it might come true. At the time, I hadn't touched a lick of cheap whisky in fifteen years. That meant that I no longer woke up next to a changeling. Their wishing well was dry. There was only dust in bucket.

I thought that Nida deserved someone other than a man who had to cut through the water drains and sewer systems to see her. Satan made sure that I had no money to elope. That would destroy his narrative. I was employed as a maintenance supervisor in a high-rise apartment building in downtown Detroit. I was blessed in 1997. When I looked for a place to reside, the building owner needed skillful help with the upkeep and overseeing of the building and gave me a penthouse apartment with a real fireplace. I lucked out again when I talked a beautiful Filipino woman named Elaine into moving in with me. I loved her, but there was just one major problem with my heart in our relationship: I could not shake Nida.

This had never happened to me before. I had been on the road, living in different cities since I was sixteen. I left my local girl in so many towns, never looking back without any regrets. I guess that I'd never known love before. But it was different that time. Music was always in my head. I had a song that popped into my conscience for every mood, situation, and occasion. With her, it was the song from the group called The Manhattan Transfer titled "Shaker Song." It was on cue so many times, repeatedly, that when I woke in the morning, I knew that I had to let every note play out in its entirety before I started my day.

When my roommate and I were out and about, doing up the town, I thought about her. During our romantic Filipino cuisine dinners, my mind drifted back to her. I tossed and turned trying to sleep at night, wishing that it was her lying next to me. Regardless of the distance between us, we were never apart. This had never happened in all my nomadic years; I could not escape. It felt like when we were having dinner at the table, she was there sitting on the sofa, winking her sparkling, enchanting eyes at me, smiling and motioning, "Come back to me."

A Spirit That Loves Football

Huntsville, Alabama. 1976. On a early evening sunny 62 degrees light breezy gorgeous weather for football day at the Redstone Arsenal Military Base. I was standing on the 35-yard line on a lush well-manicured football field getting ready to play in an intramural 9 on 9 flag football game between the different units. During the kickoff a sensation had enveloped me. It felt like a low voltage electrical shock. This was nothing unusual however, this day it had don on me that this was a feeling of des a vow, that repeatedly occurred at the kickoff of a football game. This 9 on 9 contest turned into a memorable 9 on 1 mauling. I made 30 straight plays in a row on defense and had completely shut down the opponent's offense. The results of my play making the other team never made a first down in the game Not only the spectators but, the referees were in awe. The refs simply followed me around on every play. After that football game I was conscience that I was assisted at kick off by an outside influence.

When I was very young, I had this remarkable talent for identifying and picking out the right candidate and organizations that excelled. All the way back to my stellar job that was forced up on me in Job Corps, my choice of high school football teams that I followed I flip-flopped between Birmingham Brothers Rice and Farmington Harrison.

Michigan was and is my favorite sports team from day one. I read everything about one of their safeties named Thomas Darden and his gang that they nicknamed "the den of the mellow men." I liked Michigan State also, until they played Michigan. In professional football I could watch any two teams play against each other. And because I moved around so much, I had this thing about being in Rome and acting like a Roman, even though I supported the Christians.

I rolled nothing but seven and elevens on the dice game of picking a professional football team to follow. I had my eyes on this quarterback from Stanford named Jim Plunkett. There was something different about him that separated him from the rest of the signal callers in college football. Years later it was the same thing with quarterback Andrew Luck. I would tune out and drop everything that I was doing to watch or listen to every game that Stanford's Mr. Luck and running back Toby Gerhart started in.

While I was a teenager analyzing the pro football teams, I dug up all the information that I could on the owners and general managers of the organization. I then focused on the players that they had chosen before I decided to stick with a certain team. In the year of 1971, I chose the Boston Patriots because I thought that any team that picked Jim Plunkett in the draft was smart. Good or bad, I stuck with Michigan and New England throughout the course of my life. They say that you can't beat the house, which is true in most cases, but my team broke the bank winning all those Super Bowls and sent me home owning the mansion.

There was something strange that was happening to me during a foot-ball game that I did not understand. When I was trying out of the junior varsity football team at Kettering High, Coach Tucker told me to go back and return kick offs one day. While at the goal line, I told myself that I was going to take the ball all the way back for a touchdown.

When I caught the ball, something joined me and made me feel invin-cible. I was hit six times beginning at the forty when I ran past my blockers. I cut back inside, breaking three tacklers that had me in their grips. I started up field and saw two tacklers at the fifty come at me horizontally, one from the left and one zeroing in from the right.

They had me in the crosshairs, dead to right. Like everyone else did most of the time, they had misjudged my speed. And instead of being tackled, I jetted right past them, and they collided with each other headfirst. The real action happened when I reached the ten-yard line. There, three tacklers grabbed and held a vise-lock grip on me, one on the left, one on the right. One guy had a hold on me by the neck. I somehow became stronger. I lowered the torque and put my body into four-wheel drive. The tacklers slowed me down just a little as the one that had a hold on me by the neck was flying parallel in the air. I carried all three tacklers in the end zone for the score.

The wide-eyed coaches had me do it again. I told myself that I was taking this back all the way again. That time I caught the ball on the right side of the goal line and started left. I saw a small opening at the twenty-five and hit the accelerator. I was untouched when I reached the end zone. Only then would I look back. I never looked back while I was running with the football. That time when I looked back, all my teammates and the whole defense was thirty yards downfield behind me. I was the backup quarterback, but that day the coaches promoted me to the role of the starting running back.

A lot of football players look good in shorts on the practice field. They look and preform like world-beaters, having the coaches salivating. Once the real hitting began, they showed their true colors and wasted away, making mental errors, missing tackles. They were manhandled by the opposing team. I was the complete opposite. I wasn't excitable in practice. There was nothing overtly impressive about me, mainly because I was not trying to tear my own teammates head off. And I always hid my speed. But during real game time, I was joined. I was completely focused. I didn't believe in taking a play off.

Something happened to me during each kickoff. Never, but right at the blowing of the whistle, it felt like something from the outside was entering my body. It was way too wacky for me to tell anyone about it. Also, I didn't understand it. After all those years, I had another epiphany while I was watching *The Phantom Menace*. It happened when Qui-Gon Jinn explained to young Anakin Skywalker about Midi-chlorian. The more that I thought about it, to a lesser degree, that was the same feeling that I had when I went to that church way back in Kentucky.

At kick off I had this feeling that my body turned into a whole bunch of little, tiny bubbles—small like a single cell. The strange part was that the grass that we played on turned into the same small bubbles that I now was. The air, the trees, and the bleachers, it felt like all the surrounding elements, and I were connected, and all were made of the same substance. In hindsight, the small bubbles didn't join me. I joined them. I hadn't told anyone about this because I didn't feel like I was losing my mind. I had no reference or any person that could explain what was happening to me, anyway, and I was not going to let them put a tight, white jacket on me then give me a free ride to the psychiatric hospital. The movie was the closest thing that I had to understanding my dilemma.

Once upon a time, even in the big cities at night as a youth perched on the back roof of your home, you could clearly see the stars at night. I was conscious of the fact that somewhere out there were other civilized planets, uncountable mysteries, and different dimensions. I knew that in the same space, two or three could coexist in distinct realities. I wasn't afraid of ghosts, monsters, or dragons. Because my eyes were open, I was aware that unnatural and or unpleasant entities do roam the universe. But I was honestly more scared to death of doctor's hypodermic needles.

There were astronomical trillion-to-one odds of seeing a pure energy cloud just once. Even higher odds that an over-forty ballplayer could create the conditions to uncover it once more. However, nothing is impossible for the creator of the sun, earth, and the clouds.

The Lord showed me the way and literally lead me by the hand to the time and place where I was supposed to showcase my physical skills, where the end results would give me the ability to conjure up once more my metaphysical cloud.

I was awakened by the touch of the spirit. That told me to go to the 2004 San Diego practice facilities located off Murphy Canyon Road. I dressed in sharp but casual attire and headed out the door to observe my current Cinderella team. The weather outside was tropical. There was a soft, welcome breeze of generosity off the Pacific Ocean. It was sunny with an aqueous blue background. The spattering of cumulus clouds added flavor to the complementary temperature that was typical for Southern California. The picturesque sky reminded me of a landscape painting that could easily have been created on the canvas of a Vincent Van Gogh, Jean-Baptiste, or a Martin Johnson Headey work of art. As the clouds moved on the wind, somehow the temperature and the hue outside were the same as the Easter holiday weather that I had experienced in Detroit long ago.

I parked my car far away from the practice area and walked there. My reason for doing this was that when attending concerts at Pine Knob and Meadow Brook back in Michigan, if your vehicle was parked to close, you had a hard time getting out from under the bottleneck created by exiting concert goers. It could be hours. So, I parked near the end close to the freeways and had an easier time getting home.

As I was walking, I was kind of upset with the Chargers for drafting another quarterback. In that department, I was a Purdue Boilermakers and *Street and Smith's Pro Football* prodigy. After Bob Griese piloted Miami to a perfect season, I wanted to learn what he knew from where he polished his skills. And that's what I did. I reached the practice field and watched the players go through individual drills for their specialties until the coaches called for the offense to scrimmage against the defense.

I had a habit of watching the offensive linemen first to see how they gelled together. Next, I peeked at the quarterback to determine if his delivery and zip on the ball was adequate for game management. Finally, as always, I watched the receivers to see how they got off the line of scrimmage, what kind of speed they had and how they run their routes. Do they square in or round off when they make their cuts? Do they know how to box out a defender? And primarily, can they hold onto the ball when hit? As a forever backup quarterback, I spent most of my time in practice, holding a clipboard and grading the receivers.

I knew most of the Chargers' pass catchers from the previous season and knew what they were capable of doing, but on that day, a certain receiver who I had not seen before had me mesmerized. I looked at this young man run through the defense, and I loved the way he ran and cut on a dime. I stood in awe, becoming fixated while watching him. I thought that he ran like someone that I knew. *Well, I'll be darned. He runs like me.*

I asked myself, *Is number eighty-three that Welker fellow?* This player reminded me of my brothers and other kin folk who played football. I used to smile at the beginning of pickup games when no one picked them, but I did. They were short, but they played precision, mistake-free football. And, as usual, they had their larger-sized competitors scratching their bewildered heads because those small guys outran them, scored, and literally blew them away.

I had this list of a fraternity of fast runners, and on that day, as a rare occasion, I initiated Wes Welker on the spot into this shorter list of the larger brotherhood members, which included names such as Devin Hester, Fred Biletnikoff, Herman Moore, Steve Largent, Charlie Sanders, James Lofton, Bob Hayes, Michael Irvin, Johnnie Morton, and Randy Moss. Mr. Welker was a brother of mine, and he didn't even know it. Like my other brothers, I knew that with a guy like this, there could be so many nights together when we would be putting away some ice-cold beers.

It was one catchable pass on this day that was a pivotal mistake. Me not reaching down and corralling the ball unknowingly had major ramifications for the success of the 2004 Chargers' championship run. And another unfortunate consequence was me losing my last chance of capturing the energy-whisper vapor. The next series of events was catastrophic in the Lord's walk-on plan for me and my destiny.

I believe that it was receiver Eric Parker who broke my fixation on watching that new guy. He loudly kept on shouting out, "Where's Willie?" As he left, the coaches were huddled down deep in the defensive back field. He continued to shout, "Where's Willie?" five more times before I started looking around to find which ballplayer he was talking about. He said it again, and I turned 180 degrees behind me, looking at the bleachers to see if it was someone there who he was trying to find.

Fighting with demons all the time made me forget about the meeting that I had with the scouts in my daily donut shop on Market Street. Eric shouted one more time as I turned away from the crowd in the bleachers and back toward the practice field. At this crucial moment, the new quarterback threw the ball past the fields marked sideline and directly toward me. My first thought was, *damn, he's accurate.* So, then I was thinking about how I would catch the ball. I had three ways to catch the pass coming at me with laser beam accuracy. First, I could simply dive over the fence and catch the ball in my hands. Second, I could dive over the fence, catch the ball, and, like the cats taught me, turn over in midair and land on my back. That move would not hurt as bad as the first one would because the belly flop would be taken out of the mix.

I briefly looked down at my semi-sharp clothes and shoes that I'd worn. To avoid sliding on the grass and permanently staining my clothes, I decided to simply reach my hands over the fence and just catch the ball. Simultaneously, I looked at the galvanized chain-link fence that was worn, just like the one back when my mother caught us playing football in our Sunday best.

I was ready to close my hand around the perfect pass, when, from behind, I hear my whole name, "Willie Lamarr," shouted extremely loudly in my mother's voice. It was the exact same decibel and tone that my mother used when she shouted at us in the alley for playing ball in our Sunday best. That sound stunned me, causing me to alligator arm the ball. There was no way would I not catch a clean pass like that. I probably dropped an uncontested pass once in every three games.

Satin! I thought. The premiere deceptive ventriloquist—he had triggered something. My mother would never do anything like that at a serious moment. She loved football. I had not seen or talked to her for three months. I called her during the January 30, 2000, Super Bowl XXXIV between the Los Angeles Rams and the Tennessee Titans. I was all happy to speak with her during the second quarter. I was stupefied when she told me to get off the phone if I didn't have nothing to say. I was messing up her game.

Rams great Roosevelt Grier would buy her lunch and talk football when they worked together as volunteers for an urban league center in San Diego. My mother was a regular San Diego police force volunteer. I thought, *this can't be her.* Under normal circumstances, I would have caught the easy pass, thrown it all the way back to the quarterback to show my arm strength and accuracy, jumped the fence, walked into the locker room, and gotten a uniform. I did this with so many teams: the Detroit Jets semi pro football team. The Motor City Cougars, San Diego Storm, the short-lived Detroit Titans, and Redstone Arsenal when I played army ball in Alabama.

There were over 150 professional football players, coaches, and assistant on the practice field who heard the wide receiver repeatedly shout, "where is willie" and subsequently saw Phillip Rivers throw me a catchable football.

Sitting in the bleachers and standing near the chain link fence were thousands upon thousands of Chargers fans, administrators and sport reporters who didn't know that they were witness to an ominous occasion, didn't hear what had bewitched me causing me to suddenly pull back my arm's from corralling the in-coming football.

Out of character, I was baffled and spooked, something that rarely happens to me. I stepped back away from the fence, trying to ascertain the situation. In my life I had been rendered that way only once before. As a gift for being the best of the best radar team, we were invited to tour one of Adolf Hitler's gas chambers at one of his concentration camps. With a few of my fellow squad members, I stood in the middle of the gas chamber located in Dachau. I immediately was overwhelmed with the sensation of screaming, dead souls in crossing patterns, swarming all around me. My skin itched. I swear that I could faintly see and feel the ghostly sight of dead souls during their moment of sheer terror. I lasted only about five second before I had to get the heck out of there.

Back at the practice field, thinking about why that happened was too much for me. In situations such as those, when I don't understand things, I punted. Instead of walking on to the field, I walked away feeling baffled. I had to go home and regroup. As I took three steps away, on the other side of the fence, I passed by Shane Phillips. If I thought that day could not get any stranger, it did. As we passed, something inside my head went *Phhffiiittt!* What was crazy about it was that the word came out of the left side of my head inside of a deflated balloon, just like in the comic strips.

That prompted a feeling that something was wrong. I felt like I was not supposed to leave. The guys on the team gave me a rare opportunity to join by walking on. And with those demons on my mind, I was blowing it. I had forgotten that the devil does not care for clean, wholesome, family-oriented sports such as hockey, baseball, soccer, or football. The creature loves to hang out in drug dens, poppy fields, and the VIP sections of strip clubs. The people in these places are its kind of posse.

Satin knew that if I were to join the Chargers, I would have had a much larger platform to inform the public that he was real. And that is exactly what I would have done. The farther I walked, the worse I felt. A wave of uncertainty slammed into me, trying to direct the stunned me to turn around. I was supposed to be there and be part of a championship drive. That was my 2004 Cinderella team that was Super Bowl bound. It should have nothing to do with me, but the more that I watched the games during the season, the more that I knew I was completely wrong.

Later the spirit pointed out that if I had run around with my adoptive little brother Wes Welker, the organization would not have separated the combination of the two disadvantaged rookies whose hearts were bigger than the typecasting. Because of our game-changing play-making abilities and surfacing moments of great inspirational talent that were displayed on the playing field and in the locker room, it would have been too great to mess with the dynamic of the odd couple—the two underdogs.

In essence, this was not because of faults of the Charger's organization. They were on top of their game. The owner, the manager, and the coaches, were firing on all cylinders. It was what I failed to do that was the catalyst, causing the catastrophe that had happened at the end of this walk-on story. I could feel that it was that elusive window of time when Coach Marty Schottenheimer shook off the past jinxes, misfortunes, and unlikely scoring drives to win a championship game. And the same for the championship starved city of San Diego and I would have finally gotten my cloud.

All I had to do was catch that darn ball. Those who were close and truly know me call me an alpha male, whatever that means. I knew that deep down inside of me I had best of the best, X-factor chemistry as a player, coach, or administrator than anyone saw coming. Watching the season nervously, I saw missed plays and situations on the field where I would have made a tremendous difference.

In the pickup games that I continued to play in, and when I played semipro ball, I was just having fun. After that ringer's game, I didn't care about scores anymore. I just showed up for the hitting. If I made a tackle and looked back at the referee, and he was not reaching for his yellow flag going, "Boy, I oughta," then I needed to step it up because I wasn't hitting hard enough. As an on-the-field player and coach, I always let the youngster return the kickoff so that they might gain experience because to return kicks, I never needed one second of practice.

In a meaningful game, I would have gone to the coaches to ask for the chance to showcase my return abilities. I didn't need to with the Chargers. The scouts had witnessed me live, taking the kickoff all the way to the house on several occasions when I was practically forced into preforming this duty in the spur of the moment, with absolutely no prior touches or practice. I was a world-class sprinter, 100-yard gallops were where my real money-maker resided.

At the precise moment during the very last play of the Chargers 2004 wildcard overtime playoff when they lost to the Jets, my heart dropped. I felt exactly like Dallas Cowboys tight end Jackie Smith, dropping an easy touchdown pass from quarterback Roger Staubach in the end zone, near the end of the third quarter of Super Bowl XIII against the Steelers. I was thunderstruck with a sick feeling. It took me a very long time to get over that catchable ball from the brand-new quarterback.

The spirit showed me where, how, and why and gave me everything that I needed—practically handed me an opportunity to accomplish my goal of lassoing a cloud on a silver platter. Wes and I were the only two intangible missing pieces preventing the Chargers from going for the gold in their 2004 Cinderella football season.

DANGER:
HIGH VOLTAGE

I was only six years old when the bullies started their mess. There was an attraction between someone who was looking for trouble and someone who was quietly concern only with minding their business. What I failed to understand was the saying "watch out for the quite ones." And yet they never heed of their own advice. Their aggressive nature propelled them harass, oppress, and try to do harm to those whose personalities made them look weak, meek, or introverted. Bullies do not fathom that perhaps somewhere down the line, they are going to meet their match. And what's more relevant, they do not take into consideration that they might unexpectedly mix it up with someone who, perhaps, is more dangerous than they could possibly imagine.

Class was dismissed, and I was walking home. I was in the second grade and not thinking that this could be the beginning of a lifetime of combat. Here they come. They approached me and told me that I said something about their mother. I didn't even know who they were, let alone talk about someone's mother. The crowd gathered around them. In every battle there is a point of no return where the line has been crossed, and words will not stop it. The spectators expected that the loudmouth bully, who they were secretly afraid of, was about to whip on another person who didn't say too much.

They were going to teach me a lesson about talking about their mother. I didn't believe in arguing with people. Saying nothing, I gave them my standard "oh yea?" look. What sounded good in their own minds never panned out in real time. They looked dazed after trying to lift themselves off the dirt, learning that reality got them knocked backward over a two-feet wire fence.

The very next Friday after school, the same crowd formed one block away in front of this popular bully's house. He wanted to show off for the onlookers right inside of the fence of his home. This time the challenge was that I had to knock a piece of wood off his shoulder to get the fight started. That was the kind of challenge I would not back away from. So, I knocked the small stick off. The next thing that I saw was that the young man had both hands on his mouth, trying to stop the profuse bleeding from having all his front teeth knocked out. His parents who watched from the window and could have stopped the mishap came running out of their front door in shock.

The next Friday after that, I had to cross a line drawn in the dirt also with a gang of kids watching in front of another opponent's home. His parents had to take the young man to the hospital with a concussion. The following Friday, this kid had to go to the emergency room to treat broken ribs. The bullies didn't stop completely, but they were no long taking the battles in front of their homes.

In junior high school, the bullies were still at it. However, these battles were scheduled to be held on the playgrounds and in the parks away from the schools. The fights were always over very quickly. And the excited, fickle crowds, mostly girls, followed this young man halfway home—the one who they never saw loose a fight.

The older the bullies got, the more dangerous and deadly the warfare grew. Fighting to me was just a one-on-one art form between two individuals. As time passed on the streets, it morphed into the loser bringing a gun in the mix. That blew up into deadly family brawls nowadays, like the Hatfields and the McCoy's. In the days when there was no other reason but to display dominance over their mates, I had witness, with regularity, wives being beaten by drunken husbands on the weekend, to the dismay of the younger children. Many of the boys in such families could not wait until they were strong enough to challenge their fathers. It occurred in my close family, which ended in a tragic loss of the bread winner and one of my favorite uncles.

It happened on a moonlit, gentle breeze, comfortable summer night. My very close cousins who kept on saying that they were going to get him for hitting their wise, easygoing, small mother kept their promise. The father came home from another bout of drinking and gambling all evening in a blind pig. When he and his car staggered home in the wee hours of the morning, making it to the front door, like clockwork he started to accuse his wife of engaging in activities that he himself was doing.

Two of his growing boys who were wide awake heard him spouting his misdirected anger. Unlike other nights, on that one they invited him to pick on them. He had no problem with their challenge. They took the scrimmage out back in the yard. It was a fierce fight, and for a while my knife-tossing teacher could handle them. But they were just as strong as he was. They killed him in battle. They received no punitive punishments from the court of law.

My mother and father were always traveling out of town on the weekends to Chicago or to Tennessee for a booze runs. They would spend the whole weekend away from home every time the Kentucky Derby rolled around. The last thing that my father said to me was, "You are the man of the house. Take care of your brother and sisters." We had an older uncle that lived with us, but he wasn't all there. So, they left me with the guard duty and security details.

My sister had an older boyfriend that worked at one of the many plants that had saturated the city. He treated her nice, but to the rest of the family, he was an arrogant dictator, trying to tell me what to do, demanding we get him water among other things. His character just kept on getting worse as he thought he was the king of the house. He jumped on my sister one day, causing all the little kids to panic, cry, and scream throughout the house.

Seeing this really pissed me off. As he was leaving, I stood in the doorway, half-blocking his path. He bumped into me, but I didn't move. His last words were, "You think that you could do something to me? You are too light in the pants." I answered, "Oh yea?" Steaming, I watched him get into his car and drive away.

After work he and the boys in his gang were drug dealers. They slung the white horse. He was armed with a beautiful, pearl-handle .25 semiautomatic that he showed me while bragging. I was only fourteen years old, about five feet, and weighed only ninety pounds. My sister's boyfriend was near twenty. He had that same demeanor of a cutthroat. He was six feet two and close to 185 pounds. He was right about one thing: physically, I was no match for him.

What I did have for him was a bag of tricks. I have been working with electricity since I was eight years old and could control and send power just about anywhere that I wanted it to go. Repeatedly I saw those wife beaters come back the next day sober, crying and carrying on like they would never hit her again, which lasted only a month before the woman's head was once more wrapped in bandages like a mummy. Sure enough, he came back the next day after work, and I was ready for him. I didn't believe in arguing with anyone, but I did believe in stopping a bad situation in its tracks.

I could never be a peace officer because I was one of those people who would shoot first, then ask questions. Talk crazy to me, and I would pop them in the leg, then turn around and ask my partner, "What did he say?" In the Military I didn't always totally agree with the Geneva Convention. Should I see a platoon charging at me, they didn't have to shoot at me first before I start lobbing grenades left and right. If the man next to me wanted to wait to see if they would fire first, I would tell him that I would worry about a court martial later. "Right now, let me have your grenades if you aren't going to use them."

In any event, her boyfriend brought my hidden personality traits to the surface, the dark side of me that lies deep in everyone. Only mine is packed with a short fuse and is a few bad selections of words away from popping out on the surface. A half hour before I knew when he would arrive, I went to my office in the garage. I found a very long, broken extension cord. I stripped one end back three inches and the other six inches. I went into the basement and took out the screw-in fuse in the box to my sister's bedroom. I removed a penny from my pocket and wrapped it in aluminum foil, and then I stuck the wrapped penny back into the fuse socket. I sneaked into my sister's bedroom while, as always, she was posted in front of the television watching *General Hospital* or a couple of highly talked about lovebirds named Luke and Laura. She would not leave her spot on the sofa for an hour.

I tied the short end of the extension cord on the metallic doorknob on the inside of the bedroom door. I took the longer stripped cord and spread out the copper wire on the floor. Beforehand, I soaked in water the welcome mat that she kept in front of the door for him to wipe off his dirty feet. He could not tell it was wet unless he stepped on it. I placed the mat halfway underneath the door. I plugged the cord into the wall outlet, and then I climbed out of the bedroom window.

Right on cue, he pulled up dirty and muddy after work. He got out of the car with a bag in his hand. I had a blank stare, looking at nothing, thinking, *I got something for your bad ass.* As he slithered past me, like always he took off his muddy shoes and said a few words to my sister before he headed to the bedroom to take a short nap. I sat on the porch and watched my sister so that if she goes to the bathroom or to her bedroom, I could have bolted into the house to stop her from going into her room. Women never did leave their spot while Luke and Laura were on.

Oh uh! The boyfriend didn't go directly to the bedroom. He sat on the couch next to my sister and started crying and asking for forgiveness, like they all do. He pulled some nice flowers and candy from the bag and gave them to my sister. Oh shoot! They were making up. I could not unplug the cord by way of the inside door, so I had to climb back into the window to snatch out the cord. Murphy's Law is a son of a gun. As I hurried to the side of the house underneath her window, her window slammed shut.

Damn. I frantically looked around on the ground to find something to pry the window open. I finally found a strong piece of sheet metal, got the window open, climbed in, unplugged the extension cord, removed it from the doorknob, picked up the wet mat, and jumped back out of the window. Whew! That was close.

As soon as I sat back down in the lawn chair on the front porch, he headed back to her bedroom to take his short, regular nap. He and my sister were unaware that he was seconds away from getting some permanent sleep. His aggressive, superior attitude, quick to cause strife wrong assumptions, brought out the evil inside of a severely underestimated, quite skinny kid.

I was under the impression that if I were the CEO of a company, and ten years had passed without any positive results, and there were wasted resources and we were no closer to the end than when they had begun, I would drop the cause and fire everyone. With humans, this might have been the case. However, with an immortal entity, time and money do not apply. Not only did it not forget, but the creature turned up the heat so hot that I felt like I was lodged tight in the middle of an erupting volcano.

That first volley of daily, misguided, dark recruiters that I had endured in 1991 wasn't anything compared to the lowdown greediness of a brand-new breed trying to collect on Satan's contract. They tried to entice me by showing me money, a handful of hundreds. That made my rich self-think that they were trying to entice me with nickels and dimes while I was turning down a million-dollar honest contract because of philosophical differences. They shouted out loud, sitting behind me on a city bus, about what I better do for them. They stalk me on the streets, inviting me to join their money-loving club of lost souls.

A moving target is harder to hit. Moving from place to place is what I did. Because of the demon dodging, I could not sit still long enough to focus on catching up with Nida. Every hour of the day it seemed like I was fighting for my spiritual life. My blood pressure shot up tremendously from my body being on red alert all the time because people were always wasting resources by trying to get me in a sting.

I let my guard down just for a second, and the creature got one in here and there. I was set up by some slick unclean spirits. They got their wish by having me land in jail with some trumped up charges. One summer day, enjoying the Pacific coast tropical weather, my brother and I were sitting on a bench in a park that had a sixty-five-degree pitch. After my brother lit a cigarette, suddenly a patrol car appeared from out of nowhere and zoomed up the grass of the elevated park. Two officers exited the car to searched us for contraband. One officer called in on his shoulder radio to check and see if we had any warrants.

In a matter of a few minutes, all hell broke loose. Three cars tore up the neatly cut grass, trying to get to us. On the air ways, I kept on hearing the repeated words, "We got him." I was handcuffed and sitting in the backseat of a patrol car. I was thinking backward, trying to find something that I did in the past that caught up with me.

Officers who were in the front seat spoke into the handheld mike, saying we finally caught a fugitive. I didn't have the faintest of ideas what they were talking about. I believed that I just hadn't done anything that bad that would lead to this. I was thinking about those old movies where they take a railroad prisoner to jail, and they never heard from him again.

I was nervous when the officers didn't bother to process me in the main station in downtown San Diego. In all the numerous times that I have been arrested just for being Black—and for the many nights that I spent in a caged pen for fighting at the 5th precinct that was located on the Jefferson and St. Jean in Detroit—not once in my entire life has a peace officer read me the Miranda Rights. Just like during this occasion, once more they shot me through the system.

They also skipped taking me to the local county jail. In the middle of the night, they traveled with me in the backseat of a patrol car, with shackled feet and hand-cuffed wrists, across a very dark long stretch of barren land. There were no streetlights or lights of any kind. I was really thinking that someone had done a good job of setting me up.

I knew that I would never get out because once someone tried me, my retaliatory nature easily would have had me put into solitary confinement. The first thing that I already had on my mind before I was even transported into the prison system was to make or purchase a shank. In jail and in prison, there is an unwritten rule to assault a brand-new inmate to test their resolve. In matters such as this, the devil knew that I was a sneaky lad, and some day, it was a probability of 99 percent that hypothetically I would stealthily return the favor to the unexpected bully with a direct jab into the assailant's carotid artery, no doubt resulting in me receiving an extended sentence and a private cell.

The car pulled into a creepy, heavily guarded, gated area. The place was called Wackenhut. The judge sent me back home Monday night for a lack of evidence. It was a con job from the start. The evil spirit wanted me dazed in one of his favorite hangouts. Once I was there, it could try to control and manipulate me with the help of its best followers. It screamed at me in the most horrific voice that was in a decibel way beyond the imagination of humans every time I got out of an extremely bad situation where everyone thought I had no chance winning. What's more, every time I arrived with shackled hands and feet at the county jail, a huge number of the neighborhood young men, and some that I let smoke in the garage—and I do mean so many —were there to protect me.

One of my hoodlum friends that lived around the corner named was Joey. He was knocking convicts flat out almost every day and then gladly coming to tell me that he'd gotten away with decking another one. The guards had no witness to dispute the claim coming from the one who had a swelling knot the size of a grapefruit on his forehead.

There was no time for Nida. That go round, Satan won. In dire straits again, I had to flee from San Diego. By the middle of 1973, the Player's Club had disbanded. The stars were shipped home or to different geographic locations while still in the military. The dynamic changed because of the new recruits who were mostly volunteers displayed selfishness and a significant lack of cohesion in banding together in the sorority of a brotherhood. The dap was no more, but the backstabbing increased. Blue-jean wearing college students invaded the club at night instead of the sophisticated, high-society, well-dressed officers or the officers' wives who were out looking for a different kind of excitement. It was a different world in the club, and I dropped by only every now and then.

One late summer night I went to the club with a close friend. I hadn't picked up on the fact that he constantly got in fights every time we went out together. I would be sitting in a corner with arms wrapped, holding hands while looking in the eyes of a Fraulein. A bartender or maid would come to my table and say that me and my friend had to leave. This developed into a pattern. I was a lover boy who was out only for a good time.

When I felt a little homesick, which was rare, I hung out with the boys from 11B Infantry. After two beers, someone, on cue, would feel disrespected for any little thing. Perhaps their shoelaces were not tied right. Bar fights made me feel like I was right at home around my family because after two drinks, that's what they did.

In any event, it was that night that the bar owner had had enough of this new breed of soldier, and he regularly called the German police. I was standing in the hallway near the exit steps, talking to a young lady. Out came my friend being pushed roughly in the back by two peace officers. I say, "Hey, man. You don't have to treat him like that." One pushed me out of the way. What did he do that for? It was right up my alley. I tossed them into the walls like they were rag dolls.

From out of nowhere, two more came to join the battle. They were punching, kicking, and hitting me over the head with their Billy clubs, and I didn't feel a thing. I was just getting warmed up. Two more jumped into the mix. Bodies were flying all over the small room at the base of the steps. They were punching, and I was punching and tossing. This went on for a little while before six of them finally wrestled me to the floor. I was thinking, *Now I'm going to jail.* But a Hollywood-like movie scene happened. A voluptuous redhead who used to date one of my player's brothers, who went back to the States without her, was there. I was pinned down on the hard surface, looking her right into her eyes at the entrance of the club at the top of the twelve steps. Like magic she walked down the stairs and reached her hand out to me while I was still on the floor. One by one the officers got off me and stood aside, parting like the Red Sea. They let her take me out of the club. Strange, me not going to jail. I looked back before my stairway accession, and the six German police officers looked at each other, then at me and said, "Good fight." They let me go. Before we cleared the exit doorway, it looked like the Christmas Season outside because I saw all kinds of blinking red and blue bright lights. She still had me by the hand, and I almost gasped for air as I saw about twenty police cars in full force surrounding the whole block. Whew! That situation was about to get ugly.

Later, my younger brother who was the next boy in the family after me moved in with me into my small studio apartment that was located on East Grand Boulevard near Chene Avenue. The main street was neighborly, with a mixture of single homes and apartment housing. But the whole surrounding area was a commercial setting with private and public business, four-star restaurants, banks, and factories.

On the same block, only five houses down the boulevard from where we lived, was the headquarters of the neighborhood street thugs called the Chene Gang, who, by the way, in the ended up being good friends in the end. At any time during business hours, they would hang across the street from the bank right next to the bus stop as a way of avoiding being detected by the police. They robbed and beat up people coming out of the bank or the many businesses in the area.

For a long while, they left my brother and me alone when we walked through them. They didn't harass us. One day I was coming home from a technical school on a Friday which was when they robbed bank customers. I believe it was because of the way I was dressed, with the shining diamonds and all, that they tried to rob me.

There were five of them on that day. Normally, they just parted as I passed through. Yet that time they blocked my path. I stop just short of running one over. And, as expected, they surrounded me, then told me to empty my pockets. I told the one in front of me, "You better get the fu*k out of my way." That startled them mainly because no one had resisted their bull crap before. There was talk in the neighborhood that many were frightened of them.

One suddenly reached for my pockets. I jumped out of the middle onto the curb by the street to give myself some room. In any fight that I faced, the thought of running away had never occurred to me. I was in the ready position to hurl the first man that was closes to me into the second attacker to get things started. Even a pack of animals can sense that something bad can happen to them, no matter how many of them appear to outnumber the one. I said, "You better move." They did, and I walked home past them without looking back.

The very next day the gang did the same thing to the wrong one, my brother. If people thought that I hid my short fuse very well, there was no hiding it with my younger brothers. They wore their anger on the outside of their bodies, on all their sleeves. They put their hands on my brother Reggie, pushing him into a wall. My goodness, what did they do that for? If someone wanted to know who the meanest, most brutish, and most down-right arrogant person in our entire family, it was him. Before he changed, everyone thought that the way he was conducting himself would land him not just in prison but on death row.

He stormed into the door, threw the bag that he was carrying on the small kitchen table, and explained to me why we must get them. His request was hardly unusual. On either side of our family, mention a fight, and you would have no trouble having two full carloads of combat troops coming to the battle ground.

Once my mother got into a lovers' quarrel, and her lover man decided to involve his sons. I looked out of the front window and saw his car pulling up. Three of my mother's sons were home that day. She believed that one of his sons would be carrying a gun. What was funny was the fact that my mother didn't think that we carried guns, let alone that we had one in her house. It was normal in Detroit for almost every young Black boy to pack some heat.

When his automobile stopped in front of the house, I reached back to pull my .25 automatic sidearm from the crease of my back. Simultaneously, so did my other two brothers, even the youngest one. The car took off as my mother, who was now in shock, was screaming at us to put those things away. We laughed at each other because none of us knew that the other one had a problem eliminator. No one had told the other a thing about who had what.

Meanwhile my brother and I decided to wait until night to get those bullies from the Chene Gang. We knew the bar where they mainly hung out on the weekends because we also frequented the same bar that was on the street where the Pole Town automotive plant is now located. We knew that this was the big one because inside of the bar there were usually ten or eleven gang members at one time. My brother and I felt that we would not be coming back home from this one.

So, we played the music, drank two bottles of wine, and smoked a piece pipe as the dusk approached and the sober reality kicked in that we were severely outnumbered. But this was our neighborhood also. We had to go. It was kind of a pleasant evening as we walked the four blocks towards the club in silence, trying to remember all the good times that I had in a few moments. I gulped and sucked in air like I was inhaling my last chance for living breath.

We reached the bar and my brother saw the one who pushed him, he wasted no time and struck him in the back across the neck with a pool stick that he took off the first table as we came through the door. Oh uh. The place was crawling with gang members, many more of them than we thought. One of the gang members was celebrating a birthday, and like in Western movies, inside the saloon, all hell broke out.

The melee was totally chaotic. Chairs were thrown, glass was breaking, bottles were toasted, and on went the shipwrecking, crunching, rumbling sound of property being destroyed. People who had nothing to do with the fighting were trading blows between themselves. I saw a lady sitting with a man, who she appeared to be with, fling her drink onto her date's face for no known reason.

As things calmed down, some customers hid in the restrooms, and a few hid behind the bar. And, as usual, the culprits who started the whole thing bolted out of the front door. As if things couldn't get worse than that, they did. The leader of the gang and his brother were in the bar next door where the real party was. The full squad was there. The ones that we were mixing it up with were some of the stragglers of the gang.

The bar owner stopped my brother and me from going outside where the whole street was loaded with the boys in the gang. I stopped trying to size them up. When I reached the number twenty-five, I stopped counting. The leader, who later became a good friend of mine, came to the other side of the door to see what had caused this calamity, to talk to me.

The owner blocked my path and told me to wait until he called the police. *Shoot*, I thought, *that will not work*. If we copped out then, they would never have let us live it down. We lived down the street from each other, and they would collectively jump on us for gang-stomping practice each day. We never expected to walk away from that one, anyway, and we couldn't have the police escort us home. We were going down fighting. So, I moved the bar owner aside and hit the leader directly in the mouth. His lips were moving, but I did not hear a word he was saying. I knew very well that I was going to get killed or beaten to smithereens. Either way, this gang would respect us and know that they can't rob everybody without consequence.

I stepped out of the door swinging. It made no difference in what direction that I made contact; they were everywhere. They split into two huge groups, ten or more for my brother, ten or eleven for me. My brother hung with them for a short spell until I saw them yank him to the ground, and every one of them kicked or punched him while he was on the ground.

It was my turn to be yanked to the ground but pulling me down didn't work on me. As I fell, I grabbed ahold of two of them and pulled them underneath me, still hitting them with both hands while their boys could hit me only on my back and head. They could not stomp me on the back because as I was going down, I pulled two of their boys to the ground and was lying on top of them.

Suddenly, I saw some glass fly off my head. Someone broke a full champagne bottle on the back of my head, like in the battle with those police officers back in Germany. I never felt a thing. Strangely, they stopped fighting me and were backing away, mainly because back then, we all, even the gang members, dressed up to go out on the town. We wore expensive Pierre Cardin shirt, pants, underwear, socks, and shoes. And I think that the gushing blood coming out of my head changed their minds about continuing.

However, I didn't stop. The adrenalin had me pumped up, and I felt like I could take on an army. I was yelling, "Come on, damn it. Come on." They backed away from me saying, "Go on, man." They didn't want to do battle any more or, perhaps, get their Pierre shirts bloodstained.

Years later after I relocated from Detroit, I slipped out of San Diego in the wee hours of the morning, just like the Cleveland Browns football team did to avoid detection by the night demons. There is a time in the night when they and their usual questionable characters slither back to hide in the shadows and underneath their rocks, like vampires before sunrise.

The bad girls always hung out with them because they kept some blood money in their pocket, or they were in the process of scheming about how to set an unaware person up to relieve them of their valuables. They were always dressed nicely when they showed up in church every Sunday, even sang the loudest in the choir. I know because I was sometimes in the after-hours joints with them. Never mind you that only hours before, they were partying females functioning as one of many stationaries, still-life room decorations. They had mastered the art of batting their eyes, mooching, and catching the crumbs that fell off the tables with their regular Monday-through-Saturday-night posse of deceivers, thieves, and flimflam artists.

I travelled the scenic Pacific Coast Highway all the way through to the county line of Los Angeles before taking a faster route of Interstate 5 to San

Francisco. I did that for the sheer enjoyment of this majestic view on that stretch of highway—the appreciation of the Lord's handiwork and Earth's natural conduit of water that completes the circle between man's soul, the ever-loving spirit, and the vastness of the universe. In this equation, the sum of the parts one-third each equals the whole.

Even a small stream has a magnetic, instinctive connection, and even a stubborn evolutionary scientist could agree that this invisible molecule in the combination of hydrogen and oxygen is therapeutic for meditation, calmness, and reassurance for the soul. It's just natures circuit being completed. This is the sensation of harmonious fulfillment that connects everyday people to the cosmic tunes which explain the atomic theory of the that matter which composes the make-up of humans or the Himalayan Mountains. The bottom line is that these elements are one and the same throughout the universe.

It is this linkage that I experience every time at kick off during a football game. And yet, this sensation is multiplied expeditiously when I'm driving by the awesome and unmatchable powerful waves near Pacific Coast Highway, slapping against the scattered rocks on the ocean shore.

I traveled from San Diego with radio silence for months, not using the cell phone or talking to anyone in my family. In the year of 2008, a major cell phone network verified something that I had suspected for year: my cell phone was bugged. I grew up in the early sixties when telephone subscribers had to share phonelines. And even when another person tried to hide the fact that they were listening, I could tell that they were still on the line. In the eighties, someone would call and then hang up. In the nineties, they would call and stay on the line for a long time, saying nothing until I hung up.

In the years of the two-thousands, the people became really bold with their eavesdropping. They didn't bother picking up the line quietly. They just picked up the tap in the middle of our conversation, and both person on my line would hear the unmistakable click, the exact same sound that you heard back in the days of partying phone lines when someone on the other end hung up.

One such day, when I was speaking to my middle sister, Cheryl, it was too obvious, and on a three-way line, she phoned the phone company who stated after a few moments that "yes, your phone line is bugged." However, the mind-blowing part of the conversation with the major cell phone carrier was that they indicated that could do nothing about my bugged line because it would cost them just too much money to remove. They basically suggested that I had to live with someone listening in on my telephone conversation.

From that moment on, I seldom or almost close to never communicated with family, friends, and or associates on the telephone. I don't have the luxury of ever joining a social media site because the demon workers would somehow find a way to intrude and then talk stupid to me about what they would do to me, never thinking about cause and effect. However, I knew all along who and what was misleading the greedy people and the creature who was behind the whole scheme. Not being able to communicate with people on the telephone and social media really put a damper on my lifestyle. But I sincerely believed that I didn't have any other choice. I had to punt so that I could have time to ascertain the endless madness that had surrounded me.

Once I crossed the Golden Gate Bridge, I felt a burden lift off my shoulders. I could finally take my body out of stressful red alert. I experienced fewer headaches because my blood pressure started going down to a reasonable level. As usual, my money in the mail had been diverted, but the Lord provided me daily with a brand new twenty-dollar bills, twenty-five times over the course of two months.

I started feeling alive again: enrolling in City College, learning nanotechnology, dressing nice, sight-seeing, and taking in the charm of one of my favorite cities. I started meeting good people and once more began going to church with mostly Asian lady friends. Even the freezing cold nights in the summer felt refreshing. I was living the life of Riley. It was great until I slipped and made the mistake of calling one of my talkative sisters who I was close with to let the family know that I was doing fine. The next thing that I knew the levee broke, and I was flooded by the greediness with the same impact as Hurricane Katrina.

Unlike before, they started getting antagonistic, extremely disrespectful, and quarrelsome mainly because of my beliefs. Regular folks don't know the real meaning of persecution until they are being relentlessly being hunted night and day by the spawns of the master of deception, trying to turn you into one of them.

What was even worse was the philosophy and logic that they were trying to sell me. I wanted no part of the kind of lifestyle that they lived. It didn't even register as something to think about in my mind. They had no sparkling light in their eyes like a true Christian has. I endured a brigade of lost souls trying to recruit me. Decades passed, and they still had not accomplish anything with me. They started becoming grim, pushing harder. Instead of shouting at me, they started coming closer and closer to me, getting in my face and then becoming physical. I unsuccessfully went to the authorities on multiple occasion who only stated that they would arrest me if I hurt them.

I was further handicapped by my own vow that I made with the Lord the day that I was baptized. I was born again, a brand-new person who gave up my old, un-Christlike ways of waiting in the shadows to catch my antagonist all by their lonesome, who thought that they were the big kahuna in front of a crowd.

While growing up, I repeatedly told the adversaries who were in the clubs after gaining a backbone by way of liquid courage, interrupting me trying to pull a lady, that I would see them again when they were sobber. I kept my promise every time, and I caught them by themselves in a clear state of mind and said, "Are you ready to do all of those things that you said to me?" The same one without the bottle became a sorry excuse for a man. They were terrified, about to pee on themselves when I popped up out of nowhere. And the worse thing concerning the situation was that they truly sounded as though they did not remember what they said or did the night before.

They were sending more and more adults who looked totally malnourished, many who you could tell were on hard drugs because they all looked the like the Crypt Keeper. I kept trying to warn them off. I repeatedly told them that someone was giving them real bad information about me.

During that time, at the gym I was lifting 400 pounds on my shoulders with only the use of my tip toes. To the wicked, the humbling vow that I took made me appear meek and like an easy mark on the cutthroat streets. But that was hardly the case. Back in the hood, a young skinny thug who took kids' lunch money at school dogged them around and beat on girls got caught breaking and entering homes in the neighborhood. The court ordered him to join the military service or go to jail. He went to the army, looking deathbed thin, and came back to the hood a little more than a year later in the worst way after being booted out of the service. He was much taller. puffed up, and looked stronger, like the service gave him a shot of that Captain America juice.

One fine, sunny day, when I didn't have a care on my mind, I saw him walking toward me on the same street. I crossed over to the other side as to avoid trouble that I sensed was about to come from him. He crossed over onto my side and deliberately bumped into me. They could spew nasty words at me until they foamed at the mouth, but there was absolutely no touching. Three second later, in the time that it takes to snap your fingers, I had his whole body twisted into a very painful pretzel. With a little more pressure, I could have snapped his arm completely from his shoulder blade. He was crying uncle like a little girl, yelling, "Mister, please stop."

They came and came. I found myself talking to my Father, praying for them, saying, "Father, forgive them because they know not what they do."

All were ignorant of the fact that they were a misled participant in a shaky dialogue which could change this engagement in less than a heartbeat into something violent and lethal. They were totally unaware that they were merely used as a suitable receptacle for embodying unclean spirits, but I was aware. In almost all the indefinite cases, I had the presence of mind to perceive the moment of possession and immediate changes in their personality.

It's not even worth fighting when you know what you are going to do and that you can send them to the emergency room with only one punch. However, the local authorities informed me that I would go to jail if I hurt them. I could not understand this line of reasoning. It was they who initiated the conflict. Why were my hands being tied behind my back? I found myself repeatedly praying for them. All the while, inside of me I was utterly miserable for years because I turned the other cheek and walked away from combat, instead of provoking them on the spot by saying, "I'm here your worthless piece of manure. Do what you said that you going to do." It ate me up inside like bad stress because I was now a Christian. Clobbering people was something that the Lord Jesus Christ did not do, but the dark side of me did it regularly. I was torn in two.

The persecution heated up to a very dangerous point where they made me fall off the wagon. I snapped when I was standing in a soup kitchen line to get a three-course meal. I had a thousand dollars a month in my pockets courtesy of my late ship building bob. But a thousand dollars a month in the city by the bay is nothing. I stood in the chow line which was no different than the food lines in the service. It gave me mental time to think through the days' events. Then something poked me in the back. He was a short, soon-to-be-middle-age white guy. At the same time, he whispered in my ear that "I better join them, or else he was going to kill me." My eyes opened wide like a kid on Christmas morning, not because of the gifts and toys they received under the tree but because of the handsome tables that were donned with mouthwatering cakes, pies, pecans, oranges, apples, and, best of all, lots and lots of candy. Even the candy from the Goodfellow box was something to look forward to.

"Oh yea?" Now they were in my arena. Threat talking is what they were good at. All bets were off. I was not walking away from stimulating real action. Damn the police. They just must do whatever. I turned and looked at my would-be assailant directly in the eyes. I gave him a look that said, "You threaten me, I get to sent you away from this spot on a gurney. Go ahead." I dared him to reach for his pockets. My on-call arsenal that I packed during my bodyguard years was a left uppercut to the chin. It was guaranteed to put a cerebral cortex to sleep.

My reaction was nowhere near what he expected. If he had made the slightest move, he sensed that he was going to be on the wrong end of his, or their, miscalculation. I was just as fast as Doc Holliday from the old Westerns. I wanted him to make a move so bad. I did not care anymore this guy was going to get jackhammered. I wasn't going to let no one pull me off him until he was hospitalized and unable to move with his own power.

He sensed it, got the heck out of the line, and was gone. The tables had turned. They say that hunting is no fun when the rabbit has got the gun. I could no longer keep my bad side easily contained under the name of Christianity. It was like sticking in my finger to plug one small hole in the many holes of a powerful but cracking dam. I couldn't tolerate the constant harassment, the character assassination, and the deliberate spreading of lies and vicious, misguided rumors just because I was reserved, stayed to myself, minded my own business, and didn't sleep with the kind of women they did. I could fool around and go offtrack occasionally. If you were fortunate and slept with an array of talented, beautiful women for most of your life, even if they were exotic dancers, then at time, the other breed will not do. Your heart gets too picky. It throws in the towel and just wants to go home to your stunning, gorgeous, smooth-skinned, people-friendly, intelligent women.

I used to say the same things over with my close family and friends who slept with their company that was so hard on the eyes that I had to put on sunglasses in the house at night. They would tell me that all flowers are the same, but that is very far from the truth. If you woke up in the bedrooms of quite a few radiant models all around the world, you would never fix your mouth to even make a statement like that. They questioned my slim pickings of bedmates. I retorted by saying, "Once you've lived in a penthouse, you can only move laterally to maintain the same. The only other direction you'll most likely be moving in is down."

My endless battle with the flock of the living creatures, the development of aggressive action in the food line, and the continuing barrage of fanatics getting in my face every day had me go into some serious discussions with my Father, God. I started questioning our relationship. I still knew who the father was and who the son was. And yet, I was unsure that I could continue to walk in the ways of Jesus. Turning away from strife and loving an enemy who has threatened to kill you just wasn't me. My motto was "keep it up, and you will get more than you asked for." I was really on shaky ground up in heaven. What happened next made me abdicate my vow that I made to my Father God.

Some pretentious authority figures back in San Diego made me again leave San Francisco to come back on a manufactured charge. He was taller and bigger than I was and started really pissing me off by trying to intimidate me daily. My mind was wrestling with thoughts of going back to my old ways, of waiting in the shadows. *You are a Christian now. No more can you lurk in the shadows like a predator-hungry jungle cat crouching down in eight-inch blades of grass, waiting for your prey to make a mistake.*

I became so weary of the silly man getting in my face, talking crazy. I said to him, "I will eliminate you in a public place if you keep it up. In the grocery store. At the check cashing place." I was serious when I gave him my final warning that I would kick his butt in the middle of the police station. He didn't believe me.

That was one of the most crucial and critical times that I ever had between my Father, God and myself. That was one of the rare nights when I experienced direct communication with the Lord. The line was clear; there was nothing in between us. I was so confused about who I was and how was I required to perform as a Christian. I wasn't a hothead, nor did I start any conflict. It just ripped me apart inside to keep on praying (forgive them, Father) and reluctantly walking away. They were deity controlled, not aware of who or what was really behind their conscious actions.

In my thoughts I had failed as a child of Christ. Never in the annals of humanity has a Christian asked his Father, God what I did when I'd had enough of this person. I was on my knees, pleading with my Father to "let me get him. Just let me get him this one time." The spirit reminded me of a parable in the book of Matthew when an aristocratic soldier who had dirty hands and, because of duty, could not cleanly function in the world like Jesus.

I may not look it, but I have the unmistakable Georgia Bulldog's mean spirit of a warrior that continues to percolate deep inside of me. My thoughts are never far from military procedures. I'd rather fight than talk. Perhaps it is best that I keep a sneaky, sharp mental edge and that I continue to remain a warrior throughout my antagonist battles with the father of calamity.

The next day the devil's advocate called my hand. He decided to see exactly what I would do in a public setting. He chose to perform on the second floor of the crowded city library. He was approaching me with a friend from the opposite direction. I tried to ignore him, and I moved aside on the aisle to walk past him. That action must had sounded hilarious in his mind because when I stepped aside, he had a belly laugh with his friend. Unprovoked, he stretched out his arm and pushed me.

"Oh, really?" At the same moment, before he could retract his arm, kaboom—I hit him in the ribs so hard that the echo in the hallway sounded like a dynamite blast. The concession shook all the windows on the floor. They rattled like they did during a level six earthquake.

When that man composed himself from bending over and gasping, trying to replace the air that was knocked out of his lungs, he and his astonished friend had to bum-rush through spectators, practically knocking them over while bolting into the elevator in case I decided to also give his companion a sample. I never saw either of them again.

LAST ACT:
THE PARTNER / GENERAL
MANAGER STORY

It was I who informed the Oakland Raiders football organization that their high-priced franchise quarterback was not coach able. Al Davis. Legendary owner / partner / general manager of the National football's Oakland Raiders football team. He was well known for his unorthodox ways and business decisions by not following parodical and hiring practices in the league. Because of my search for a professional football organization that showed potential or was already play-off ready, I had my finger on the pause on the behind the scenes off the field climate of the entire pro football league. Also, the health and well fare of those in the areas of administration and management of those teams. I was aware of the declining health of the owner of the Oakland Raiders; however, I was unaware that Al Davis wanted to shake up the NFL again by hiring an unknown black guy from off the streets to coach two of the most important position on a pro football team: The quarterback coach and the offensive coordinator. This simple fact during this era hiring a black person to coach these positions was a rare occurrence that merit major attention and that event most likely dominated the sports talk shows and football fans in general for months. The aging Oakland Raiders Owner's health was fading. My being hired by Mr. Davis would have been one of his final acts in the life and times of the maverick owner to shock once more the National football League.

Denny McLain was the last baseball thirty-game winner after the Detroit Tigers won the 1968 World Series. Since then, growing up, every time I told someone my last name was McClain at a store, job, or business meeting, the person across from me would joke and respond, "Are you a relative of Denny McLain?" This continued up until the year 2000 in just about every city and town in the United States that I had visited. The funniest part about that was even overseas, the Germans even said, "Are you a relative of Denny McLain?" I was never a thirty-game winner, but I was gifted with one pitch—his ninety-five-mile-per-hour fast ball.

In elementary school, there were two other very young boys along with me who were crowned the dodgeball kings. When that ball left my hand, no matter the distance, it was immediately on its target. There was no time to duck, nowhere to hide, and no escape. On most of my football teams, I was the backup quarterback. I never argued too much with the coaches' decisions because starting meant that I could not play on special teams, a unit that I loved to participate in because I was crazy, and I liked hitting at full speed.

I was just launching passes to some college students in the city-block wide Panhandle Park in San Francisco, completing passes accurately for sixty-five, seventy yards. A few days later, I got a visit from the professional football team that I was trying to play for all the while. The problem was that I won't do anything just for money. I must be somewhat enthusiastic about whatever livelihood or mission I'm undertaking. It was not unusual for me to decline or slide past a suspect job offer. This was the third time in my life that I had declined a million-dollar pay day because, in my sober mind, I was already rich. And it wasn't about money to me. It was all about winning.

I was stepping into a no-win situation where I knew that after every game, all I would be doing on stage is facing bright lights and television cameras, explaining why and how we lost again. When I already knew the answer to the question. The quarterback that they were trying to have me mold into was a top-notch NFL player who, in my opinion, was a bum at the professional level. I told the organization that he was just not coachable.

They kept on barraging me for six weeks to take the money. My reasons were sound. I believed in the former Green Bay Packers' coach's motto: "Winning is the only thing." I just could not live with myself getting paid to lose because I was working with an above average college football quarterback who was in over his head competing at the professional level.

I had a letter from the player personnel director of the Oakland Raiders, Michael Lombardi. The letter was about my inquiring for a quarterback position. His respond was more hopeful where I was placed on his rolodex up next list in case the organization need a body.

In any event, I was soliciting the organization for a quarterback position. I wanted to go out of the game of football the way that I came in. I evaluated the roster and knew exactly that they were severely handicapped in the passing department. Out of all seventeen positions that I played on the field, quarterbacking was the easiest for me to perform. I could sling the rock to everyone who was eligible to catch a pass. Playing as a lineman on the line of scrimmage, I really didn't have to do much thinking. I only had run a few yards and make sure that I won two out of the three plays on a series while beating up the man across from me. Except on a rare occasion, with legs that had the ability to lift 700 pounds multiple times in a set, I normally won three out of three plays while holding down the line.

At quarterback, I did have to think a whole bunch in a very short time. What is unique about my mind is that the more information I must process, the more clarity and clear consciousness I have. It was like playing chess, and I kept two slick moves ahead of the defense. I beat a computer once playing a game of chess. When I checkmated it, the darn thing frantically searched around the board for mistakes, thinking that it was not possible. The computer was a sore loser and would not acknowledge that I won, so it just blinked and blinked until the owner shut it off. Sometimes it might have taken a quarter and a half before I got that great feel for the strengths and weaknesses of the opponent in order to make some adjustments. And then, like a skilled surgeon, I would cut them into pieces.

I was a deep ball passer, deadly between the fifty- and seventy-yard range downfield. I don't remember when or how I developed an uncanny knack for pinpoint accuracy in measuring distance and azimuth by sight.

I remember when I was very young, while visiting a relative's farmhouse in Inkster, Michigan, back when the city was mostly wooded area and green wet land, I was just throwing an apple in the back of the house. It struck a telephone line some sixty-five yards down slope in the valley and stayed stuck there on the line that stretched horizontally across the lower part of the valley.

One of my favorite uncles was watching at the time. He said, "I don't believe that happened. Let me see you do that again." I casually picked up another fat, juicy red apple and flung it at an arch high in the air, knocking the other one that was lodged there completely off the line. He was amazed. So was I.

Twice while scrambling during a heavily contested game, from the twenty-yard line I heaved a pass that had reached the white chalk line of the end zone, eighty yards right into the receiver's arms. One was caught for a touchdown. The other was knocked out of the receiver's hand after the ball, from that great distance, had dropped into his hands.

I did the cartography for all our scouting missions while I was in the service back when I could draw and paint on a canvass. I visually mapped out the range and azimuth to the power sources of the enemies, to the accuracy of a plus or minus of only ten meters, making the gang from artillery and mortars look good when just their second volley annihilated the targets.

Back home, my own teammates had band me from quarterbacking in pickup games because when the score reached forty-two to seven or forty-eight to fourteen in only the second quarter, the safeties and corners had to play so far back from the line of scrimmage that they could not even give a tiny bit support for the run defense. I had boat load of five-star running backs on my team. One touch of the ball for them, and it was nothing but green grass and end zone.

Come up to support the run game, and the receivers left burn marks on the grass for a scorching behind the whole defense touch down. The other team would just quit and go home. Sometimes the games would be scheduled to be played months in advance, and we would travel great distances to get across town to the field, only to have teams say, "to hell with this" and get back into their cars after twenty minutes of playing time, truncating a three-hour game.

It was a pleasant fall sweater-wearing Sunday afternoon in the Motor City, right around the same time of the year when, like clockwork, the *Wizard of Oz*, who really didn't give anything to the Tin Man, came on TV. The date was October 25, 1970. I was watching a thrilling football game between the Pittsburgh Steelers and the Oakland Raiders on a beautiful, finely crafted, burnt brown TV set that I had found tossed away in the alley. It was a one of the few Magnavox color TV sets that people could afford back then in the neighborhood. All I did was replaced two hidden fuses and three vacuum tubes, and then it worked liked brand new.

The starting quarterback, Daryle Lamonica, was injured. His replacement was an old guy, and the game announcers kept reminding us of viewers of his age. What was even more remarkable was that in that era, the opposing defensive didn't have one hand tied behind their back. The quarterbacks were fair game to them, and they usually annihilated them.

I watched a game when all three quarterbacks—the starter, the backup, and the reserve—were knocked out of one game. A wide receiver had to finish the contest. This Hall-of-Fame, seemingly ageless quarterback came off the bench and won the game. For a five-game stretch, he manufactured late game theatrics all the way, earning an opportunity for his team to play in the elusive championship game. George Blanda, who was forty-three at the time, was the oldest quarterback to start in a championship game, and I watched them all with interest. Since that October game, what stayed on my mind was that I believed that I could also do what he did, perhaps a tad better.

The old argument that the male body was finished and that every football player's skill declined as soon as they reached thirty was foreign to me. I was a freak of nature who didn't reach my football prime until the age of fifty-five. Whoever made that determination, logic, or conclusion didn't jive with me at all.

We shared many similarities. He played in the National Football League for a career of twenty-six years. I called it a day after playing for twenty-three years, although in the minor league, the road trips and wear and tear on the body is all the same. Nevertheless, for years I continued to play in pickup games anywhere, any time. He was comfortable as a linebacker as was I. There was nothing on the field that he didn't do. I was comfortable playing seventeen positions and could start in at least fourteen. We called our own plays and did real-time strategy on the field. And mainly, all things considered, we both appeared to be resilient on top of being ageless.

During the same time that the Chargers gave me an opportunity to walk on, the personnel department of the Raiders asked me for a resume. The scouts for the Chargers found out that I was not joking about my speed and/or all the things that I could do on the field. For reasons that only I knew, I didn't have an agent. All I could highlight on my resume to the Raiders was that I had a major-league arm. And what was more, I was an accurate deep-ball passer.

There were two standard operation procedures that stood out about me: sooner or later I was going to start and in all things in life, especially at the helm of a football team, when I positively absolutely cannot make a mistake, I don't.

I was patient and always bid my time in games because the laws of averages stated that sooner or later an injury or substandard playing will send a ballplayer to the bench. Once I replaced the player, his job was finished, and I never had to go back to wait on the sideline. That is why I didn't get a break and wound up playing in all three facets of the game—offensive, defensive, and special teams in every game. I knew that if or when I had the opportunity to run the scout team for the Raiders. I would make the cut.

I ran the scout team for our first game when I played junior varsity at Kettering High. This was also another reason why I quit and went to the army. At our last practice before the scrimmage, Coach Tucker had us take a knee, and he talked about how proud he was concerning his defense. He stated that they had the makings of shutting out lots of teams that season. As the second-string quarterback, I waltzed the offense through his valiant defense like we were Fred Astaire on a polished dance floor.

They were discombobulated trying to stop our drive of one big play after another. Coach Tucker didn't like that one bit. He was furious, and once more he started yelling at me. That time he told me to deliberately throw an interception. I carried out his command. It was against my nature to make mistakes on the field and lose on purpose. I was one who could never take a dive as a boxer. I knew then, at that moment, I was a goner.

I was persistent in contacting the Raiders about even making the practice squad as a backup quarterback as I continued to insinuate that I had the makings of a George Blanda 2.0. But, in essence, they would have had on their roster a mentally tough, Hall-of-Fame Steve Young prototype, an extremely efficient left-handed passer who was intelligent and with elite physical gifts. We were identical in height at six feet two (1.88m) and weight at 215 pounds (98 kg).

What separated us from many other quarterbacks was the footlocker full of the unseen intangibles. I was never flagged for an offside or false starts because of my clear peripheral vision. I didn't have to turn my head while on the line of scrimmage. I could look at my opponent directly in his eyes and still see the hiking of the football. At quarterback, while looking straight ahead at the deeply posted free safety, I had a clean vision of where both cornerbacks lined up and how far they played off the receivers. I didn't do target fixation, locking onto one receiver. I quickly went through my progressions and hit whoever was open. I turned my head only to bait the safeties and linebackers to freeze them or move them into a spot where I had no intentions of throwing to.

Courtesy of Coach Tucker, I instinctively knew, on any given play, where everyone on the field was supposed to be. And yet, the greatest of all my intangible gifts were the "spirit that loved football" and truly loved to join me when I played the live game-time quarterback. I didn't learn until after I was sixty years old, before I was enlightened, that every quarterback didn't have the slow-motion factor at the beginning of every play. I took it for granted that when someone said that they were a quarterback, this intangible skill was automatic. I always assumed that it came with the job.

When the ball was hiked, ever since I was a kid, the action became surreal, like I was playing inside a vacuum—I heard absolutely no sound. It was eerie when everyone else on the playing field moved like time had stood still. It was supernatural how they moved as if they had taken an extra helping of Prozac. It looked so slow that I used to joke to my teammates that on every live play, I had enough time to drink a shot of Jack and get a couple of pulls on a cigar before I had to pass the ball.

That did not happen in practice. It didn't come there. I was only joined by the spirit after kicking off during a real game. I was astonished when I found out that I was in exceptional company because only five or six known quarterbacks have ever had this gift.

It was a delightful spring day in the city by the bay where the weather was warmer and more pleasant to me than during the summer months. I was not camping in Panhandle Park by choice. I had to blend in with the natives. I was hiding because I had to flee from the multiple deranged contract collectors that had infested San Diego. This was around the same time that professional football teams conducted their mandatary minicamps.

At the park, four college football players from Stanford were passing the football around. I never had any problem asking to join in the gathering to pass the ball to play catch. As always, we started near each other, completing short passes to loosen up. For me it usually took ten erratic passes before I could knock the rust off my arm, then I would crank up the trajectory, and I could fire the ball around accurately and effortlessly. As the guys began to spread out in the park, by my seventh pass the ball was missing its target forty yards downfield, traveling over their heads, going behind their backs some ten to fifteen yards too deep. The college boys started backing up before they could catch my passes. I had to come in and step up twenty yards to catch their best passes. By my eleventh pass, I put a lot of air and an extremely high arch on the ball that was accurately dropping right into their bread baskets sixty-five to seventy yards downfield. Even the college young men were impressed as my final bomb dropped right into the not-breaking-stride running receiver's arms for a touchdown.

The very next day for breakfast I grabbed my donut, coffee, and the *San Francisco Chronicle*. I read the sports section first when I noticed something odd about the Oakland Raiders. They stated that the maverick managing general partner had something special planned for the upcoming season. *Was the controversial owner back at it with his old tricks, stunning the entire National Football League once more with his off-the-wall antics?* I wondered.

A legal issue forced me back to dreaded, nightmarish San Diego, my goose was once again being cooked. The solar flare caused by the temptation of an unethical cult had me overflowing out of the frying pan into the fire. They started with that "join us mess or else" again as soon as I returned there. In the spring of 2008, I was standing outside of a place that I considered to be my third home, the law library, working on my case, when an older, wise, gray-haired and bearded newly met acquaintance stood next to me in the finest of Brooks Brothers suits and Oxford shoes.

Their mannerisms and posture literally smelled like he was unmistakably from an Ivy League school like Harvard or Yale. In a very dignified and professional speaking manner, he directly stated to me that that owner of the Oakland Raiders wished that I would come on board for the team as a quarterback coach and offensive coordinator.

At first, I thought that it was a joke to have such an honor bestowed upon me. It had been years since I had any contact with the organization. I had put cloud chasing out of my mind, something that I completely forgotten about because of my constant battle with the devil. With humbling gratitude, I wanted to accept the proposition. But I had one serious reservation: I did not think that the highly overpriced person that was supposed to be a leader of the team was not what he claimed to be based on my personal opinion from all of my years of playing and studying football and evaluating the performances of all thirty-two NFL teams while looking for job to play on the roster of an organization that had turned right onto the on ramp that leads to the rugged road of a championship.

I had watched the quarterback in question at his onset of his NFL career. I saw no progression during his whole rookie year. Game management was suspect, and by this, I mean that up and down had no consistency—a big physical presence, but not mentally tough. And, most importantly, he rarely showed the ability to perform under duress or buoy the team to play at a heightened level to force a win.

In college where many teams hoard a majority of five-star high school recruits and then play against inferior, less talented teams, of course they tend to look deceptively great. The fully developed, grown men on every team in the NFL with a mortgage, kids and a wife who's a shopaholic tend to hit extremely hard on every play, unlike college football where the big boys are still growing, and the quarterback takes very little pounding, maybe being on the bad side of a good lick only three or four times a game. On most occasions, they can shake that off with ease.

One hit in the NFL can send a quarterback to the sidelines or hospital for good. In my travels over a few decades, I witnessed quarterbacks getting knocked out for the season on one play. Tragically, that also happened to sometimes be his premiere in the position for the new season. Destiny had me close to rubbing shoulders with the Raiders organization on three occasions in my lifetime. Wayne Valley, one of the three general partners of the Raiders, was also in attendance at the 1972 summer Olympics in Munich where my qualifying timing in the 100-meter sprint was a barely missed opportunity for hitting the record books as the fastest man on the planet.

Other previous track stars were recruited to play professional football: 1988 Olympic gold-medal winner James Jett was drafted by the Raider. Dallas Cowboys drafted 1964 Olympic winner Bob Hayes. Willie Gault was drafted by the Chicago Bears and was also a 1980 Olympic gold-medal winner, who also finished his football career as a Raider. This organization placed a primum on pushing the ball up field with the deep pass and speedy receivers to catch it. More than likely, that year I would have gotten a great chance at being a bright blinking beep on Mr. Valley's Raiders' radar as a wide receiver.

The circumstances were more direct through the postal service for the second occasion. The correspondence was from the personnel department of the organization. It was a "maybe we will see you later" letter. During this time period, I was playing football on the minor pro football league team called the Great Lake Raiders, starting free safety of course. To them it was a great big deal. It gave the young ball players hope that anything is possible.

The Patriots' organization was my first and only professional football team as a fan, yet my game-playing heart belonged to the Raiders. They carried a mystic roster full of misfits that was right up my alley. Those sanitary, sane, squeaky-clean teams didn't fit my after-hours lifestyle, like the times when I was regularly hanging out with my dysfunctional family members or the infantry units in the army, listening to music by Seals and

Crofts' "Diamond Girl" and Paul Simon's "Tenderness." Those Raiders were my kind of road dogs.

As fate would have it, the third contact was a direct face-to-face with someone from their personnel department who offer me a historically tremendous job that was handed to me on a silver platter. As usual, I had paid close attention to the activities that surrounded the off season, during the season, and after the game. I was aware of the owners' declining health. As a last act, he wanted to once more shake up the National Football League with something unique. The league would have been in a uproar had destiny been fulfilled, asking, "Where in the heck did you get this unknown fellow to coach? Who in the hell is he? Why did you pass by all the other available coaches that were primed from the college and professional ranks?"

Me accepting that fabulous opportunity would have been a burning-hot topic on all the sports talk shows throughout the entire 2008 football season.

And yet, there was this one important and very significant reason why things did not work out between us. It was called winning. There was absolutely no chance of this happening with their current quarterback who was slated to be the starter. I was not concerned with things like fame, notoriety, prestige, or money. When it came down to who was the quarterback under my direction, I asked them to give me another one before I would take the assignment. I told them point blank that I did not believe in playing bums just because I paid them a lot of money. What I thought was ironic was that I had the exact same argument over two decades before with the Detroit Lions' general manager Russ Thomas I believe in biting my bottom lip until it bleeds and cutting my losses before I keep playing an overpriced, ineffective ball player.

I had this phenomenal gift for choosing the right personalities for a specific assignment since the Job Corps. I knew quarterbacks, or more specifically, great signal callers. I watched them mature in college and knew from the very first minutes that Peyton Manning, Tom Brady, John Elway, Andrew Luck, Joe Montana, Phillip Rivers, Brett Favre, and Steve Young were a few quarterbacks that had what it takes.

The real reason that I moved to New York in 1994 was that I saw the makings of a great quarterback in that Phil Simms fellow. I was only going to play for a championship-bound team. I figured that if or when the New York Giants saw me run, they would get hooked and couldn't resist because to coaches, pure speed is like a narcotic. My argument about why I could not coach franchise quarterback JaMarcus Russell was that I believe in winning, and the law of diminishing returns is going to catch up with you. Getting it over sooner is better than later.

When you coach another person, you expect that they would share a few of your talents, characteristics, and have some similar thought processes. I looked the defense off and threw to a spot where the receiver could catch the ball on the run. He tended to focus on where his pass was going and threw to a pausing receiver, for a second that allows the defense to make a play on the ball. I watched him for the whole rookie season when I realized that he had a slight advantage on the field because of his physical height. With powerful arm strength and under ideal circumstances, he could be programed to manage a clean drive.

However, in professional football, there are not that many ideal circumstances. He didn't perform very well when the play broke down. His fragile ego could not handle the pressure when hit hard by the defense. He was not strong enough to just shake it off. For me, being on the receiving end of a violent hit just woke me up. It was "game on." Any residual cobwebs were knocked off.

He started thinking about how far the passes had to go instead of just cutting the ball loose. I let it fly. There was no grit, no grim passionate determination there to gain tough yards. He seemed to accept losing as a matter of fact. Great quarterbacks are bothered by losing. They are determined to change the status quo. You will see them hanging around the playing field after practice, talking after hours to teammates, studying game film, trying to fix what has gone wrong. This one magically disappeared after a head-scratching performance. With two minutes left in the game, his mind was probably thinking about rushing to take a shower so that he could hit the club early. There would have been no continuity between us. We certainly would not have meshed from the start.

Beginning in the early spring months of 2008, I counted approximately six weeks when I was bombarded with the words "take the money." That was probably high on the list of one of the hardest things in the world to decline—an offer from a person that you have nothing but genuine respect and admiration for since you were a child.

I had to keep explaining that "it takes on to know one. He maybe a football player, but he is not a great quarterback." Personally, I thought that he was still valuable to the team in another capacity. Although the speed of the game was a bit too much for him, he still possessed the ability to read plays. I believe that he could have made some top-ten money on the defensive-weak side-linebacker position.

Take the money. Like a prism, sometimes I can interpret some of the things that lie outside of the visual spectrum. He had no X factor, intangibles, or pocket presence that can feel defenders swarming on your backside, trying to decapitate you, the unseen ability that will let you know when to step up in the pocket. The man's peripheral vision was questionable. Instead of looking the defender off, they knew that he had a problem with target fixation. His eyes would lock onto a receiver, hitting the first one in the progression. The defensive backs baited him by playing off. When he delivered the pass, they would move in to intercept the ball or, for the most part, level the receiver to the ground so hard that they would need smelling salts to remember who and where they were.

For weeks I tossed and turned at night, wrestling with trying to figure out drill that would enhance Mr. Russell's performance. I thought about letting him have a taste of the Oklahoma Drill to toughen him up. I even entertained the thought of blindfolding him and brush blocking him at drop of three, five, and seven steps to see his if we could correct his mechanics, his throwing motion, and sturdy his game rhythm.

However, no matter what I came up with or which game scenario I placed him in, at the end of each day, my mind kept on drifting back and seeing myself at the end of each game, standing behind the podium where a myriad of microphones was pointed at me. Dissatisfied while addressing the media, I repeated my favorite, classic one-liner expressed by former Detroit Lions coach Bobby Ross: "I don't teach that stuff."

There was an incident that occurred in the middle of my teenage years that made me stick with my final decision. I was involuntary recruited to engage in another fight; this time with a martial-arts expert. He was a neighborhood kid who grew up on the block during nostalgic times when people could fall asleep on their front porches all night unbothered. Everyone knew just about everyone. And the police officers lived in the hood and walked the beats—only their screen doors were locked summer nights. There were even a few trusting residents who left their parked cars with the keys still in the ignition.

As children, 90 percent of the time we took advantage of the privilege and opportunity to go into each other's cribs, except for that special man's home that always seemed to be located on the corner of the block. If the timing was right, we would wind up being seated at the kitchen table by a hospitable mother, for a tasty, refreshing glass of Kool-Aid and a tuna fish sandwich. Ronnie was a friend of the family. He grew up with and around us. Since he was ten years old, he was into martial arts, going to classes twice a week. He had the only garage on the block that many young and old in the hood envied.

It was outfitted to harness his skills: there was a stack of mats, a weight bench, a heavy punching/kicking bag, different sized weights that were scattered around the dusty cement floor, boards of different sizes and thickness that he constantly used to show off by breaking them in two, a large bowl of rice that he daily pounded his fist into, and various five-by-eight pictures of Bruce Lee, Chuck Norris, and body builder Mr. Universe of 1968, Arnold Schwarzenegger, were tacked to the studs on the unpaneled walls of the single car garage.

Absolute power corrupts absolutely. Once he received a fifth-degree black belt in karate, or something like that, his demeanor changed. He became head strong, arrogant, and irritating, talking forcefully and mean to people who were his friends. Sometimes I thought that it was those weird color looking protein drinks he downed regularly that maybe had something to do with it.

In any event, it was a gorgeous autumn afternoon. It was pleasant enough that you could wear a sweater or not. The leaves hadn't begun to change colors just yet. I was relaxing in the prone position, hands interlocked underneath my neck on the pillow. I was on the bottom bunk of my cousin's bed where I was in a peaceful and tranquil mood, when suddenly in comes one of my male cousins who some called "the rain maker" because he also, at times, was an instigator that brought dark clouds of trouble, and folks ran in all directions to get out of the way of his rain.

On that occasion, it was he who was being agitated. While his hyperventilating chest expanded and collapsed, breathing heavily in between the words, he explained what had happened. On the way home from school, he had run into Ronnie who stopped him on the street. He called my cousin names, and then he physically assaulted him, shoving him around. Oh yea? My eyes enlarged to the size of a Susan B. Anthony silver dollar. It was my first reaction after Derrick, in between slobbering, slipped in the highly relevant information that Ronnie was already outside waiting for me.

My cousin told him that I was upstairs in the house, and I was going to check him. I never said no. I always answered "let's go" to anyone asking this kind of request of me. That was one reason that compelled me to continue to engage in challenging bodyguard work until my late forties. Way back, in the very old days, I would be one of the ones who the villagers would come to when they needed someone to fight the fire-breathing dragon.

SHIFTING SOCIAL ENGAGEMENTS

Five years into the twenty-first century, the dazzling, head-spinning dating game had switched direction dramatically like Earth's magnetic poles. Baby boomers' courtship, traditionally, was set in stone. Your choice of mate was decided in high school. They were a permanent fixture in your life. There were no dating others in the open, anyway. The whole town knew who couples were, and after graduation or when you reached the age of eighteen, the kids left the nest and married, creating their own families.

There was a job waiting for you in one of the Big Three automobile plants or at Great Lakes steel mills, or you took over your father's business, that is, if you were not drafted into the military. A young lady having a baby outside of marriage was scorned, and at thirty, those who were not married were called an old maid. If she fooled around, she was called a Jezebel. With this kind of template, there were no room for mate shopping. You were stuck with your high-school sweetheart. And the men in the homes were primarily bread winners.

There was some real ugliness in this limited development. Every weekend I witnessed an awful lot of abuse between the husbands and wives. For absolutely no reason at all, the women were beaten, sometimes to a pulp. Society said that it was OK for a man to have a mistress outside of the marriage if they took care of home first, which meant dropping off their paychecks to pay the bills. Then they were gone mentally for the weekend.

They were in and out of the house physically, and if the wife spoke on the subject, they were immediately jumped on. But let me remind you that many of the same man would chicken out if another man challenged them to do the same to them. The women were stuck in loveless marriages primarily because of their financial status. They had no money to escape. The ones who did get away to live with their sisters or mothers were lured back in a very short time with fake tears and promises of never drinking again. There were many women who didn't have an alternative route, so they stayed in this madness.

It wasn't always the man's fault. Some had a barracuda at home who sat on the couch watched soap operas all day. And when the dirty, worn-out man came home from work, instead of cooked food and ready bath water like it was in the beginning of their marriage, the woman no longer dressed nice. They dressed like old hags. They nagged, picked on the tired man, and did nothing but complain. When the man got a sip of liquid courage, and she opened her nitpicking mouth, it was pow, right in the kisser.

I didn't follow the script. I was a bookworm and daydreamed about traveling to all the fantastic places I read about and viewed the breath-taking, scenic pictures in magazine.

Because our family was mixed with wives of different races—white, Koran, Italian, Mexican, and Black—I, along with those in my immediate family, knew absolutely nothing about prejudice. Any race was treated with the utmost respect and invited to live with us. The very first time that I had experience prejudice was shocking. I was sitting in an off-the-beaten-path, side-street club in Erlangen, Germany, in one of the small, intimate spots where I retreated to get away from military personnel. One night there, I walked past a table where, strangely, four Black men were sitting. In most cases, like everywhere that I visited normally, I was the only Black person in the building or neighborhood. I stopped at the table to greet and acknowledge their presence. I stuck out my hand as a good gesture and could not believe the reply I received. They were hostile and told me to get away from their table.

I froze on the spot, feeling baffled and wondering why. I politely asked why they wanted me to leave them alone. In unison they answered that it was because I was Black. Now I was really confused. I looked at my hands, then I turned them over to look at the palm side. I looked back at the four men at the table who were Black like me. Again, I asked why. They answered that they were from Africa and did not associate with Black Americans. "We don't like them." OK, I walked away and let them be. But that night haunted me for a very long time, mainly because I was naive in believing that this race-hating issue was between people of different colors.

The very first girlfriend that I fell in love within high school was named Janice. She was extremely attractive: petite, high yellow, with a touch of brown in her black hair, and she had a cheerful, unassuming personality. We were a perfect match, and our courtship headed to that point where the village said that it was now time to follow tradition and make plans for our wedding. It was a gut-wrenching time for me. My how I love her. But I loved hanging out at the city airport even more, dreaming of owning my own plane and lifting off to places and spaces unknown. I never once thought about taking anyone with me on my unrestricted journeys.

Robert Frost's poem "The Road Not Taken" summed up my whole young love life. I pondered the two pathways that lay before me. Do I follow my father's footsteps by marrying and heading to the factory? Or do I head to the airport and catch the next flight to an uncharted territory. Frost wrote, "Two roads diverged in some wood, and I— / I took the one less traveled by / And that has made all the difference." I wasn't going to work thirty years in a factory like all my cousins and family members did.

I really was painfully hurting inside as I sabotaged my relationship with Janice and packed my bags to go on my flight of fancy out of town to the Job Corps. I was extremely happy for all the ladies who were forced or stuck in bad marriages when the no-fault divorce was passed into law. Prior to that, divorce was a no-no in all faction of society. They were frowned upon at the mere mention, and now they had a chance to correct the mistake of jumping into the hot water of a love bath too soon.

But there was still the matter of finances. There were not many gainful employment opportunities for women, that is, until affirmative action came to be. This was game-changing legislation. That shook up the stranglehold that the men had over women. They were more independent and no longer had to hang around to get beat up after a couple of pints were had on a Friday night. And, what's more, they now had the chance to explore their own sexuality. I overheard many housewives talking about they never experienced an orgasm with their mates.

Freedom at what cost? The sexual revolution had inadvertently caused a schism between men and women, opening Pandora's box. The more independence they gained, the more they started taking on all the bad characteristics that they hated in a man: cheating on their mates, lying, stealing, robbing, abandoning their children, and using people to satisfy their lust for power. Homemaking classes in public school turned into empowerment classes for self-fulfillment, and that they did. Prison, once thought of as a hard place where mostly men was sent to by the justice system to be reformed, now saw an expeditiously increasing level of hard, heartless women with criminal records if a coast-to-coast Greyhound bus ride.

By the turn of the century, the rules of the player's brotherhood no longer applied. Especially rule number three: treatment / attention. Perhaps one out of twenty-five women during those times took us treating them like the queen of Egypt to heart. Shower them with gifts and attention these days and they will think of you as a sucker, a trickster, a mark fresh off the slab to be had. Young ladies thought that a young man draped with white gold around the neck, wearing 200-dollar gym shoes and pants hanging down to their knees is the norm because TV and/or society has them figuring that bad boy in the hood is the norm.

Rather than being spoken to nicely, these days, in their individual clicks, they feel normal being addressed as bitches and hoes, like they carry on in the rap-artist game. If you were a goody-two-shoes, sooner or later you will be set up. Once, in previous times, you could meet a nice lady at a club or wherever, take them home, let them spend the night, leave them there while you go to work, return home, and the house would be clean, and a meal would be cooked with items that you didn't know were in the refrigerator. Nowadays, if you do this and come home from work, everything in your house would be gone. They would even rip the carpet off the floor, taking that and your dog with it them.

Rule number five said that marriage equaled run. A lack of home-making skills made the fast-food joints financially bloated because women do not even know how to clean or cook. They expect to be given to, but they're too selfish to return. They twiddle their thumbs, trying to figure out why they can't find a good man. Primarily because of the kind of crowd the hang out with all night —those who've got to get over no matter who they step on—don't know the first thing about caring and sharing.

A person must have very thick skin and must be able to tolerate multiple personalities all wrapped up in just one person and, perhaps, doesn't lose heart after so many costly failed relationships. There weren't any cell phones back in the day. It's a bad sign when you are out on a date, one that you canceled all your important appointments for, and throughout the evening your companion prefers to constantly have their cell phone attached to their ear, even though they don't own a business or practicing medicine and are only talking on their cell phone to insignificant others about their hair, stylish nail polish, or the clothes that they are wearing.

In the years of 2000, the level of difficulty for dating was an eight out of ten. Homemaking, pottery, debate teams were tossed out of the life-skills window. As was typesetting and learning how to operate the Carver printing press, just for the sheer enjoyment of learning the basics of how old newspapers were printed. If a young man or lady is not careful, eating fast food, constantly dinning out, and eating all your meals can bloat the body and bring on an assortment of medical issues such as food poisoning, diabetes, and high blood pressure. Listening to only one side of an argument is the devil's doing. Pure justice—she hears both sides.

. Back in the day, at eighteen you were gone, moving into your own home. Arbitrarily, the moving age leaped to twenty-five in the late nineties. By the year of 2015, they may never leave Mom. For a beginner young person dating these days, player's club rule number five would be changed. If you truly want to enjoy playing the field and indulge in some less stressful romantic adventures in your young lifetime, of course there are exceptions to every rule, but rule number five might mean run faster.

TRIAL BY FIRE

To the delight of my moisture-eyed cousin, I calmly rose off the bottom bunk, put on my PF Flyers, and headed to the backyard where the karate master was waiting for me. We left the house through the side door and turned left toward the alleyway where Ronnie was on the nicely cut green grass high kicking, squatting, and shadow boxing, darting his arms back and forth quickly in the air. He stopped to turn and look at his latest conquest. Or so he thought.

To get in his head, I asked him where he wanted to fall. I said, "You can pick your spot where you'd like to hit the ground." I did this as a psychological move, to show him that I was not afraid of him. Growing up a young Black man in Detroit, there were three things that you could just about count on that were going to happen to you: One, you are going to jail multiple times for something or nothing. And number two, it was common that 45 percent of young Black men are going to get shot by a gun at least once. My younger brother and I were shot twice. For me it was once in the stomach by the security guard that was supposed to keep me safe. He robbed the store and took the money during closing time. And once in the head by a wayward Frank Nitti wannabe. It was a mistaken identity assassination attempt. I was shoved out of the way by an unseen force and avoided being seriously harmed. And three, you are going to get robbed by gun point. I was during being robbed, always by four gun-toting young Black guys, at least five times in the city.

I clearly remember the very first time and the second, third, and fourth time, but it was during the Christmas holiday shopping season when I was walking down the street, out and about looking for gifts. A car pulled up along the curbside near me to ask for directions. The driver rolled down his tinted window and asked me to come closer because he could not hear what I was saying. I moved closer toward the car, and he act like he could not hear from that distance either. I was asked to come closer, and before I knew it, I so near that I rubbed the driver's side door. Suddenly, the tinted back driver-side window was rolled down, and one of the passengers stuck a .38 caliber into my chest and said get in.

Ronnie, who most times always carried a pair of nun chucks with him, didn't that day. He chose to fight across the street, in front of his house. To begin the fight, he drew a line in the grass and said to step over it. I never waste time. I quickly stepped over it. His first mistake was that he tried a 360-degrees roundhouse kick but only made it 180 degrees, hitting the ground awkwardly after I kicked the back of his planted leg. His torso was twisted, and his split legs were off center. Then the back of his head hit the ground. In most cases, I let the opponent get off the ground to give them a chance to think about what they are getting into. Still determined, he lifted himself off the ground and began swinging.

Holy smokes! The guy was fast. I always had a three-to-one punch advantage in most contests, but not this time. Uh oh. The number of excited spectators grew on the boring block as they came out of their homes to watch. And what's more, my girlfriend lived directly across from Ronnie and came out of her home to watch. Blurring blows was traded. I was thinking that I might lose this one, and I better do something quickly. I did: I let go.

I was always in control of my three-to-one punches. When I was at quarterback, during a live game and in the heat of a battle, I let go of my conscience mind and gave in to my subconscious that preformed without a thought. During these moments, I had perfect clarity of my surroundings, a crisp clearness of thought, and could engage in actions that I wish that I could access all the time, but I can't.

A lot of those sayings in a Star Wars movies about letting go are true, only I call it the spirit. In a trial by fire, when the spirit takes over, instead of a three-to-one punch advantage that I controlled, the spirit can manufacture an explosive flurry and let loose a six-to-two punch advantage. I did this in my second amateur boxing match while I was in the Job Corps during Friday night fight.

Two of those six blows packed a wallop. The first one that connected rocked Ronnie's head backward. The second jarring blow knocked the martial arts expert three feet backward, onto the hood of his father's car. After all those years of discipline in the martial arts and all those tournaments that he participated in over the course of many years, he became unglued. He began to swing wildly with no control whatsoever. I continued to pound him as his head was bouncing off the hood of the car.

He was in a survival mode when he said, "I give. Please stop." The front porches were packed like sardine cans with spectators in the uneventful, nothing-exciting-ever-happens neighborhood. No one on the entire block expected me to win that fight. As always, my challengers got the outcome of the battle, which was predetermined in their minds, wrong again. That was the number one reason I believed that I could not win many football games coaching Raiders quarterback JaMarcus Russell. I watched all the game where he was at the helm during the 2007 football season. I saw a pattern. I observed that whenever the defense lit a fire under him and turned up the heat by blitzing, he became unglued after the fourth or fifth hit.

Reverting into a survival mode, like the martial art expert did, he started hurrying his throws, hearing footsteps, and ducking instead of stepping up in the pocket. I rarely saw him make the crucial, calculated sacrifice in the last two minutes of a game to connect on a pass that will keep a potent offense off the field of play and/or give his worn-down defense a rest like I did against the Lions' great Jerry Ball. When I stepped up into his rush and he literally knocked me into the stratosphere, my decision was not personal because I have no animosity against the brother. However, no coach can teach grit or toughness. Either the ball player has it in his heart or, he doesn't.

END GAME

I wrestled for months about making the decision to coach or not coach the quarterbacks and offensive linemen for the Raiders. It was gut wrenching, mainly because I loved Al Davis. He was a father figure to me. I was sympathetic in the way that I thought about him. His instinct about me coaching was right on the money. I had been calling my own plays since I was twelve years old. He had no idea that I had been a head coach before at any level, let alone an athletic director, which I found out was a formidable task, fielding teams of multiple sports and dealing with the haphazardness of logistic—the weather and the mixture of different personalities and races all at the same time. I was aware of the owner's declining health. He was one of the two coaches that I would have played for, for minimal wages, not concerned about money. The other was the San Diego Chargers' head coach Marty Schottenheimer.

I loved his coaching style when he coached the Cleveland Browns and the Kansas City Chiefs. He had two cornerbacks that played the position the way that I played in Cleveland: number twenty-seven, left cornerback Frank Minnifield and Hanford Dixon, number twenty-nine, right cornerback. They were not afraid of the blazing fast receivers that were saturated throughout the NFL. Those two got right into the face of the receivers during a time when most corners backed ten yards off the line of scrimmage.

I tried my best to resolve our philosophical differences about playing overpriced bums. I pleaded with them to give me another quarterback to coach. I found that the offensive linemen on the roster were adequate. Nevertheless, being one myself, I felt that I could come up with something maybe as simple as an attitude adjustment to improve the lot. The organization would not bulge. They wanted me to turn a lump of charcoal into a diamond. I could not envision this happening.

I was not a cocky person. Nor could I dance to make it rain. My teammates growing up and I didn't celebrate when we scored a touchdown. Our reasoning was that if you thought that was something, "just give us a few minutes, and we will be right back down here." At one time, I possessed the gift and ability to see talent at its finest or worst depending on the situation. I was not a person who was afraid to lose. Losing isn't so bad when your team put up a good fight. I have played on many losing football teams and took it all in my stride. Beating yourself because of miscues, lack of routinely taught discipline, and not being aware of down and distance is unacceptable.

If I were to be beat in a fight, I would be a good sport about it, get up, shake the victor's hand, and ask him if I could I buy him a beer. Because if you beat me, then you must be damn good. But that never happened. It was always my opponent who quickly threw in the towel.

I showed up to play in a ton of semiprofessional football games, not concerned about the score but only for the love of hitting. But if I oversaw any of it, I became a changed person, a stickler for details. Prior to a football game, you might catch me at 3:30 a.m. with a measuring tape on the field, checking the length of a blade of grass, when just a few hours before, at midnight, I was on the field, checking it a first time.

It was never about money. Everyone in America knows that the coach takes the blame for losing games. Even if the overall team's talent is substandard, the coach is the first to be fired. I didn't take the job coaching in professional football because I was a sore loser—perhaps it may have been true—but it was because these games will be written in the history books for hundreds of years. If I were placed in a book on the shelves, in an archive, then I wanted a "W" posted by my name. I could accept losing, just not on my watch.

There are only thirty-two teams that don the field in professional football. Out of billions of people that roam this planet and thousands of coaching positions at the PAL league, high school, college, semipro and professional level, only a select few have had a golden opportunity to coach in a lucrative occupation on a professional team each year, let alone the scrawny ranks of a Black coach. Although titles, gesticulation, and token positions do not become me, my mind is wired to do or do not. If you had the right formula to win, then I was in. Owner and general manager Al Davis, in seeing me as the cream of the crop, in essence, placed me in the category of being one of "the best of the best."

ZEPHANIAH:
WHAT THE LORD HID

Colossians 1: 25–27. On the eve of December 24, 1985, it was a mild winter night in the sub-city area of Detroit called Palmer Park. The magic occurred right after sunset. I had the privilege of viewing the most spectacular, stellar phenomenon that mankind has read about but could not even possibly imagine. The sheer beauty and the massive size of this sighting was awesome. Over two-thousand years ago, three wise men saw it and traveled toward it. This behemoth was unmistakable—the second observation of the Christmas star, located in the southeastern sky. It was shaped into a huge, glorious cross, sparkling like polished diamonds, majestically designed, on display that entire Christmas Eve. What was unusual about this sighting was that on the very top was a large Star of David formed in diamonds. On both arms were smaller Stars of David, also formed in diamonds. It was exquisite and took up a large quadrant of space. As blindingly bright as it was, the general population could not see it.

There is a reason the Lord often keeps blessings and signs hidden until he unexpectedly reveals something that was thoroughly foretold. The cryptic way the Lord reveals critical information concerning man's salvation is done in a short-story fashion, to teach a moral lesson encircled in truth. Unknown is the reason why, in that period, the Holy Spirit chose to divulge the crux sighting.

Many, over the course of millennium, have faithfully adhered to reject the truth or simply may not be prepared to see the word's authenticity. What the nonbeliever dismisses as rubbish will make perfect sense to a Christian.

The word alias is little Christ. As a messenger, is it better for me to deliver it to ears that listen and hear timely, gently? It is the Lord's soft way, making known the second sighting, avoiding jarring people into a dreadful panic.

I am understanding this need to not cause the entire human race into bedlam and pandemonium. In the book of Matthew 25: 1–13, "Parable of the Ten Virgins" was told in a thoughtful, clear, well-explained manner about preparing for the time of salvation. It was serious, not heavy-handed or frightening. However, it told people to get their acts together or be left behind. Intercession—the gift that can only come through the Lord. Intercession by way of man's repentance can only be accessed through the cross in this universe. The cross is the only way to defeat the finality of death. It is the staging area for man to purge and decontaminate his sinfully acquired traits. It allows, through passage from death to the destination of sharing, for an infinite joyful reunion with departed loved ones in heaven. The cross seals and secures the severed bond between God, His son, Jesus Christ, the Holy Spirit, and his wayward children forever.

I was a senior at Wayne State University. I also worked for the university part-time as a veterans' recruiter/counselor for the Veterans Educational Opportunity Program (VEOP) program. A brainchild, upward-bound program of its creator, Mr. Paul Rease, who was also a Vietnam veteran and friend who taught me how to write a feasible proposal that works almost anywhere. I had two private offices, one on the eastside campus and one at the Northwestern Activity Center, located on the westside of Detroit.

I did it again after telling myself that I would not put myself in that predicament anymore. My problem was that I waited two weeks before finals, when I started reading and writing reports on the three 495-page, four- and-five-hundred level books that were required reading. That was due along with other assignments in the other classes. And yet, since my freshman year, I always got the job done. But there was a cost called burnout. Every time, for four college years when the holiday season came around and after the office Christmas party, I was pooped, so much so that I only wanted to catch up on sleep.

I didn't want to visit anyone because during finals, you did not sleep. You crammed, reading and writing until your hand and brain became numb.

Up until finals, you saw many nights becoming day, going to work having had not one hour of sleep. I got the job done, but I still received three Xs on my report card after all that hard work. That was mainly because during the earlier part of the year, I received the worst letter from the Department of Defense. One that I never wanted to see.

The letter stated that I had reached a ten-year time limit to use my VA benefits. They cut me off cold turkey. Suddenly, I had one thousand dollars a month less to work with. Along with my regular benefits, I was doing work study and math, tutoring geometry, trigonometry, and precalculus. The more I tutored Pythagorean theorem and other mathematical models, the sharper my memory became in those subjects.

In any event, the government sponsored me in all those endeavors, and now it was a ragged rug snatched right out from me. It affected my thinking. And from the fall 1985 semester onward, my grades in all my classes went south. I was sitting at my now visible kitchen table. On it was a crystal drinking glass, a pint of Hennessy, and a whopper with fries. Prior to that, the table was covered with books stacked in piles of threes and fours and loose-leaf paper and spread sheets surrounded the table legs like carpet. There was nowhere to put any food. After I had done my homework and cleared the table and floors, it was Miller time.

"Wow!" was the first word that came out of my mouth as I peeked out of my rear kitchen window. This supernatural sighting was breathtaking. It was gorgeous. Stars perfectly aligned vertically and horizontally in the night sky and formed into the shape of a cross. I had this divination gift and have seen unseen forces coming from the spirit world ever since I picked up that broken piece of mirror as a child in the alley. However, this was completely different because it did not disappear in a few moments. I had to get a better look at it, so I put my shoes and coat on to go outside.

Once on the street, there was this certain feeling the permeated the air. It was the holiday festive sensation that made the day feel like back-in-the-day Sundays—calm, easy, laid back. Those times when the population didn't have to work so much on a Sunday. There were three shifts instead of just two, and people had time after work to entertain and enjoy life, not having to work split shifts seven days a week. Unfortunately for me, I didn't have the luxury of taking in the Christmas day to its fullest. My looking forward to Santa didn't last long because when I was nine years old, the mystery and gleefulness of the holiday season was shattered when my earth father said, "Son, there is no such thing as Santa Claus." This broke my heart because all the other kids my age got the opportunity to believe.

Since the day my father discovered that I could take everything apart and put it back together again, and it worked, he had me go to the locked room in the basement where the gifts were stored and put together a boatload of toys and electrical items such as an Easy Bake Oven and doll houses, which were the hardest to put together because you had to work on it like a real house. By this I mean moving in the furniture, setting up bedrooms, putting the plates in the kitchen, and sometimes sitting little people in their chairs.

I rarely looked at the instructions in the following years as I stitched together Big Wheels, Radio Flyer wagons, bikes, trains, planes, and toy cars that looked good on television but at home only ran in circles. You name it, and I had to put it together. I started working on these gifts the day before Christmas Eve. That was the day all the adults in our immediate family, like clockwork, traveled to Tennessee and Kentucky every year to visit family and friends out of state. My mother and father always came home around 3:00 a.m. Christmas morning to help me wrap up the presents and take upstairs to spread them around the Christmas tree and then wake up my just-fallen-asleep sisters and brothers who were trying to see if they could catch Santa coming down the chimney.

In any event, I went outside a stand next to a crowd of people and looked up at the cross. What was significantly different about these exquisitely crystallized stars from the one that had attracted the three wise men. On the very top of this one, formed in diamonds was the unmistakable Star of David. On both sides were smaller Stars of David. I had my head tilted so that they would look up to see what I was seeing. I did this on the other side of Woodward Street to see if they could see the majestic sighting. With a few folks, I pointed at the glistening crucifix that appeared in the southeastern sky, primarily to verify that I wasn't going mad.

First that solar system flight, and now this. After an hour or so, I was stumped and wondering how it was possible. It occupied a large quadrant of space and was just too massive. And as luminous as it was, others could not see it. Maybe the reason they couldn't was to prevent public hysteria because, even then, they simply could not handle seeing such a deracinating spiritual sighting. I know not the Lord's reasoning. I thought about Proverb 13, then I headed back home. I slept for only twenty minutes off and on that night because I kept looking out of my kitchen window to see if it was still there. It was. At the break of dawn, on Christmas, I stood at my kitchen window and watched as the cross started dissipating. The way that it started turning into a drifting fog floating away was also glorious.

I started writing a sports book about my adventures in football in the year of 2018. In 2016, I walked into a hospital and underwent a botched, painful lower-back surgery that afterward, made me unable to walk out of the hospital. Surgery left me struggling just to walk to my bathroom without assistance.

I was sidelined due to a repetitive employment where enough was never enough, and we need more, six days a week, twelve hours a night. So, I start writing as a method for convalescing from an idle mind that only thought about pain from dusk to dawn. I was wide awake, and it was early morning when the spirit of the Lord commanded me to write about the cross. There were two reasons why I wrote: The second reason I will mention later in the epilogue story. The first reason was because I was a faithful servant and a child of the Lord God and Jesus Christ.

EPILOGUE

I don't fly around the planet in my phantasmagoric state like I used to when I was much younger. Every now and then, I take a quick flight to keep in practice. These days I travel straight to the moon. In a few seconds, once there, NASA has three storage bunkers on it where I'm waiting for them, and I'm always asking why it took them so long to get there.

Counting the loose change mainly due to my philosophical differences, I walked away from some $11 million, perhaps more, in salary and performance bonuses to play or work in professional football. That was back when a million bucks spent like a million bucks. I really didn't think too much about how much my football salary was, anyway. I knew that I could make five times as much doing commercials, selling all kinds of products that could make you run fast and jump higher after the age of forty. And if I really needed money, they exact change seemed to always fall out of the sky.

My check was delayed for a week as usual, and I ran out of the weekly 200 dollars for a week of hotel rent. It was 3:30 p.m. when I had enough thinking about it. So, I headed outside to got to the store to get a brew. It was crowded outdoors, with people and school buses going every which way. As I walked perhaps forty feet up ahead, I saw some strange looking paper on the ground. There was a man ten feet in front of me who walked past the funny looking paper. When I reached down to pick up the two small papers, it had 100 dollars on the corners. *This cannot be real because the man just walked past it*, I thought. *I will take the funny money to the bank to verify that it is real.*

Always my check in the mail seemed to be diverted to someplace else for weeks sometimes for six months. I had been completely broke, and yet just about every morning after I woke and do the bathroom, I walked outside and would find a five-dollar bill to buy my coffee, newspaper, and donuts. But this was not a once or twice occurrence. This happened to me automatically over six decades.

I was never worried because as a gift from heaven, I got my newspaper, coffee, and donuts every day. After more than half a century, I can count on my hands and feet the few times when I didn't get a five spot. Could I have taken the football money? Yes! Could I live with myself? No! I witnessed some bad football games that would have made me give them all their money back plus an extra five dollars to get away from them. The players took losing three mind-bogging games in a row with a grain of salt. They would shower and one or some of the homeboys would take them to a club, and they might have gotten a lap dance. As a coach, after losing three horrible games back-to-back with a gun-shy quarterback, they would have had to take me to the emergency room because I would have lapsed into a coma.

I was mindful that it was an honor to be recognized by one of the greatest football minds in the business, an exceptional man who has a bust of him sitting in the Hall of Fame in Canton, Ohio. He helped orchestrate the merger between the National Football Conference and the American Football Conference that turned out to be a financial bonanza.

Mr. Al Davis believed that I, a man off the streets, had enough football smartness to formally instruct, educate, and improve the young talent on the playing field. I was also aware that this skill was transferable, meaning that it should also work for another professional football organization. It took mostly all the football experts in America and the scouts for the organization another entire football season to agree with me and to see what I saw in their franchise quarterback a year earlier.

However! Draining fatigue erupted in my heart and soul like a sleeping volcano coming to life. Years of constantly fleeing, leaving all my possession behind, fighting with disrespectful, greedy demons, and constantly sleeping with one eye open from one town to the next caught up with me. I felt like Comet Shoemaker–Levy 9 missed the planet Jupiter and leveled me. I was living out of suitcases, taking care of my hygiene like a cowboy on a cattle drive, washing up at any waterhole, eating at all the fast-food restaurants for breakfast, lunch, and dinner so many times that the regular and dollar menu selections started tasting bland, like some of the flavorless army ready-to-eat field rations.

Too many times I had sung Willie Nelson's "On the Road Again." And I sung way too many renditions of "Guitar Man" by the group Bread. The people in my company could sing the song along with me: "He just got to find / Another place to play." I just wanted to go home and rest, wherever that was. I knew that should I chose to coach for another team. I would not get any rest at all.

I would spend night and day in the film room. I was an obsessive stickler for details (OSFD). I knew me. Sooner rather than later, even if I lived in a million-dollar home, in the middle of the night I would purchase a cot from the army navy surplus, grab a coffee pot and a hot plate from Walmart, and sleep off and on at the stadium in the film room, going over plays. No rest there—that is why I ended my pursuit of chasing the cloud. And it's the reason I didn't pursue employment for another play-off bound football organization.

I enjoyed the exhilarating adventures during my football-playing years: the camaraderie, traveling by convoy, and, most importantly, the free beer and hot dogs. I thought that it was fitting because the last professional football player that I kicked it with was also an iron man and offensive line man—Lomas Brown Jr., a Super Bowl champion, seven times Pro Bowler, and blocker for the elusive running back Barry Sanders.

We were both outliers in the sport, respectively. Mr. Brown played for eighteen seasons in a sport where the average length of career for a rookie who obtains a spot on the opening-day roster was six years. He cranked out three times the pro-football-playing length. I muddled through twenty-three years in minor league football, six times the average length of the amateur ballplayer's participation. We met at a veterans Christmas function in Detroit where former Detroit Lions fame kicker Eddie Murray and quarterback Eric Hipple were also in attendance. Of course, I shot the breeze with Eric first. We both got excited as we reminisced about his debut Monday Night Football game against the Chicago Bears. Eric continued to remind me that after getting hit viciously, "he kept on getting back up."

I didn't have an opportunity to spend time with the kicker because when I reached Mr. Brown, we chewed up a lot of time talking about the Lions' offensive line over the years. Our meeting was so natural because linemen were the ones that I hung out with, anyway. It seemed like I was always invited to dinner in the home of the National Football League. However, it was I who never sat down at the table to enjoy the handsome meal.

One sore spot that haunts me about my pro football endeavors is not the declined money or the endorsements that fell off the silver platter, it is not catching the perfect sideline pass from rookie quarterback Phillip Rivers. To this very day, it still bothers me. Seems like I will never have any football peace until I apologize to Mr. Rivers for not dropping it but simply not catching it because, I admit, for the second time in my life, I was spooked. Thinking back, perhaps I should have attended one of coach Sam Wyche's football camps, if only to make a friend that I could trust who was on the inside of pro football. Things might have been different. Maybe?

It was one of those carefree summer days where the weather was just right. The temperature was in the lower eighties with a slight cooling breeze and not a cloud in the sky. Sitting under an old oak tree in my backyard and enjoying an ice-filled glass of lemonade, I began to reminisce about the elusive damsel who I described in the beginning of this story, the one I could never catch up to. For some reason, I began to think about my longtime girlfriend Nida, who I couldn't bring all the way into my circle of family and friends because I had to hide her from a multitude of despicable spirits.

First, I thought about her hair, then I remembered that it was the same length and color of the disappearing maiden. Next, I compared their height and weight, which were the same. Then I remembered the eyes, age, and skin complexion. Those were also the same. And my goodness! She was identical to Nida in all her intoxicating essence. And her family migrated from somewhere near the Mediterranean Sea. The resemblance was way too uncanny. *Is this omen?* I asked myself. My relationship was playing out in the way that it did so long ago with the disappearing goddess. Yet the irony in the forecast was that I realized that it was I who was the elusive one—the mysterious person in the incomplete relationship, never staying put in one place long enough to where she could catch up to me.

The sixteen-year-old hoodlum whom I called Frank Nitti Jr. was apprehended as was the other assailant who gave me the gift of a cone-shaped little piece of lead with my name on it. He was caught after another assassination attempt, charged as an adult, and given a twelve-year vocational vacation in the pen with the big boys. His father found me and apologized for the almost fatal mistake brought upon me by his son. The security guard that robbed his own duty station, sending me to the floor with a bullet, I thought was the smarter assailant. He, along with his girl, spent all the money that he took from the hold up. When his high wore off, out of all the many possible scenarios, he and his companion decided that he should go back to the scene of the crime and ask for his last check. His employer told him to come and get it. The police were waiting for him. They gave him a year for every thousand dollars that he took. He had to serve five years.

Shortly after I was baptized, my helicopter advocates would not let me get away with any of my lustful habits. They slowed my player's brotherhood rule number three to a grinding halt. I did this mainly because I believed that I took so many females for granted. In my home, I paid attention to them and treated them like queens. They felt as if they truly belonged to me. However, in my ungrateful mind, once they left my home, I felt that they belonged back to the world. Thinking back, I realize this was not nice. I never thought of them as disposable pleasure, but it was close because they were using me also. They all left happy campers, leaving my home satisfied because they had gotten everything that they wanted. All would gladly return with quickness when or if I called.

It had gotten so bad for me that I threw in the towel when the angels wouldn't even let me pay for an escort or date. They pounded me until I got it through my brains that I was different. I could not do what regular mortal men do. It wasn't enough that I knew I was number five of the Lord's favorite children. I had to consider my conduct and old tendencies, like hanging out and partying (I was a neutral civilian with the Crips and Bloods gang members), even though I was only in their cars during the times when they were shifting their money. They all said the same thing when they asked me to ride alone with them. They "just wanted to talk with someone who made sense." To me they were only entrepreneurs. I never saw them twist anyone's arms to buy something from them. It appears they did things that were no different from what Joseph Kennedy did in his bootlegging days.

One of my late best friends in Southern Cali named Juan Carlos was a big shot in the MS 13. I could not pass his house without drinking at least one Corona beer with him, which always resulted in going back to the store to get a refill after knocking off a six pack. They loved my brothers' and my seductive, swaggering, good-times spirit. They never asked me to sling anything for them. I liked kicking it with gangsters was because they were blunt and didn't hide or pretend what they were thinking. In a way, it was refreshing because they spoke what was on their minds. They were the ones who didn't trigger my sixth sense of deception. The siren didn't ring that loud around them like it does around normal people. You knew beforehand what they were up to. They all said that they only had their words and wouldn't break them for anyone. They told you point-blank if they were going to rob you and wouldn't befriend you for five or more years, then unexpectedly stab you in the back.

The sexual exploration during skirt chasing, the hanging out with scandalous scoundrels, and excessive hankering for retribution had to be put to rest. Mostly at the homes where I had resided and a short distance around my surrounding neighborhood, my conduct and personality were nearly that of a preacher's son. I was easy going and quiet as a kitten. But boy oh boy, on the other side of town, out of sight, I was a good-time Charlie, reckless, carefree, and wild as Friday nights, not looking but looking for a fight. I had to mature like I was a wise servant, with all the teachings since childhood about seeking revenge, wisdom, and knowledge provided by the Lord. It was only then that the angels cut the taut umbilical cord.

I often wondered why, after I escaped from another close-call scheme initiated by the prince of darkness, Satan (who is realer than or perhaps not as the Wendigo, a spirit-possessed human from the Minnesota area who was a terrifying monster myth) choose to reveal itself to me. Was this a blessing or a curse? Is it because my parents' names were prominent figures in Genesis?

Sarah, my mother's name, is in the Old Testament and in Hebrew means "lady, princess, noblewomen." Or was she the Black servant of Mary Magdalene? My earth father's name was Moses, who is of Hebrew origin and means "savior." To me it was uncanny that those two Moses were the only people who I knew who had the exact same speech impediment.

Or perhaps Lucifer decided to make it personal by choosing me as its recreational boy toy to try and kill and destroy me or yank the rug of blissful life right out from under me. Was its attempt to block me from reaching and of the three degrees of heaven? Or maybe the Lord allowed the original master of illusions to visit and test me under too many of the same circumstances as Job?

I was born as close to the Lord Jesus Christ as humanly possible, without transcending over to the nether land. Numerous times, as bad and counterculture as my character was, I was still told by different angels that my place is with the "prophet, preacher, and saints in the divine hierarchy."

As I started writing this story, the serious nature of those insignificant meetings with Lucifer, its cohorts, and/or the creature's endless number of unclean human's associates, it struck me that perhaps it wasn't just about naive me. What it asked of me concealed a purpose that was considerably more mysterious and had solemn ramifications that were greatly more catastrophic than I could possibly imagine. My refusals to cooperate blocked something unknown, and only heaven knows what.

The subconscious voice inside of my head said, "Remember every time that the evil one shows up and asks a sanctified human to join him. After each had resisted the allure and temptation when the bribery, blackmail, and, in my case, bullying didn't work, the demon had a temper tantrum. It was followed by great wrath and pure pandemonium that intensified within all territories of principalities and the social and economic stratum of societies on this side of the Orion Constellation."

When the spirit of the Lord Jesus Christ commanded me to give a written account about the breathtaking cross that I witnessed on the eve of Christmas 1985, I was not required to disclose my spiritual connection. Be that as it may, if I did not, something relevant would be missing. I'm the enigma, one of the eleven. I stood apart as a messenger in these darkening hours, chosen specifically to deliver the good news of the encouraging prophesied signs indicating the return of our only savior, the Lord Jesus Christ.

Everyone cannot be placed in a black or white box. Greater are the mysteries of the universe. The writer of Ecclesiastes says that there is nothing new under the sun. So many in the general population see with squinting eyes, open wide enough only to view what the snake oil salesman Satan shows them. The whole thing is a set up. The popular state of civil, political, and legal due process is being misled with Polynesian dreams by the rebellious archangel, all while the unparalleled divergence that separate current leaders is incubating in an oven of superfluous, blinding hate.

This hostile emotion has filtered down, with the help of the internet, into the hearts and souls of the disheartened villagers, who are witnessing the eradication of their religion while simultaneously seeing the building structures that bond the communities, and members of innumerable parishes are being watered down, dismantled, and destroyed at an accelerated pace that was never recorded before. Gloating and unseen are the one who is foremost responsible in arranging the prophesied collapse of the natural evolution and progression of mankind as we know it. This creature is the architect of the often-used military tactic of "divide and conquer." Any person who is in an influential class has an inherited duty to help his fellow man, and the one who dose so is a great statesman and a servant to humans.

On the other side of the street, there is a blooming number of those in elite positions who exhibit a lack of compassion for helping the peasants, and they make things worse by also practicing in bearing false witnessing, manufacturing lies, and spreading propaganda in a covert, social-engineering attempt to change the natural evolution of man into something abnormal.

You just cannot change someone else's children. All are the Lords kids. Trying to convert and indoctrinate them without the consent of the parent will result in untold consequences. Shrouded is the masterful scheme that is too powerful for humans to mount a winning defense. And without divine intervention, man has no chance in this battle against a conglomerate of self-centered individuals who came into power or received the ill-gotten treasures by bartering with the devil. And yet still unknown to those who have sold out for glory, fame, or money—they also will be deceived and ensnared with the rest of society's purging. This creature feeds off the venomous, uncalled for hating for sheer enjoyment. It is only fattening up the beef by dividing and preparing it for the calamity of Judgement-Day slaughter.

Prophets, preachers, and saints are not ancient nobleman that once roamed the planet. Just as evil spirits, demons, and the original puppet master who is immortal are all still here in the now. Nothing has changed. The shutters that cover nonbeliever's eyes allow them to see only this one visible physical dimension of the multitude that exist.

I have always believed in other dimensions, sanctioned beings, and inhabited solar systems. We have a short life span, and nothing was impossible for the Lord to guide us through it. The very first vision that I had was a frightening experience. I was awoken from a peaceful sleep when I was twelve years old. I looked out of my bedroom window and saw the moon. It wasn't orbiting the earth 384,000 kilometers away. Its orbit was only 100 meters away, and the color was wrong. It was covered crimson red, like the color of blood.

The main reason I talked about my spiritual adventures and did care what others conjectured is because once a person was visited and has looked directly into the eyes of the living serpent or has been shown the astronomical size and sheer speed of the cylinder sphere that this planet's caretaker travels in, I guarantee not another person alive would care what a human male or female thinks about them. No one would go on an ego trip or pat themselves on the back if they saw what's out there. Nevertheless, it is happening.

Here on planet Earth, almost everyone unwillingly, and at critical moments, experienced some level of conflict with an invisible presence, a dark spirit they cannot see or feel (psychic and telepathic excluded). And yet like gravity, even nonbelievers are keenly aware that it is there. And right now, at this very moment in the shrouded dimension, the one that exists slightly outside of ours, there is a ferocious battle that's been going on for millenniums with the same angry, raging spirit. The fighting is near its conclusion. The creature is losing. The great Babylon is free falling. And mankind has entered the seventh stage of the period called Revelation.

The end-time prophecies that speak of the wrath of God, repercussions of pestilence, famines, earthquakes, and the raging of the seas I can honestly say, as His messenger, that these things are not my Father's preference.

His law is personal, and at the same time, this breaks His heart that these things are written. Therefore, these things must be done. "If only mankind would sincerely repent and be baptized." This would halt all the resulting catastrophic chain reactions of being born into the bondage of sin. We all know the answer to this solemn pleading. My friends, we are going down.

This spiritual fighting, bit by bit, is beginning to leak into the visual realm of our existence. In the year of 1981, as a star gazer with my naked eyes, I saw that sphere which was the size of the planet Jupiter. (See April 7, 2021, Patriotsnetworknews.com: An enormous UFO has been discovered hovering around the sun!) Darting back and forth, covering the many parsecs between the eleven o' clock and the one o' clock positions in the sky in half a second, paused for a moment as if it was posing and then returned to the previous vacated point, suddenly I was aware that the occupants wanted me to see it.

I had seen some very strange, unexplainable happenings so many times that this wasn't scary to me. And yet I was astonished as I watched this spear with my mouth wide open. As soon as I stopped squinting and my night vision started focusing, even at the great of a distance I could clearly see that the configuration was that of a considerably fast, gigantic spear. It gyrated not in an ecliptically movement but changed position in a straight linear motion, unaffected by the gravitational pull of the nearby stars. At this precise moment is when I realized that this was a powerful, well-illuminated vessel. Simultaneously who, what, why, and how information about the bewildering crew's responsibilities that I believed to be worthwhile had abundantly gushed inside of my head. Could it have been telepathically, perhaps? I was privileged to learn that they were not a menacing or threatening species. They were simply just the planets' caretakers.

They thought that mankind's gallant efforts to be good stewards of the earth were commendable; however, the planet called Earth, is a living, breathing, aging, self-healing astronomical body and one of the first templates in the design of humanity. For a fraction of a second, I thought about the book of Genesis 2:7.

The entire encounter was very brief, no longer then eight minutes, and it didn't frighten me at all. But the last piece of information made me feel vulnerable, frail, and completely defenseless. I was overwhelmed, so I stopped looking to break the contact and looked for a place to get out of their sight to comprehend, especially after it had left me with the knowledge that they have the sovereignty, intelligence, and mastery to make Earth's time stand still, whether it be in minutes, hours, days, or months.

What really sunk me into avoidance was that they could put everyone here to sleep for a hundred or more years while the planet heals itself. And when they awaken, as they carry on as usual, not one person, time piece, or machine will realize that a fraction of a microsecond will be missing from their daily lives. They somehow knew that at some point in time I would write about this unforgettable encounter. I felt like this thing drafted the entire human race, rendering us tiny, like the size of an ant.

This sphere primarily exists just outside man's view. It is much too large to travel inside of our solar system because it will disturb the gravity well. They don't have to come inside to see what we are doing. And now this has leaked into our view as a preview to let man know that more from the other side is coming.

Although I feel like I'm just a character or messenger that's playing out a scripted part in the Book of Revelation, what I cannot deny is that these fits. I'm not an ancient historical figure from 2000 years ago that Christians read about. I have seen the crux in the midnight sky, and I have looked the Devil close, directly in the eye. This time around I live not in the past, but I live here, in the now, to tell those who have listening ears about these leaking events.

True Christians are mindful and are not fooled by the current pandemic forecasters. They are acutely aware of the consequence of opening Pandora's box, of the snowballing growth of impressionable members of worldwide society who follow the teachings and misinformation word for word, straight out of the graphic crimson color of the devil's bible. The book that I read twice a long time ago.

The biggest whopper of a lie in its book was that "there is no God. There is no such place as heaven. There are no laws of nature that govern the sexes. You can do whatever you feel like doing with whomever you want. No one else matters. Man serves no purpose while they are here. Have unrestricted fun and enjoy because there is no afterlife." The second reason I didn't hesitate to comply when the spirit asked me to write about the millions of winking and shimmering glowing stars that transmogrify into the Christmas Eve crux was that I was undaunted when it came to fighting fire-breathing dragons. I stood ready to take on quarrelsome space aliens from the six dimensions and put on my best suit of armor when it was time to battle with those disreputable, shady automotive mechanics.

I shudder every time I think about what the prophet Jonah did not do. I like eating fish, but I'm sure that I couldn't handle the occurrence of winding up being like the Japanese raw fish dish Sushi, flopping around inside the belly of a whale. What's my interpretation or assessment of the transcendental sighting of the Christmas Eve cross composed of a hundred thousand sparkling stars? My first thought was that the timing, hours, and date validated the accuracy of what was passed down over two thousand years ago: that only this eve was the day of Jesus Christ's birth. Only a few were privileged with the honor to view the sighting. The three wise men from the east did see the star that pointed them to Bethlehem during the birth of Christ.

I strongly believe that most of us are bioluminescent beings, children of light. I have been in the presence of those beings created from the alternate region of darkness. It was sometime during the year of 2013, perhaps, in the city of Detroit. A single mother whose occupation was that of a health-care worker was on her way to work. While crossing the street of East Grand Boulevard near Jefferson Street, she was tragically gunned down. The victim was a childhood and still-in-contact friend of my late wife. The vigil was held on the street where the murder occurred and was attended by a substantial crowd of heartbroken family, friends, and well-wishers, all who wondered why the senseless assassination took against this strong, good-natured, well-liked person in the community mother.

We let fly those cute, small, little floating kites up into the air and decided to finish the vigil at the victim's house. As soon as my wife and I crossed the threshold of the front door, I was smacked with a malodorous, ugly scent that rushed in tingling waves over me. It took me so many years to learn how to suppress sudden disturbing emotions from people. I whispered in my bewildered wife's ear that "something is terribly wrong in this house." During the evening, the victim's only child, the son, was acting unusually strange, not in the usual bereavement manner of allowing his relatives and friends to share their condolence with him. Instead, he hid alone in the basement.

The beer was kept in a freezer in the basement, so I went downstairs to grab one or two. The moment that I saw the cowering son jolt like the loud, unexpected, one o' clock Saturday afternoon civil-defense warning siren jolts, it suggested to me that the unsettling evil that I felt while coming into that house was being emitted from him. I gingerly walked back upstairs and told my wife, "I suspect that the son killed his own mother." She turned and said that I was imagining things because she had known the boy since he was born, and it was not possible.

Civic pressure in the next few days routs out the gunman who is also found murdered as his body was set on fire. In the days before the son was due to collect the money from his mother's insurance policy, Detroit police arrested the emotionless, greedy child of darkness for double murder charges for hiring an assassin to kill his mother for the insurance and for killing the trigger men and then burning the body to cover his morbid tracks.

On this planet Earth, there's not a single human, animal, or creepy species that is of the light is capable to willfully turn around and kills their own birth mother. This was a dark demon action. Astronomer, educator, and author Carl Sagan was correct in his exposition of the progression of civilization. He traced the cosmic evolution, which centers around the hypothesis that all the essence of humans were brought into being in very far away, extinct stars over fifteen billion years ago.

Everything in the origin of life and the history of the earth points back to light, or more specifically, to the infinite numbers of stars that continue to multiply expeditiously. There's one reason humanity enjoys warming their hands, standing over a crackling fire coming from the insides of a fifty-five-gallon drum or a bonfire and enjoys basking in the soothing warmth while sitting in front of a lit fireplace. It is the same stimulus or response that's achieved while sitting on the rocks of a beach, watching the roaring ocean's waves.

In the same way that moths are attracted to flames, humans are also attracted to astrophysical plasma (stars), our sun, and flames; it is an instinctive response of a primate returning to its roots. It's the stellar-terrestrial plasma connections, the shining stars from where we are another unseen spectrum of light, luminous beings, and part of the whole. Energy never dies, only the state of matter changes.

Most importantly, that cross signaled hope in the return of the Lord Jesus Christ. The ornamentation of the Star of David with the largest one on the head, three times the size of the smaller versions positioned on each arm, completely tied in the factualness of the story explaining King David's offspring. This crucifix was a behemoth, unlike the guiding star that the wise men saw. This version, should the shroud have been lifted for the laymen to see, would have been viewed at some point on all the different continents.

Ephesians 4:7 He has given each one of us a special gift. Yet it's hard to stay grounded when in the spiritual realm everyone including God says that you're special. I believe that love, moderation, and meditation in everything that you do is the key to longevity. I chose to pursue the traits of love, gentleness, faith, righteousness, endurance, and godliness.

Brothers, sister, and little Christ who are of the Lord. Take a break. Read the Book of Revelation again before it's too late.

Revelation 22: 21 The Grace of our Lord Jesus Christ be with you all. A-men.

The scripture quotations in this book are from the Holy Bible, King James version, printed in the Republic of Korea.

ACKNOWLEDGEMENT

One evening during the winter 1983 semester in college at Wayne State located in Detroit, Michigan, the class geography instructor B. Thompson scheduled a field trip to the campus library. The class size was about twenty-five students. Once there, after we sat down around two tables squeezed together, at the end of the table, nearest to a row of books, he held up two books that he had written, published, and sold, He enlightened us with his knowledge about writing a book: when to have it copy written and how to sell it in a certain market. Right then I knew that someday I would write a book to share my stories and anecdotes about my rich life that was much crazier than the normal life. I was living as if I was a reincarnation of a character like an ancient Hebrews scribbler memorizing and writing down phenomenon that he has seen. At times the shroud which cloaks the space between the spiritual and physical dimension was completely drawn back for me so I could clearly view and interpret what exists here on this planet and what also exists unseen here on this planet. The last time that I spoke with the inspirational Mr. Academic Advisor was during a conference call. The memorable date was January 28, 1986. The time was exactly 11: 39 a.m. EST. On the landline telephone, I suddenly paused mid conversation and shouted "wow!" into the phone, as out of the corner of my right eye, on cable television, I witnessed the space shuttle Challenger exploding.